A Theory of Multicultural Counseling and Therapy

About the Authors

Derald Wing Sue received his Ph.D. in counseling psychology from the University of Oregon. He is currently professor of psychology at the California School of Professional Psychology, Alameda, and California State University, Hayward. He is a Fellow of the American Psychological Association, the American Psychological Society, and the American Association of Applied and Preventive Psychology. Dr. Sue was a founding member and first president of the Asian American Psychological Association, past editor of the *Personnel and Guidance Journal,* and author of numerous texts and articles in counseling and psychology. A five-year study by a Fordham research team concluded that "Derald Wing Sue is without doubt the most influential multicultural scholar in the United States."

Allen E. Ivey received his Ed.D. from Harvard University. He is currently Distinguished University Professor at the University of Massachusetts, Amherst. An ABPP in counseling psychology, Dr. Ivey is a past president of the Division of Counseling Psychology of the American Psychological Association. The originator of microcounseling and developmental counseling and therapy, he has won wide recognition and national and international awards. His works have been translated into at least 13 languages. He did original work on multicultural implications of microskills in 1968–1974 and has been increasing his work in multicultural studies ever since. His most recent writings have focused on "psychotherapy as liberation."

Paul B. Pedersen received his Ph.D. in Asian studies from Claremont Graduate School and an M.A. in counseling from the University of Minnesota. He is currently professor of counselor education at the University of Alabama at Birmingham. Dr. Pedersen was director of a NIMH project, "Developing Interculturally Skilled Counselors," at the University of Hawaii and was a faculty member at the University of Minnesota and Harvard Summer School. He taught at universities in Indonesia and Malaysia for five years. He is a Fellow of Divisions 9, 17, and 45 of the American Psychological Association.

A THEORY OF MULTICULTURAL COUNSELING AND THERAPY

Derald Wing Sue
California School of Professional Psychology
and California State University, Hayward

Allen E. Ivey
University of Massachusetts at Amherst

Paul B. Pedersen
University of Alabama at Birmingham

BROOKS/COLE PUBLISHING COMPANY
I(T)P® An International Thomson Publishing Company

PACIFIC GROVE ■ ALBANY ■ BONN ■ BOSTON ■ CINCINNATI ■ DETROIT ■ LONDON
MADRID ■ MELBOURNE ■ MEXICO CITY ■ NEW YORK ■ PARIS ■ SAN FRANCISCO
SINGAPORE ■ TOKYO ■ TORONTO ■ WASHINGTON

 A CLAIREMONT BOOK

Sponsoring Editor: *Eileen Murphy*
Marketing Team: *Margaret Parks and Connie Jirovsky*
Editorial Associate: *Patricia Vienneau*
Production Coordinator: *Fiorella Ljunggren*
Production: *Greg Hubit Bookworks*
Manuscript Editor: *Molly D. Roth*

Permissions: *Catherine M. Gingras*
Interior Design: *John Edeen*
Cover Design: *Terri Wright*
Typesetting: *Susan Benoit*
Cover Printing: *Phoenix Color Corporation*
Printing and Binding: *Quebecor Printing, Fairfield*

For more information, contact:

BROOKS/COLE PUBLISHING COMPANY
511 Forest Lodge Road
Pacific Grove, CA 93950
USA

International Thomson Publishing Europe
Berkshire House 168–173
High Holborn
London WC1V 7AA
England

Thomas Nelson Australia
102 Dodds Street
South Melbourne, 3205
Victoria, Australia

Nelson Canada
1120 Birchmount Road
Scarborough, Ontario
Canada M1K 5G4

International Thomson Editores
Campos Eliseos 385, Piso 7
Col. Polanco
11560 México D. F. México

International Thomson Publishing GmbH
Königswinterer Strasse 418
High 53227 Bonn
Germany

International Thomson Publishing Asia
221 Henderson Road
#05–10 Henderson Building
Singapore 0315

International Thomson Publishing Japan
Hirakawacho Kyowa Building, 3F
2-2-1 Hirakawacho
Chiyoda-ku, Tokyo 102
Japan

Printed in the United States of America

10 9 8 7 6 5 4 3 2 1

Library of Congress Cataloging-in-Publication Data
Sue, Derald Wing.
    A theory of multicultural counseling and therapy / Derald Wing
Sue, Allen E. Ivey, Paul B. Pedersen.
        p.   cm.
    Includes bibliographical references.
    ISBN 0-534-34037-7
    1. Minorities—Mental health services.   2. Cross-cultural
counseling.   3. Minorities—Mental health services—United States.
4. Cross-cultural counseling—United States.   I. Ivey, Allen E.
    II. Pedersen, Paul, [date].   III. Title.
RC451.5.A2S92   1996   95-42616
362.2'08'693—dc20   CIP

To my wife, Paulina, and my children,
Derald Paul and Marissa

D. W. S.

To my colleague and valued coauthor of
many of my books, Mary Bradford Ivey

A. E. I.

To Anne Bennett Pedersen, Deborah Kai,
Karen, and Jon

P. B. P.

ABOUT THE CONTRIBUTORS

Patricia Arredondo holds a doctorate in counseling psychology from Boston University. She is president of Empowerment Workshops, Inc., of Boston, an organizational development firm specializing in diversity management. Since 1985, Dr. Arredondo has led a multidisciplinary consulting team in both private and public sectors. She has served as president of the National Hispanic Psychological Association and the Association for Multicultural Counseling and Development. Her publications in the multicultural counseling field address gender and culture, Latino cultural considerations, multicultural competencies and education, and training.

Mary Ballou, who holds a Ph.D. in counseling psychology from Kent State University, is an ABPP Diplomate in Counseling Psychology and a Fellow of the American Psychological Association. She is an associate professor of counseling psychology at Northeastern University in Boston and also has an active professional practice in counseling and consulting. She has authored numerous articles, chapters, and books, several about feminist therapy. Currently she is committee coordinator in the Feminist Therapy Institute.

J. Manuel Casas received his Ph.D. from Stanford University, with a specialization in the areas of counseling and cross-cultural psychology. Currently he is a professor at the University of California, Santa Barbara. Recognized nationally as one of the leading experts in the cross-cultural and diversity areas of psychology, he has published widely and served on numerous editorial boards. As president of JMC & Associates, one of the few Hispanic-owned diversity consulting and research companies, he serves as a consultant to various agencies and organizations.

Madonna G. Constantine received her Ph.D. in counseling psychology from the University of Memphis. She is currently an assistant professor in the Counseling Psychology Program at Temple University. Dr. Constantine is very active in the American Psychological Association, particularly in the Division of Counseling Psychology. Over her professional career, she has published and presented in the areas of ethnic minority psychology, sports psychology, and the training and supervision of psychologists and other mental health professionals. She has also served as a consultant to numerous organizations in multicultural diversity.

Gerald Corey, Ed.D., NCC, ABPP, is professor of human services and counseling at California State University, Fullerton. He is a licensed psychologist; a Diplomate in Counseling Psychology, American Board of Professional Psychology; and a National Certified Counselor. Dr. Corey is a Fellow of the American Psychological Association (Counseling Psychology) and a Fellow of the Association for Specialists in Group Work. Among the many books published with Brooks/Cole Publishing Company are: *Theory and Practice of Group Counseling, Theory and Practice of Counseling and Psychotherapy,* and *Case Approach to Counseling and Psychotherapy.*

Michael D'Andrea received his Ed.D. in human development counseling from Vanderbilt University. He is an associate professor in the Department of Counselor Education at the University of Hawaii, Manoa. Dr. D'Andrea has published extensively in the areas of multicultural counseling and human development counseling. He is the co-author of the Multicultural Counseling Awareness, Knowledge and Skills Scale (MAKSS), which has been identified as the most widely used instrument of its type in the United States.

Judy Daniels received her Ed.D. from Peabody College of Vanderbilt University. She is currently an associate professor in the Department of Counselor Education at the University of Hawaii, Manoa. Dr. Daniels co-founded, and subsequently became the first state president of, both the Hawaii Association for Multicultural Counseling and Development and the Hawaii Association for Counselor Education and Supervision. Her research and scholarly interests are in the areas of multicultural counseling; diversity counseling, with a particular focus on homeless children and their families; and development psychology.

Pamela Highlen received her Ph.D. in counseling psychology from Michigan State University. She is currently associate professor of psychology at The Ohio State University. Her theoretical and research interests include transpersonal and multicultural psychology. Recent work includes development of the Self Identity Inventory, based on the Optimal Theory Applied to Identity Development (OTAID) model, and the application of transpersonal psychology to vocational assessment with racial/ethnic minorities.

Margo Jackson is currently a doctoral candidate in counseling psychology at Stanford University. She co-founded —with D'Youville College, daVinci High School, and the School and Business Alliance of Buffalo, NY—a multicultural mentoring program to further college and career aspirations of African-American, Hispanic, and Anglo high school students paired with trained college student mentors. Her former positions include director of an urban college career center, counselor/instructor with the Educational Opportunity Program, and president of the board of directors of the Greater Buffalo Counseling Centers.

Teresa LaFromboise received her Ph.D. from the University of Oklahoma. She is currently associate professor of education at Stanford University. Dr. LaFromboise is a counseling psychologist concerned about Native Americans' stress-related problems. Her research topics include interpersonal impact of interviewing strategies in multicultural counseling and the evaluation of social skills interventions for Native American bicultural competence. She teaches seminars on counseling theories and intervention from a multicultural perspective and Native American mental health. She has also held seminars on the impact of race and gender in therapy in the Soviet Union and East Africa.

Courtland C. Lee received his Ph.D. in counseling from Michigan State University. He is professor and director of the Counselor Education Program at the University of Virginia. His areas of research specialization include multicultural counseling and adolescent development. He has published numerous articles and book chapters on counseling across cultures. He has also written, edited, or co-edited four books on multicultural issues in counseling and human development. Dr. Lee is the former editor of the *Journal of Multicultural Counseling and Development* and serves on the advisory board of the *International Journal for the Advancement of Counselling*.

Frederick T. L. Leong obtained his Ph.D. from the University of Maryland in counseling and industrial/ organizational psychology. He is an associate professor at The Ohio State University. In 1993, he received the Early Career Scientist/Practitioner Award from the Division of Counseling Psychology of the American Psychological Association. Dr. Leong has published numerous texts and journal articles on vocational psychology, cross-cultural psychology, and organizational behavior.

David Mann received his B.A. from the University of California, Los Angeles, his M.A. in counseling psychology from the University of California, Santa Barbara, and is currently a Ph.D. student in the Combined Counseling, Clinical, and School Psychology Program. His research interests include the impact of acculturation on the lives of Hispanic adolescents, as well as on the nature of gender schemas among Hispanic children. Over the years, he has served as a teaching assistant for a variety of classes in the area of Asian American studies.

Ena Vazquez Nuttall obtained her doctoral degree in school psychology and counseling from Boston University. She is currently associate dean and director of the Graduate School at the College of Pharmacy and Health Sciences at Northeastern University. She was recently elected treasurer of Division 16 (School Psychology) of the American Psychological Association and has been on several APA committees, including the Commission on Ethnic Minority Recruitment, Retention, and Training. Multicultural issues, including assessment and intervention, are some of her major areas of scholarship; and she has also co-edited a book on assessing and screening preschoolers.

Thomas Parham received his Ph.D. in counseling psychology from Southern Illinois University at Carbondale. He is currently director of the Counseling Center and the Career and Life Planning Center and is an adjunct faculty member of the University of California, Irvine. Dr. Parham is the 1995–1996 president of the Association of Black Psychologists and a past president of the Association for Multicultural Counseling and Development (American Counseling Association Division). He is the author of numerous texts and articles on psychological nigrescence and therapeutic approaches with African-American populations.

Donald Pope-Davis received his Ph.D. in counseling psychology from Stanford University. He is an associate professor in the Counseling Psychology Program, Department of Counseling and Personnel Services, at the University of Maryland, College Park. He is currently on the editorial boards of *The Counseling Psychologist* and the *Journal of Counseling and Development*. Dr. Pope-Davis has published in the areas of multicultural education, training, and competencies, as well as identity development.

William Sanchez received his Ph.D. in clinical psychology from Boston University. He is currently assistant professor of counseling psychology, rehabilitation, and special education at Northeastern University in Boston. Dr. Sanchez was formerly the director of the Latino Treatment Team at Children's Hospital in Boston. He is a member of the American Psychological Association's Committee on Children, Youth, and Families. His research and teaching interests include multicultural training and Latino studies.

Jennifer Joyce Webber received her B.A. in psychology from the University of Notre Dame and her M.A. in applied educational psychology, with a specialization in school psychology, at Northeastern University. Her interests include providing assessment and therapy to a multicultural population of children and their families and working with teachers and families to promote literacy in children and adults. She is currently doing her year of internship in Hawaii, where she hopes to work with children from preschool to high school ages.

CONTENTS

CHAPTER 8

MCT THEORY AND IMPLICATIONS FOR TRAINING   123

Ena Vazquez Nuttall, Jennifer Joyce Webber, and
*   William Sanchez, Northeastern University*

CHAPTER 9

MCT THEORY AND IMPLICATIONS FOR RESEARCH   139

J. Manuel Casas and David Mann, University of California,
*   Santa Barbara*

CHAPTER 10

MCT THEORY AND ETHNOCENTRISM IN COUNSELING   155

Judy Daniels and Michael D'Andrea, University of Hawaii, Manoa

PART III
MCT THEORY AND SPECIFIC POPULATIONS 175

PREFACE

The field of multicultural counseling and therapy (MCT) has matured and become influential in the helping professions. A long time in the making, this maturation was fueled early on by the social unrest and political turmoil of the 1960s. The demand by racial/ethnic minorities and women for equal access and opportunities; the increasing awareness of the pervasiveness of racism, sexism, and oppression; and the Third World, Women's, and Civil Rights movements coalesced to confront society with an unpleasant question: Are we an integrated nation that believes and practices equality for all, or are we a nation segregated and unequal? The honest answer to this question has raised numerous others as well. If we truly believe in the democratic principles we claim to hold so dearly, what must we do as a nation to achieve these goals?

Our intent in this brief introduction is not to provide a history of the last 35 years but to indicate that the social upheavals of society have also influenced the field of counseling and psychotherapy. Just as the inherent biases of the economic, political, educational, and justice systems were challenged by various racial/ethnic minority groups, the field of mental health came under attack for being culturally encapsulated and unhelpful to many groups composing the population.

Reluctantly, the mental-health profession has been forced into some serious soul-searching. The findings from this journey have not been pleasant: Educational materials and research have portrayed minorities in negative stereotypes; an implicit equation has been made between pathology and different lifestyles of culturally different groups; mental-health services have often culturally oppressed minority clients; and counselors and psychotherapists have failed to recognize the biased assumptions present in theories about human behavior.

An unprecedented number of presentations, papers, and symposia on aspects of multicultural psychology have filled professional conferences and conventions. Indeed, during the past 10 years, most major professional organizations at the local, state, national, and international levels have held conferences on multiculturalism and diversity. Similarly, the number of publications devoted to the topic has dramatically increased. Though it has been rewarding to witness these changes, we believe that a conceptual and theoretical void continues to exist in the multicultural counseling and therapy literature. Our current work is an attempt to address this deficiency.

HOW OUR PROJECT CAME ABOUT. For some years, the three of us have written consistently about the serious limitations of current theories of counseling and psychotherapy. In particular, present theory and practice fail to consider the influence and importance of cultural and sociopolitical forces. All three of us, in different ways, have sought to address these issues. In one of those rare moments when our paths crossed—in both Atlanta, Georgia, and New Zealand—we had an opportunity to share our thoughts and ideas concerning the development of MCT theory. Surprised but pleased to discover how much our thinking converged, we decided to undertake a joint project, from which we have written the first three chapters of this book.

These chapters represent our conceptualization of a theory of MCT. Though we had originally planned to publish it in a major journal, it became obvious that such publication would limit our editorial freedom; furthermore, the article would be much too lengthy. Thus, we submitted our manuscript to several publishers, who responded with much enthusiasm. We chose Brooks/Cole because of its stature as a producer of high-quality professional texts, as well as its excellent marketing experience and history.

THE NEED FOR DIFFERENT PERSPECTIVES. No matter how much we, as authors, strive to be unbiased and culturally sensitive, we are products of our history. We recognized that what we proposed might be limited by our own biases and thus would need different perspectives to act as a counterbalance. No individual or group can completely understand the broad ramifications of any theory for a particular population or discipline. For example, even though we would like to perceive ourselves as enlightened and sensitive to the life experiences of other groups, our theory of MCT is based on the conceptualization of one Asian-American and two Euro-American men. We realized that we needed input from individuals who had worked in multicultural research, training, practice, organizational development, etc. Furthermore, we felt the need to obtain perspectives from the several chosen groups—African Americans, Asian Americans, Native Americans, Latina(o) Americans, and women.

As a result, our project would also involve two separate parts in which multicultural counseling/therapy experts commented on the proposed theory. We felt that two different foci were important: the first on broad theoretical issues and the second on applications to specific populations.

We carefully identified the leading experts in the field of multicultural counseling/therapy and asked them to consider either a particular topic (i.e., practice, research, training) or a specific population. Assuming that these individuals would be the best judges of how to approach the task, we purposely allowed contributors considerable freedom in how they would respond. However, we did ask them to be guided by three questions: (1) What were their general reactions to our MCT theory? (2) How does the theory relate to their topics or specific populations? (3) What did they see as the future direction of MCT, and what recommendations did they have regarding the development of an adequate theory of MCT? Within these parameters, the contributing authors could move in whatever direction they considered important for the topic or population being discussed.

HOW THE BOOK IS ORGANIZED. The text is divided into four major parts. Part I, "Toward a Theory of Multicultural Counseling and Therapy," consists of three chapters in which we propose and develop a theory of MCT. We have attempted to integrate our major works in the multicultural field and take the first steps of constructing a comprehensive theory of MCT. Though we have probably been overly ambitious, we consider such a contribution long overdue and necessary to begin a major paradigmatic shift in the counseling field.

Chapter 1, "Shortcomings in Contemporary Theories of Counseling and Psychotherapy," actively critiques current theories and argues for the need for the development of MCT theory. Chapter 2, "Basic Assumptions of a Theory of Multicultural Counseling and Therapy," presents propositions and corollaries related to MCT theory. Chapter 3, "Research, Practice, and Training Implications of MCT Theory," discusses our view of the implications of MCT theory in these three areas. As much as possible, we have tried to interpret the implications of our MCT theory for certain selected broad topics.

Parts II ("Implications of MCT Theory") and III ("MCT Theory and Specific Populations") present the contributors' views on our proposed theory, both from a theoretical perspective and from the perspective of how it applies to specific populations.

Part IV, "The Future of MCT Theory," consists of one chapter, which we wrote in response to the contributors' reactions to our original treatise. Chapter 16, "MCT Theory Development: Implications for the Future," is an attempt to summarize and organize these authors' reactions, suggestions, and recommendations in regard to the future of MCT theory—specifically, how it may potentially change the helping professions.

HOW TO USE THE BOOK. This graduate-level textbook is geared for courses in psychology, counselor education, and social work, among others. Specifically, instructors of courses that deal with multicultural counseling, psychotherapy, or social work will find this book an excellent conceptual and practical resource. In addition, students in courses that deal with theories of counseling and psychotherapy not only would find MCT a valuable theory in itself but would also enhance their understanding of other Euro-American theories because of the unique challenges presented to those perspectives.

We encourage instructors who use *A Theory of Multicultural Counseling and Therapy* as their main text to have students read the book from cover to cover. Those instructors who view it as a companion text to other books (as in a traditional course on theories of counseling/psychotherapy) have considerable freedom in selecting those parts related to the issues or concepts being addressed.

In either case, the first three chapters present the main treatise and should be thoroughly mastered by students. Instructors can then pick and choose from the response chapters. For instance, one course may emphasize population-specific issues, while another may explore the implications of practice, research, and theory development. In all cases, however, we have found that students need time to consider and digest the richness of ideas presented by authors. Because the ideas and concepts presented may be quite controversial, allowing time in the class to process these reactions will enhance learning.

Acknowledgments

There is no way we can adequately express the depth of our appreciation and gratitude to our friends and colleagues who agreed to contribute their thoughts to our book. We appreciate the time and effort they put into their respective chapters, and we are even more impressed with their candor, honesty, and expertise. Interestingly, not a single person whom we contacted declined our offer. We feel fortunate to have them not only as professional associates but also as friends. To that end, we extend thanks to Patricia Arredondo, Mary Ballou, Manuel Casas, Madonna Constantine, Gerald Corey, Michael D'Andrea, Judy Daniels, Pamela Highlen, Margo Jackson, Teresa LaFromboise, Courtland Lee, Frederick Leong, David Mann, Ena Vazquez Nuttall, Thomas Parham, Donald Pope-Davis, William Sanchez, and Jennifer Joyce Webber. We are also grateful to the reviewers of the manuscript for their valuable and helpful comments. They are Jesse Aaron Brinson of the University of Nevada, Doman Lum of California State University, Sacramento, and Ronnie Priest of the University of Memphis.

On a more personal note, the three of us would also like to acknowledge the support of our families in the undertaking of this project. This has truly been a family affair in more ways than one!

Derald Wing Sue
Allen E. Ivey
Paul B. Pedersen

PART I

TOWARD A THEORY OF MULTICULTURAL COUNSELING AND THERAPY

In these first three chapters, we propose and outline a theory of multicultural counseling and therapy (MCT). Chapter 1 discusses the inadequacies of current theoretical formulations, Chapter 2 outlines the propositions and corollaries of MCT theory, and Chapter 3 discusses implications MCT theory may have for the helping professions. Because these chapters form the basic treatise to which other chapters are linked, and because the ideas and concepts are quite compact, we encourage you to actively involve yourself in the reading process—allow yourself time to critique our approach. What do you like? What would you change?

All theories of counseling and psychotherapy operate from both explicit and implicit assumptions that guide their formulations. We have found that doing an "assumption audit" is a helpful way to approach the material. Therefore, we have outlined some of the assumptions contained in the first three chapters, though we have not spelled out all of them. You will see in later chapters that we have also listed selected assumptions made by contributing authors. We suggest that you scan the list of assumptions prior to reading the chapters, even though you may not understand them until you have digested the chapters. After reading the chapters, return to these assumptions, identify and formulate additional ones, then think through their implications. In other words, conducting a critical and independent "assumption audit" on your own will enhance your understanding.

Underlying Assumptions
Contained in Chapters 1–3

- Current theories of counseling and psychotherapy inadequately describe, explain, predict, and deal with current cultural diversity.
- Culture is complex but not chaotic.
- Diversification is occurring at such a rapid pace that mental-health professionals will increasingly come into contact with clients or client groups who differ from them racially, culturally, and ethnically.
- Mental-health professionals are not adequately prepared to engage in multicultural practice.
- The traditional training models of professional schools contribute to encapsulation.
- A major paradigm shift is in process.
- Multiculturalism provides a fourth dimension to the three traditional helping orientations (psychodynamic, existential-humanistic, and cognitive-behavioral).
- Asian, African, and other non-Western progenitors of counseling and psychotherapy have been trivialized.
- Individualism has dominated the mental-health field and is strongly reflected in counseling and psychotherapy.
- A culture-centered metatheory is viable.
- All learning occurs and all identities are formed in a cultural context.
- Cultural identity is dynamic and changing.
- Unintentional racism is as serious as intentional racism.
- Multicultural training increases a counselor's repertoire of skills and perspectives.
- Informal as well as formal counseling is important in many cultural contexts.
- Culture should be defined inclusively and broadly rather than narrowly.
- Understanding the cultural and sociopolitical context of a client's behavior is essential to accurate assessment, interpretation, and treatment.
- An adequate research methodology for incorporating culture must include both qualitative and quantitative elements.
- Increased self-awareness is an essential starting point in developing multicultural competence.
- The accumulation of relevant cultural knowledge depends on a well-developed cultural awareness.
- The appropriate application of skills in multicultural settings depends on both cultural awareness and relevant knowledge.

CHAPTER 1

SHORTCOMINGS IN CONTEMPORARY THEORIES OF COUNSELING AND PSYCHOTHERAPY

Current theories of counseling and psychotherapy inadequately describe, explain, predict, and deal with the richness and complexity of a culturally diverse population (Ivey, Ivey, & Simek-Morgan, 1993; Pedersen, 1994; D. W. Sue, 1995b). This weakness is glaring when one considers the rapid diversification of the United States, in which racial/ethnic minorities will become a numerical majority within several decades (Atkinson, Morten, & Sue, 1993). Given these facts, mental-health professionals are ill prepared to provide culturally appropriate mental-health services to a diverse population. Despite a recent survey of counseling-psychology graduate programs, which indicates that 89% offer at least one multiculturally focused course on counseling (Hills & Strozier, 1993), we are concerned that such courses may (1) continue to be ethnocentric and monocultural, (2) rely on unsophisticated attempts to adapt current Eurocentric theories to a diverse population, (3) lack a conceptual framework that incorporates culture as a core concept of the therapeutic relationship, (4) fail to make clear or explicit the cultural basis and assumptions of the various theories, and (5) potentially propose a technique-oriented (eclectic) definition of the helping process devoid of a meaningful conceptual framework.

Many of these criticisms arise because theories of counseling and psychotherapy are culture-bound (Atkinson, Morten, & Sue, 1993; Pedersen, 1994), and a serious vacuum exists in theoretical and conceptual formulations that integrate culture, personality, and interventions (Marsella, 1979; Pedersen, 1994). Pedersen (1991) has noted that because contemporary theories cannot be easily adapted to a wide range of cultures, the helping professions need a theory of MCT. D. W. Sue (1995b) makes a strong case that the mental-health profession seems poised for a major paradigm shift.

In his review of the theory and practice of counseling and psychotherapy, Sue points out major weaknesses, biases, and culture-bound factors in contemporary theories, processes, and goals; he further indicates how the multicultural perspective seems best positioned to accommodate the existing data related to culture, ethnicity, race, and gender. Furthermore, Kuhn (1970) has expressed the belief that a major paradigm shift occurs when (1) the science and theory of the day cannot adequately account for ideas, concepts, and data and (2) a new and competing perspective better accommodates the existing data. We believe that multiculturalism potentially represents what Pedersen (1991) calls "the fourth force in psychology" and is well positioned to fill this void. In the next sections, we shall discuss the following issues: (1) the culture-bound nature of current theories, (2) how theories of counseling and psychotherapy represent differences in worldview even within a Eurocentric perspective, and (3) epistomological difficulties in current eclectic attempts at integration. This information will help you better understand the need for a theory of MCT.

THE CULTURE-BOUND NATURE OF CURRENT COUNSELING THEORIES

Multicultural specialists have criticized counseling and therapy as culture-bound because they arise from a predominantly Eurocentric perspective (Ivey, 1993b; Katz, 1985; Parham, 1993a; Pedersen, 1987, 1994; Ponterotto & Casas, 1991; D. W. Sue & D. Sue, 1990; D. W. Sue, Arredondo, & McDavis, 1992; White & Parham, 1990). Some African-American psychologists (Nobles, 1986; Parham, 1993a; White, 1984; White & Parham, 1990) point out that psychology did not arise from the laboratories of Wilhelm Wundt in the late 1800s; they trace its roots back to African-Egyptian civilizations, which defined it as the study of the soul or spirit. In Western culture, however, psychology became equated with the study of the "mind," "knowledge," and "behavior." While one can debate whether this evolution occurred or not, the Euro-American approach to psychology and mental health is imbued with a worldview quite different from its African counterparts (Ivey, 1993b). Similarly, Lee (1993) points out that extreme bias in psychology is manifested in the educational emphasis on Greek scholars such as Socrates (469–399 B.C.), Hippocrates (460–370 B.C.), Democritus (460–370 B.C.), Plato (427–347 B.C.), and Aristotle (384–322 B.C.); minimal importance is placed on the psychological theories of Chinese scholars such as Lao Tzu (571–447 B.C.), Confucius (557–479 B.C.), Mo Tzu (325–238 B.C.), Chuang Tzu (369–286 B.C.), and Mencius (372–289 B.C.).

Theories of counseling and psychotherapy—whether psychoanalytic, behavioral, humanistic, or cognitive—that arose from Euro-American culture reflect the values, mores, customs, philosophies, and language of that culture (Ponterotto & Casas, 1991; D. W. Sue & D. Sue, 1990). That is why many have accused counseling and psychotherapy as "handmaidens of the status quo" (Halleck, 1971; Szasz, 1961), "transmitters of societal values" (D. W. Sue, 1981), and "forms of possible cultural oppression" (Katz, 1985; D. W. Sue, 1978; D. W. Sue et al., 1982). These accusations are especially true when mental-health professionals believe that the values and assumptions of counseling and psychotherapy are universally shared by their culturally different clients, and naively seek to impose them on racial/ethnic minorities.

Several excellent reviews explore the culture-bound basis of mental-health theory and practice (Ivey, 1986; Ivey et al., 1993; Pedersen, 1994; Ponterotto & Casas, 1991; D. W. Sue, 1995b; D. W. Sue & D. Sue, 1990; D. W. Sue & S. Sue, 1972). In general, these reviews and analyses suggest that counseling and psychotherapy as practiced in Western civilizations possess certain generic characteristics that reflect the values of society. These culture-bound values are often antagonistic to the values and experiences of culturally different groups.

One of the most obvious and important values present in Euro-American cultures is that placed on individualism and the separate existence of the self (Kluckhohn & Strodtbeck, 1961). Theories of personality, for example, stress the self as separate from others and the world. Decision making and responsibility rest with the individual and not the group. Indeed, there is an implicit assumption that a group is an aggregate of individuals. Theories of human development (Piaget, 1965; Erikson, 1963) place importance upon individuation as the foundation for maturity, healthy functioning, autonomy, and problem solving. Pedersen (1987, 1988) notes that U.S. societal emphasis on individualism may translate into individual competition for status, recognition, and achievement. Through socialization and education, one is taught the importance of individual identity and personal achievement.

Many psychologists fail to realize that the majority of societies and cultures in the world have a more collectivistic notion of identity; they do not define the psychosocial unit of operation as the individual (D. W. Sue & D. Sue, 1990). Indeed, these cultures may perceive individualism not as a positive orientation but as a hindrance to attaining enlightenment and spiritual goals (White & Parham, 1990). Many non-Western cultures reflect this emphasis. For example, Japanese has no equivalent for the personal pronoun *I*, and in India the term *atman* defines existence as participation with all things in the universe (Pedersen, 1988). One can understand how a different psychology of human existence may arise from such an orientation.

In counseling, the concept of individual autonomy appears in the following ways: (1) individual counseling, in which the I-Thou relationship is valued; (2) the responsibility for change rests with the individual; (3) problems reside primarily in the person; and (4) the road to mental health is intimately linked to increased autonomy, independence, and personal self-actualization. Ethnocentric helping professionals may potentially label their culturally different clients who possess a collectivistic worldview as "immature," "excessively dependent," "avoiding responsibility," "needing to break away from their family or group," and "not taking personal control of their own lives." Besides being inappropriate to the lifestyles and cultural values of such clients, such counseling practice may actually do great harm (Katz, 1985; D. W. Sue, et al., 1982). What appears to be needed is an approach to counseling that acknowledges the value of "individualism" as culture-specific, or representative of only one cultural group.

We have purposely chosen "individualism" to illustrate the culture-bound nature of Euro-American theories of counseling and psychotherapy because this value seems to particularly affect how Western psychologists view the world. However, other important culture-bound values have been identified as well (D. W. Sue, 1995b; D. W. Sue & D. Sue, 1990). First, counseling and psychotherapy is embedded in the paradigm of the physical sciences. Asking and answering questions about the human condition comes from valuing rational empiricism and symbolic logic (Goldman, 1976; Ponterotto, 1988b; Ponterotto & Casas, 1991). This quantitative, atomistic, linear, and reductionistic cause-effect approach clashes with many cultures that value a holistic, nonlinear, and harmonious approach to the world (Atkinson, Morten, & Sue, 1993; Ho, 1987; LaFromboise, Trimble, & Mohatt, 1990; Nishio & Bilmes, 1987; White & Parham, 1990). Second, openness and intimacy (self-disclosure) is often a prerequisite for effective treatment. Unfortunately, cultural and sociopolitical factors may make minority clients unwilling to reveal much about themselves or their families. For example, Asian Americans may consider it inappropriate to reveal personal matters because of strong cultural sanctions against such behavior (Nishio & Bilmes, 1987; Root, 1985; Sue & Morishima, 1982), and some African Americans may harbor a healthy distrust toward unconditional disclosures (Grier & Cobbs, 1968; Ridley, 1984). When the helping professional encounters such behaviors, he or she may draw invalid conclusions: The client is "paranoid," "guarded," "overly sensitive," and "suspicious." Third, the therapeutic process works best for clients who are verbal (use standard English), articulate, assertive, and able to express their feelings and emotions. A thorough review of cultural bias in these characteristics has been well documented, especially as they are applied to Asian Americans and Native Americans, who may well value restraint of strong feelings, indirectness, and subtlety in dealing with conflicts, and reliance on nonverbal communications (D. W. Sue & D. Sue, 1990). Other culture-bound values pointed out by numerous multicultural specialists include "insight processes and goals," "linear-static time emphasis," "competition and achievement," and even certain "definitions of the family" (Ho, 1987; Kluckhohn & Strodtbeck, 1961; Paniagua, 1994; Ponterotto & Casas, 1991; D. W. Sue, 1981).

THEORIES OF COUNSELING AS WORLDVIEWS

Multicultural psychologists have also noted that theories of counseling and psychotherapy represent a variety of worldviews, each with its own values, biases, and assumptions about human behavior (Ibrahim, 1985; Ivey, et al., 1993; Katz, 1985; D. W. Sue, 1978; D. W. Sue & D. Sue, 1977). A *world-view* has been defined as "how a person perceives his/her relationship to the world (nature, institutions, other people, etc.)," "one's conceptual frame-work," "our philosophy of life," and "the way we make meaning in the world." Worldviews are the reservoirs for our attitudes, values, opinions, and concepts; they influence how we think, make decisions, behave, and define events (D. W. Sue & D. Sue, 1990).

It has been suggested that worldviews are highly correlated with cultural upbringing and life experiences; for racial/ethnic minorities, experiences of oppression and the subordinate position assigned them in society plays an important role (Atkinson, Morten & Sue, 1993; Cross, 1971, 1991; Freire, 1972; Helms, 1984, 1990; Jackson, 1975; Jones, 1972). Given that schools of counseling and psychotherapy have arisen from Western-European contexts, the worldview they espouse may not be shared by racial/ethnic minority groups either in the United States or in different countries.

Ivey (1986) has proposed an especially intriguing concept: Contemporary theories of counseling represent "temporary cultures" even within the Western cultural milieu. Each has its own interpretation of reality, offering a different emphasis on the nature of people, the origin of disorders, standards for judging normality and abnormality, and therapeutic approach. The cultural context of each theory shapes the definition of the problem and influences the appropriate therapeutic response. Alternately, just as race, culture, ethnicity, and gender may influence and shape worldviews, the theories of counseling held by mental-health professionals may also influence their conceptions of the world. Ivey (1981, 1986) believes that different cultures generate different concepts, values, and belief systems, which are most likely to be reflected in language. Indeed, much evidence supports the contention that language is the carrier of one's culture (Chomsky, 1977; Freire, 1972; Padilla et al., 1991; D. W. Sue et al., 1992). Since counseling and psychotherapy as practiced in Euro-American societies are highly verbally oriented, they not only reflect the cultural values of that society, but may also generate verbalizations that allow one to interpret the differences and nuances that set them apart from one another.

One can find much support for this conclusion in the mental-health literature. For example, the generation of verbalizations (language structure and concepts) of clients considered to be "improving" begins to resemble those of their therapists (Ivey, et al., 1993). Studies of the two classic film series on counseling—*Three Approaches to Psychotherapy* (Shostrom, 1966) and *Three Approaches to Psychotherapy: II* (Shostrom, 1977), featuring such luminaries as Carl Rogers, Fritz Perls, Albert Ellis, Everett Shostrom, and Arnold Lazarus—make it clear that their counseling styles differ from one another in meaningful ways. Though internal consistency has been questioned in some cases, the overall conclusions are that theoretical orientations can be distinguished from one another and that the styles and skills (transcript analysis of the language used by the therapist) of the counselors appear highly correlated with their theoretical orientation (D. W. Sue, 1990).

If one accepts that (1) different theories represent different worldviews, (2) they affect communication and response styles, and (3) they generate their own language and constructs, then it is clear that a theoretical orientation may clash with the worldview of the culturally different client (Berman, 1979; Ivey, 1986; Ivey et al., 1993; Nwachuku & Ivey, 1991; D. W. Sue, 1990). For example, one may characterize the psychoanalytic worldview as stressing the importance of unconscious forces as determinants of present and future behavior; that is, the past determines the future, and problems reside within the person and can be abated only through insight and instrapsychic exploration. Culturally different clients who see problems residing in sociocultural variables (oppression, racism, and sexism) may find the assumptions surrounding the intrapsychic approach antagonistic to their worldviews. Existential-humanistic approaches stress the need for growth, attaining one's potential, self-actualization, client awareness of the present, and autonomy (freeing oneself from the expectations of others). However appropriate for many groups, the emphasis on "self," "independence," and "personal goals" may be at odds with groups that value the importance of family, community, or tribe (Ponterotto & Casas, 1991). Likewise, cognitive-behavioral theories assert that behaviors and cognitions are learned and that maladaptive ones can be unlearned. The approach is action oriented, focusing on time-limited treatments, and promotes a student-teacher relationship. While viewed favorably by some multicultural scholars (Casas, 1976; Ponterotto, 1988a) as possessing some relevance to minority groups because it stresses a person's active role in the environment, the cognitive-behavioral theories also reflect the Euro-American value system, with its emphasis on cause-effect, linear analysis, and the future. Those groups, such as Native American Indians, who view time as flowing, harmonious, and circular, may experience conflicts with such an approach.

In summary, these theories not only share a common Euro-American cultural context, but they may also represent "temporary cultures," each with their own distinguishing features. Ironically, the differences among contemporary theories of counseling seem to again reflect the Western proclivity toward analytical reductionism rather than a holistic integration. D. W. Sue (1992) believes that a major weakness of current counseling theories is that they concentrate on only one aspect of the human condition, minimizing or neglecting other dimensions. There are theories that emphasize the *feeling self* (humanistic-existential), others the *thinking self* (cognitive), while still others the *behaving* (behavioral) or *social* (family systems) selves. Most theories still need to address the possibility that people are all of these—*feeling, behaving, thinking,* and *social* beings—and probably much more—*biological, cultural, spiritual,* and *political* beings as well.

THE NEED FOR A METATHEORY

Given that traditional theories of counseling and psychotherapy have arisen from a Western cultural milieu, with each emphasizing an important but narrow aspect of the human condition; given that client populations vary in their cultural identity, requiring a more integrated and holistic approach; and given that the majority of people reside outside the Euro-American hemispheres, it is little wonder that current theories of counseling may have limited applicability to culturally different populations. Thus, continued belief in the universality of counseling theories does not only deny social reality, but also limits the availability of helping approaches to a culturally diverse population. Interestingly, most practicing clinicians seem to recognize the folly of following only one theoretical orientation. In a survey of clinical psychologists, 64% identified their approach as eclectic (Garfield & Kurtz, 1976, 1977). These therapists claim to remain open to all perspectives; they borrow diagnostic techniques and treatment strategies from all approaches and use them selectively with clients.

On the surface, it would appear that eclecticism might settle the diversity issue. Multicultural psychologists have consistently expressed the need to increase the repertoire of helping responses (Ivey, 1981, 1986; Pedersen, 1994; D. W. Sue, 1992; D. W. Sue & D. Sue, 1990) and recognize the legitimacy of alternative healing systems. Yet, the three most prevalent methods of integration pose problems. According to Arkowitz (1989, 1992), attempts at integration fall into three classes: technical eclecticism, theoretical integration, and common factorism. We shall now take a brief look at all three approaches.

Perhaps the most visible of the attempts to integrate varying perspectives is the *technical eclecticism* of Arnold Lazarus (1967). This approach has now been refined into a theoretical model called *multimodal behavior therapy* (Lazarus 1976, 1984). Although behavioral in basis, it embraces many cognitive and affective concepts as well. Therapeutic eclecticism has been defined as the "process of selecting concepts, methods, and strategies from a variety of current theories which work" (Brammer & Shostrom, 1984, p. 35). What is used in therapy should be supported empirically; attempts at theoretical integration are fruitless. It is possible, according to Lazarus, to work within one's theoretical framework and import other techniques without subscribing to the competing theory.

While technical eclecticism calls for openness and flexibility, it can also encourage the indiscriminate or inconsistent use of therapeutic techniques and concepts. As a result, therapists who call themselves eclectic have been severely criticized as confused, inconsistent, contradictory, lazy, and unsystematic (Patterson, 1980). The resulting negative reception of the term *eclecticism* has led to other terms (including *creative synthesis*, *masterful integration*, and *systematic eclecticism*) that are more positively associated with attempts to integrate, to be consistent, to validate, and to create a unique and personalized theoretical position. Indeed, evidence indicates that practitioners prefer the term *integrative* to *eclectic* (Norcross & Prochaska, 1988).

In a well-publicized debate between Lazarus and Messer (Lazarus & Messer, 1991), the latter argues in favor of *theoretical integration*. According to Messer, the theories one adopts affect how one views the world and defines reality. One cannot adopt a disembodied technique, free of its theoretical underpinnings. In any attempt to do so, some aspect of the theory or the therapeutic technique is changed; otherwise, the strategy proves ineffective.

This position has been dramatically demonstrated in the business world, where the concept of "quality circles" imported from Japan and applied to the U.S. business sector became a fad during the 1980s. Touted as a reason for Japanese business superiority, it was offered as a panacea to U.S. companies. Unfortunately, few recognized that a business strategy used in one culture might prove ineffective in another. Just as business practices arise from a cultural framework, therapeutic practices arise from a theoretical one (worldview). Thus, the position we take is more consistent with that of Messer; it is impossible to import a theoretically disembodied technique from any theory of counseling and psychotherapy without changing some aspect of the technique itself or the theory to which it is imported.

However, theoretical integration is not without its critics. The recognition of the limited nature of any one single approach to therapy has led some psychologists to attempt theoretical integration. See, for example, the recent attempts at rapprochement between psychoanalysis and behavior therapy (Goldfried, Greenberg, & Marmar, 1990. But even these sophisticated attempts have come under fire as empirically and theoretically inconsistent. Indeed, many theories and techniques seem almost diametrically opposed, and we have serious reservations whether true philosophical-epistemological integration can be attained. When one considers the difficulties of integrating theories *within* a culture, the problem increases astronomically with attempts to integrate helping systems developed in *other* cultures.

The *common factors* approach attempts to identify characteristics of helping strategies that schools of counseling and psychotherapy share (Kleinke, 1994; Schofield, 1964) or other cultures (Das, 1987; Kakar, 1982; Lee, 1993). For example, "naming" the disorder, the "credibility" attributed to the healer, and the "special relationship" that exists between the client and helper are a few commonalities identified. However, there are two difficulties with this attempt at integration. First, attempts to extract commonalities may lead to an overly general and ambiguous characteristic that one cannot translate into practice. Second, such an approach must still deal with the multiplicity of differences among the systems of helping.

Though technical eclecticism, theoretical integration, and common factorism may broaden the application of counseling to a diverse population, we believe that the most fruitful approach to counseling and therapy is the development of a comprehensive theoretical structure, a metatheory (Ivey, 1986; Ivey et al., 1993; D. W. Sue, 1995b). Such a development would offer several advantages. First, it would provide an organizational framework that would allow psychologists to outline the theoretical, philosophical, ethical, political, and professional underpinnings of the many counseling/helping approaches. We believe that the metatheory would be *culture-centered* (Pedersen & Ivey, 1993), allowing one to view each theory from its cultural perspective. In that manner, professional helpers would be in a better position to unmask and demystify the values, biases, and assumptions about human behavior made by each theoretical orientation. Second, epistomologically conflicting positions could be readily accommodated into such a framework, because the integrity of each theory would be preserved. Differences in worldview among the theories would not be viewed as antagonistic but as potentially complementary or as describing a different aspect of the human condition. Third, the evolution of established theories, direct attempts at integration, or the development of new theories would be continuously acknowledged and reclassified in the metatheoretical framework.

Last, our "theory of theories" would apply not only to Euro-American culture, but also Asian, African, Latin-American, and other world cultures. To do so, however, would require the study of indigenous systems of healing and their inclusion as legitimate forms of helping (Das, 1987; Harner, 1990; Kakar, 1982; Lee, Oh, & Mountcastle, 1992).

CHAPTER 2

BASIC ASSUMPTIONS OF A THEORY OF MULTICULTURAL COUNSELING AND THERAPY

It may seem presumptuous of us to propose a theory of multicultural counseling and therapy (MCT), but it appears that the field has matured to the point where doing so would prove beneficial for theory, research, practice, and training. We are aware, however, that our metatheory of MCT represents only one of many possible paradigms. We have chosen to work with some of the MCT propositions originally proposed by D. W. Sue (1995b), who suggests they be refined with the development of corollaries and basic tenets. As much as possible, we have attempted to ground the propositions and corollaries in the available research and theory of multiculturalism.

PROPOSITION 1

MCT theory is a metatheory of counseling and psychotherapy. A theory about theories, it offers an organizational framework for understanding the numerous helping approaches that humankind has developed. It recognizes that both theories of counseling and psychotherapy developed in the Western world and those helping models indigenous to non-Western cultures are neither inherently right or wrong, good or bad. Each theory represents a different worldview.

Corollary 1A

MCT theory has evolved from a method of helping members of one cultural group relate to members of different cultural groups into a metatheoretical perspective that recognizes the centrality and primary importance of culture as an internalized, subjective perspective. It rests on the assumption that all theories of counseling are culture-specific and that their values, assumptions, and philosophical bases must be made explicit.

Corollary 1B
Each theory of counseling and psychotherapy was developed in a particular cultural context, and, to the extent that each theory is appropriate to a particular cultural context, it will likely be biased toward contrasting cultural contexts. MCT theory uses the theoretical approach most consistent with the life experiences and cultural perspectives of the client, although at times it may be useful to draw on perspectives from other cultures.

Corollary 1C
Different worldviews lead toward different determinations of client concerns. For example, in traditional Western psychotherapy, psychodynamic approaches may view client issues as generated in unconscious developmental history while cognitive-behavioral approaches may see the same issues as a result of social learning. This difference in worldview has tended to result in vastly different modes of conceptualizing and treating clients. Furthermore, both of these systems focus on the idea that the "problem" lies in the individual. Recognizing the usefulness of this Eurocentric view, MCT theory would point out the importance of seeing the individual in context, considering the cultural background of the client, and finding culturally appropriate solutions that may vastly change the way that therapy is conducted.

Specifically, MCT theory might help the individual see his or her problem in context, draw group or family members into the treatment, and use non-Western therapeutic approaches as appropriate to the client. Historically, traditional Western diagnosis and therapy (e.g., the DSM-IV) see the "problem" in the client and fail to consider contextual issues.

Corollary 1D
MCT theory combines elements of psychodynamic, behavioral, humanistic, biogenic, and other perspectives to the extent that the person's culturally learned assumptions shape the unconscious in the psychodynamic view, act as reinforcing contingencies in the behavioral view, and define the meaning of person-centeredness in the humanistic view. They are also influenced and limited by the biogenic view and meaningfully impacted by other views.

Corollary 1E
Traditionally, as a result of counseling or therapy with counselors of differing theoretical orientations, clients tend to generate sentences (language) resembling those of their therapists or counselors. MCT theory seeks to work with and learn from clients, thus minimizing this potential problem. In coconstruction, helping professionals work *with* the client rather than *on* the client. That is, the client is viewed as an active and equal participant in defining both problems and solutions.

Corollary 1F

MCT theory is ultimately concerned with freeing individuals, families, groups, and organizations to generate new ways of thinking, feeling, and acting—living with intentionality—both within their own cultural framework and with understanding and respect for other worldviews.

Corollary 1G

Given that theories of human behavior are defined by their ability to predict future behavior and explain past behavior, MCT theory qualifies as a theory by predicting failure from the overemphasis of either cultural differences or cultural similarities and success from a combined perspective. Overemphasizing cultural differences produces a stereotyped, exclusionary, politicized, and combative perspective based on zero-sum assumptions. Overemphasizing cultural similarities results in exploitation of less powerful by more powerful groups and the pretense of a melting pot that disregards essential features of cultural identity.

PROPOSITION 2

Both counselor and client identities are formed and embedded in multiple levels of experiences (individual, group, and universal) and contexts (individual, family, and cultural milieu). The totality and interrelationships of experiences and contexts must be the focus of treatment.

Corollary 2A

All people possess an individual, a group, and a universal level of identity. People are unique, share commonalities with their reference groups (race, culture, ethnicity, religion, gender, sexual orientation, etc.), and share at least one level of identity (*Homo sapiens*). Because these levels of identity are fluid and ever changing, the salience of one over the other also changes. Though individuals and groups may show preference for one over the other, the effective helping professional validates all levels and strives to relate to that which is most salient and important to the person at a given time. Unfortunately, counselors and psychotherapists have traditionally tended to relate to clients at only the individual or universal levels, thereby negating group identities.

Corollary 2B

The importance of the person-environment interaction is basic to MCT theory. A person's identity is formed and continually influenced by his or her context. Working effectively with clients requires an understanding of how the individual is embedded in the family, which in turn requires an understanding of how the family is affected by its place in a pluralistic culture.

Corollary 2C
The complexity of cultural identity presumes that each client will be able to identify shared features of comembership with each counselor no matter how different they may appear from one another and that this common ground will provide a useful point of reference in developing a successful counseling relationship.

Corollary 2D
The complexity of cultural identity presumes that each client will be able to identify cultural assumptions unique to the client and/or the counselor no matter how similar they may appear to each other and that these subtle or obvious cultural differences provide a potential for misunderstanding in the counseling process.

Corollary 2E
Culture is a complex construct that one can define in multiple ways but is defined here as any group that shares a theme or issue(s). Language, gender, ethnicity/race, spirituality, sexual preference, age, physical issues, socioeconomic class, and survivors of trauma are a few examples of cultural groups with whom counselors and therapists work. Virtually all clients who come for help have cultural issues underlying their concerns.

Corollary 2F
Counselors and psychotherapists bring their own cultural background to the session, and the worldviews associated with their cultural groupings deeply affect the way they conduct therapy. For example, an English-speaking, Irish-American, Catholic, heterosexual, 55-year-old, blind, and upper-middle-class woman who is a cancer and rape survivor brings an important store of cultural wisdom to the session. This hypothetical therapist may practice eclectically from the psychodynamic frame of reference. Though her worldview offers much to clients, it has many potential limitations for clients with different life experience and worldviews than hers.

Corollary 2G
The salient cultural feature (individual, group, or universal) will change for the client during the interview and a skilled counselor will be able to track accurately that changing salience from one cultural referent to another. That is, the importance of the client's various cultural affiliations will change over time.

Corollary 2H
Cultural identity constantly evolves for both client and counselor, each shaped by their experiences over time. Cultural identity is defined as a dynamic rather than a static concept.

PROPOSITION 3

Cultural identity development is a major determinant of counselor and client attitudes toward the self, others of the same group, others of a different group, and the dominant group. These attitudes, which may be manifested in affective and behavioral dimensions, are strongly influenced not only by cultural variables but also by the dynamics of dominant-subordinate relationships among culturally different groups. The level or stage of racial/cultural identity will both influence how clients and counselors define the problem and dictate what they believe to be appropriate counseling/therapy goals and processes.

Corollary 3A

Developing a cultural identity represents a cognitive, emotional, and behavioral progression through identifiable and measurable levels of consciousness, or stages. Though theorists vary in the specifics, these stages appear to follow this sequence: (1) naiveté and embedded awareness of self as a cultural being, (2) encountering the reality of cultural issues, (3) naming of these cultural issues, (4) reflection on the meaning of self as a cultural being, and (5) some form of internalization and multiperspective thought about self-in-system. With each stage comes a different attitude toward oneself (self-identity) and others (reference-group identity or differences).

Corollary 3B

Each client (individual, family, group, organization) has multiple cultural identities, which most likely will not progress or expand at the same rate. For example, a man may be quite aware of his identity as a Navaho but less aware of himself as a heterosexual or Vietnam veteran. As such, comprehensive MCT may focus on helping him and others like him become ever more aware of the impact of cultural issues on their being.

Corollary 3C

Given Corollary 3B, it seems appropriate to change the traditional wording *self-concept* to *conceptions of self-in-relation*. MCT would suggest that treating the individual, family, or group in isolation may ultimately defeat interconnectedness.

Corollary 3D

Professional helpers to date have insufficiently considered issues of dominance and power in their helping theories. The very words *counselor* and *client*, or *therapist* and *patient* imply an important hierarchy of power. Historically, much of traditional Western therapy has served a racist, sexist, homophobic, and classic culture. MCT recognizes the problems inherent in the power imbalance present in current counseling and therapy and works toward power sharing and mutual construction of therapeutic strategies and goals between therapist and client. Much feminist therapy and culturally sensitive therapy offers this egalitarian approach.

Corollary 3E
MCT counselors or therapists constantly seek to expand awareness of cultural-identity issues for both themselves and their clients. There is no end to cultural-identity development.

Corollary 3F
Culturally learned assumptions are the primary features of each person's identity or concept of self as a learned perspective. Theories of identity that disregard the cultural context are therefore likely to misinterpret the basic, culturally learned assumptions that form the foundation of identity.

Corollary 3G
Because power differences influence each group's view of itself and others, MCT theory recognizes the importance of these differences among culturally defined groups.

Corollary 3H
Misunderstanding will likely occur when a client's behavior is interpreted or assessed outside of its cultural context and without regard to shared positive expectations of common cultural ground between therapist and client. Identical behaviors may express different or negative expectations while behaviors different from one another may express similar or positive expectations.

Corollary 3I
Cultural identities are complex but not chaotic; culturally learned patterns provide orderly and systematic narratives in which each part of the client's identity relates dynamically to the whole. The client's perspective must be understood historically and comprehensively, according to these narratives.

Corollary 3J
Two people from culturally different backgrounds may disagree without one necessarily being right and the other wrong. Because clients respond in ways consistent with their culturally learned assumptions, their logic may lead them in a different direction than others' reasoning.

Corollary 3K
Because culture influences both the process and the content of thinking in counseling and therapy, linear thinking may be appropriate for understanding some clients, while nonlinear thinking may be appropriate for others.

Corollary 3L
Individual differences and cultural differences are not the same. Skin color at birth is a clear example of an individual difference, while the meaning of that skin color to self and others as it has evolved over time is a clear example of a cultural difference.

Corollary 3M
MCT theory recognizes the dangers of unintentional racism as well as overt and intentional racism. The unintentional racist suffers from misattribution toward culturally different people and settings that reduce those people's effectiveness and efficiency as well as cause pain to others.

PROPOSITION 4

The effectiveness of MCT is most likely enhanced when the counselor uses modalities and defines goals consistent with the life experiences and cultural values of the client. No single approach is equally effective across all populations and life situations. The ultimate goal of multicultural counselor/therapist training is to expand the repertoire of helping responses available to the professional, regardless of theoretical orientation.

Corollary 4A
At least two valid approaches to culturally sensitive helping exist: the universal and the culture-specific. MCT uses the universal approach. However, focusing on broad, universal issues can become too general and dilute efforts for individual, family, group, or organizational change. For example, with clients who suffer the extremes of racism or homophobia, or who struggle to cope with cancer, it is appropriate to focus on the most salient area for the client. Or, if a client identifies more with her lesbian than her Asian issues, a culture-specific approach may be beneficial.

Corollary 4B
One can generate new theories and strategies by starting from a cultural frame of reference. At this point, helping theory is dominated by the creations of white male Europeans. New ideas from Asia, Africa, Latin countries, and the Native-American tradition can and will expand treatment alternatives, not only for people from those cultures, but for all others as well. Even a theory generated in one cultural context may prove useful for culturally different people; however, the theory and technique must be engaged in from a culturally sensitive and respectful frame of reference.

Corollary 4C
A system of knowledge and belief results from the interplay of innate

mechanisms, from genetically determined maturation processes, and from interaction with the social and physical environment. The task of the counselor is to account for the system constructed by the mind in the course of this interaction. The particular system of human knowledge that has so far been most accessible to understanding is the system of human language. Because counseling and psychotherapy are language-based, and worldviews exist in language, it is vital that awareness of the power of a dominant language (whether that of a therapeutic theory or that of a culture) over a client or client system be fully recognized.

Corollary 4D
To the extent that the client differs culturally from the counselor in status, affiliation, or ethnographic or demographic variables, the counseling process will prove difficult, and to the extent that the counselor and client are similar the counseling process will be facilitated.

Corollary 4E
In matching a client with a counselor, considerations of cultural similarity must come second to client preferences, which may be for a culturally different counselor. An assumption that clients will prefer culturally similar counselors is itself an example of stereotyping and should be avoided.

Corollary 4F
Counselors culturally different from their clients can learn multicultural skills to become effective with those clients. Under these conditions, cultural differences may actually enhance the counseling relationship.

Corollary 4G
Each intervention may be appropriate for one client in one cultural context and inappropriate for another client in another cultural context. Counselors must increase their repertoires of variations for each counseling skill to match the right skill in the right way with the right client at the right time.

Corollary 4H
Sympathy—how the counselor would feel if he or she were in a particular situation—is less appropriate than empathy, which focuses on how the client actually in that particular situation feels. Do not do unto others as you would have them do unto you—they might want something different.

PROPOSITION 5

MCT theory stresses the importance of multiple helping roles developed by many culturally different groups and societies. Besides the basic one-on-one encounter aimed at remediation in the individual, these roles often involve larger social units, systems intervention, and prevention. That is, the conventional roles of counseling and psychotherapy are only one of many others available to the helping professional.

Corollary 5A

Community resources can enrich therapy. A network of treatment alternatives can and should be used to support individual or family therapy. These may include the extended family, people in the neighborhood, spiritual advisers, and government officials. No one person or group has a monopoly on the helping process.

Corollary 5B

In multicultural counseling, formal methods in formal settings are supplemented by informal methods and/or settings, which counselors use when appropriate. For instance, talk therapy may not be the therapy of choice.

Corollary 5C

Though the Western meaning of *counseling* developed from a Euro-American academic setting in the 20th century, counseling has been available historically whenever individuals have helped other individuals with personal problems.

Corollary 5D

Because counseling and counselors have frequently been stereotyped as protecting the system and the status quo against the minority, individual counseling sometimes suffers a stigma in certain cultural settings. That is, in some cultures, individuals sought out as experts in helping solve personal problems may be offended if called "counselors."

Corollary 5E

Because contemporary ethical guidelines are based on a culturally narrow perspective of counseling, the multicultural counselor might need to violate or reframe particular ethical guidelines in order to counsel in an ethically appropriate manner.

Corollary 5F

Because problems usually develop in a cultural context, the definition of counseling as one-on-one problem solving may be superficial. Problems may be defined as residing in the family, group, or community. Counselors must recognize each problem in its cultural context and attend to the network of support systems surrounding the client.

Corollary 5G
While a one-directional description of counseling might emphasize outcome measures of pleasure, happiness, or other good feelings, a two-directional description of counseling might stress the importance of meaning that incorporates both pain and pleasure, happiness and sadness, and good and bad. In addition, a successful outcome will usually consider the individual-in-context specifically, as a result of counseling that includes the whole system of individuals, families, groups, and communities.

Corollary 5H
A multicultural perspective in counseling contributes to accurate assessment and diagnosis in every therapeutic setting, not just for minority populations.

PROPOSITION 6

The liberation of consciousness is a basic goal of MCT theory. Whereas self-actualization, discovery of the role of the past in the present, or behavior change have been traditional goals of Western psychotherapy and counseling, MCT emphasizes the importance of expanding personal, family, group, and organizational consciousness of the place of self-in-relation, family-in-relation, and organization-in-relation. This results in therapy that is not only ultimately contextual in orientation, but that also draws on traditional methods of healing from many cultures.

Corollary 6A
The process of *conscientizacao* or critical consciousness is a constant dimension of the helping process. Rather than focus on individual, family, group, or organizational change solely, the MCT counselor constantly considers the relation of clients to their entire context.

Corollary 6B
There is a strong psychoeducational component to MCT theory. The role of the counselor or therapist often includes teaching the client about the underlying cultural dimensions of present concerns. Concomitantly, the counselor or therapist follows strict ethical standards not to violate the present cultural awareness of the client.

Corollary 6C
MCT therapists or counselors draw on both Western and non-European systems of helping. They constantly attempt to adapt techniques and theories respectfully to the client's cultural background and special needs. There is no end to such development.

TABLE 2.1
PROPOSITIONS/COROLLARIES UNDERLYING MCT THEORY

PROPOSITION 1
MCT is a metatheory of counseling and psychotherapy.

Corollary 1A
MCT theory assumes that all theories of counseling and therapy are culture centered, the values, assumptions, and philosophical bases of which must be made explicit.

Corollary 1B
Each theory of counseling and psychotherapy was developed in a particular cultural context. To the extent that each theory is appropriate to a particular cultural context, it is likely to be biased against contrasting cultural contexts.

Corollary 1C
Different worldviews lead toward different constructions of client concerns.

Corollary 1D
MCT theory combines elements of psychodynamic, behavioral, humanistic, biogenic, and other perspectives to the extent that the person's culturally learned assumptions share these salient features.

Corollary 1E
MCT theory seeks to work with and learn from clients through the process of coconstruction, thus minimizing potential problems of oppression.

Corollary 1F
MCT theory is ultimately concerned with freeing individuals, families, groups, and organizations to generate new ways of thinking, feeling, and acting—living with intentionality—both within their own cultural framework and with understanding and respect for other worldviews.

Corollary 1G
MCT theory qualifies as a theory by predicting that failure results from the overemphasis of either cultural differences or cultural similarities, and that success results from a combined perspective.

PROPOSITION 2

Both counselor and client identities are formed and embedded in multiple levels of experiences (individual, group, and universal) and contexts (individual, family, and cultural milieu). The totality and interrelationships of experiences and contexts must be the focus of treatment.

Corollary 2A

MCT theory acknowledges that all individuals possess individual, group, and universal levels of identity that are fluid and varying in salience.

Corollary 2B

The importance of the person-environment interaction is basic to MCT theory. A person's identity is formed and continually influenced by her or his context.

Corollary 2C

The complexity of cultural identity presumes that each client will be able to identify shared features of comembership with each counselor no matter how different they may appear from each other.

Corollary 2D

The complexity of cultural identity presumes that each client will be able to identify cultural assumptions unique to the client and/or the counselor no matter how similar they may appear to each other.

Corollary 2E

Culture is a complex construct that one can define in multiple ways.

Corollary 2F

Counselors and psychotherapists bring their own cultural background to the session; the worldviews associated with their cultural groupings deeply affect the way they conduct therapy.

Corollary 2G

The salient cultural feature (individual, group, or universal) will change for the client during the interview, and a skilled counselor will be able to accurately track that changing salience from one cultural referent to another.

Corollary 2H

Cultural identity is a constantly evolving perspective for both client and counselor as each is shaped by different experiences over time.

PROPOSITION 3

Development of cultural identity is a major determinant of counselor and client attitudes toward the self, others of the same group, others of a different group, and the dominant group. These attitudes are strongly influenced not only by cultural variables but also by the dynamics of a dominant-subordinate relationship among culturally different groups.

Corollary 3A

Developing a cultural identity represents a cognitive/emotional/behavioral progression and expansion through identifiable and measurable levels of consciousness, or stages.

Corollary 3B

Each client (individual, family, group, organization) has multiple cultural identities, which most likely will not progress or expand at the same rate.

Corollary 3C

Treating the individual, family, or group in isolation may ultimately defeat interconnectedness.

Corollary 3D

Issues of dominance and power have been insufficiently considered in helping theories.

Corollary 3E

MCT counselors or therapists constantly seek to expand awareness of cultural-identity issues for both themselves and their clients.

Corollary 3F

Culturally learned assumptions are the primary features of each person's identity or concept of self as a learned perspective.

Corollary 3G

Because power differences influence each group's view of itself and others, MCT theory recognizes the importance of these differences among culturally defined groups.

Corollary 3H

Misunderstanding will likely occur when a client's behavior is interpreted or assessed outside of its cultural context and without regard to shared positive expectations of common cultural ground between therapist and client.

Corollary 3I
Cultural identities are complex but not chaotic; culturally learned patterns provide orderly and systematic narratives in a dialogical perspective where each part is related to the whole of the client's identity.

Corollary 3J
Two people from culturally different backgrounds may disagree without one necessarily being right and the other wrong.

Corollary 3K
Because culture influences both the process and the content of thinking in counseling and therapy, linear thinking may be appropriate for understanding some clients, while nonlinear thinking may be appropriate for others.

Corollary 3L
Individual differences and cultural differences are not the same.

Corollary 3M
MCT theory recognizes the dangers of unintentional as well as intentional racism.

PROPOSITION 4
The effectiveness of MCT theory is most likely enhanced when the counselor uses modalities and defines goals consistent with the life experiences/cultural values of the client.

Corollary 4A
MCT theory recognizes at least two valid conceptual frameworks for culturally sensitive helping: the universal and the culture-specific.

Corollary 4B
One can generate new theories and strategies by starting from a cultural frame of reference.

Corollary 4C
Because counseling and psychotherapy are language-based phenomena, and worldviews exist in language, it is vital that awareness of the power of a dominant language (whether that of a therapeutic theory or that of a culture) over a client or client system be fully recognized.

Corollary 4D
To the extent that the client is culturally different from or similar to the

counselor in status, affiliation, or ethnographic or demographic variables, the counseling process will be blocked or facilitated.

Corollary 4E
In matching a client with a counselor, considerations of cultural similarity must come second to client preferences, which may be for a culturally different counselor.

Corollary 4F
Counselors culturally different from their clients can learn multicultural skills to become effective with those clients.

Corollary 4G
Each intervention may be appropriate for one client in one cultural context and inapproriate for another client in another cultural context.

Corollary 4H
MCT theory recognizes that sympathy—how the counselor would feel if he or she were in a particular situation—is less appropriate than empathy, which focuses on how the client actually in that particular situation feels.

PROPOSITION 5
MCT theory stresses the importance of multiple helping roles developed by many culturally different groups and societies. Besides the one-on-one encounter aimed at remediation in the individual, these roles often involve larger social units, systems intervention, and prevention.

Corollary 5A
Community resources, which include the extended family, people in the neighborhood, spiritual advisers, and government officials, can enrich therapy.

Corollary 5B
In multicultural counseling, formal methods in formal settings are supplemented by informal methods and/or settings.

Corollary 5C
Though the Western meaning of *counseling* developed from a Euro-American academic setting in the 20th century, counseling has been available historically whenever individuals helped other individuals with personal problems.

Corollary 5D

Because counseling and counselors have frequently been stereotyped as protecting the system and the status quo against the minority, individual counseling has sometimes suffered a stigma in multicultural settings.

Corollary 5E

Because contemporary ethical guidelines are based on a culturally narrow perspective of counseling, the multicultural counselor might need to violate or reframe particular ethical guidelines in order to counsel in an ethically appropriate manner.

Corollary 5F

Because problems usually develop in a cultural context, the definition of counseling as one-on-one problem solving may be superficial. Problems may be defined as residing in the family, group, or community.

Corollary 5G

While a one-directional description of counseling might emphasize outcome measures of pleasure, happiness, or other good feelings, a two-directional description of counseling in an asymmetrical balance perspective might stress the importance of meaning that incorporates both pain and pleasure, happiness and sadness, and good and bad.

Corollary 5H

A multicultural perspective in counseling contributes to accurate assessment and diagnosis in every therapeutic setting, not just for minority populations.

PROPOSITION 6

The liberation of consciousness is a basic goal of MCT theory. MCT theory emphasizes the importance of expanding personal, family, group, and organizational consciousness of the place of self-in-relation, family-in-relation, and organization-in-relation. This results in therapy that is not only ultimately contextual in orientation, but also draws on traditional methods of healing from many cultures.

Corollary 6A

The process of *conscientizacao* or critical consciousness is a constant dimension of the helping process.

Corollary 6B

There is a strong psychoeducational component to MCT theory. The role of the counselor or therapist often includes teaching the client about the underlying cultural dimensions of present concerns.

Corollary 6C

MCT therapists or counselors draw on both Western and non-European systems of helping.

CHAPTER 3

RESEARCH, PRACTICE, AND TRAINING IMPLICATIONS OF MCT THEORY

Any theory of counseling and psychotherapy must meet certain important criteria. First, it must state its assumptions and premises. We have presumably met this criterion for MCT, although the addition of new propositions and corollaries, and revisions of old assumptions, will continue for some time. Propositions and corollaries need to be internally consistent, and clinical and research data over time will, no doubt, lead to new assumptions and revisions.

Second, a good theory should allow one to generate a set of hypotheses from it that one can test empirically and clinically. Because they are so new, our six propositions and their corollaries have not been the direct focus of research. Even so, because we formulated them from a review of multicultural-counseling literature, we believe they show promise as an integrating force in the field.

Third, an effective theory should have implications for organizing existing knowledge and for placing it in a context meaningful to researchers, practitioners, and training programs. We shall address this issue in this chapter.

Finally, we add a fourth criterion which seems to us necessary as we consider the idea of a culture-centered theory. Culture-centeredness requires one to realize that each theoretical statement is a construction, a set of concepts developed in relation to environmental contingencies. For example, we use English, still often rely on Western concepts of theoretical and research validity, and may even, at times, fall into Cartesian dualism (although our intent is to be inclusive, we tend to occasionally place MCT theory against traditional theory). As such, we consider this contribution itself culture-bound and necessarily open to continued criticism and evaluation.

RESEARCH IMPLICATIONS
OF MCT THEORY

The six major propositions and their accompanying corollaries contain clear implications for counseling research. They suggest that past and current research on culturally different populations is culture-bound (Ponterotto & Casas, 1991; D. W. Sue & D. Sue, 1990) and, at best, leads to an extremely narrow view of the meaning and importance of culture in the helping process. At worst, research on racial/ethnic minorities, for example, has been characterized as (1) portraying racial/ethnic minorities as pathological, maladjusted, deviant, or delinquent because of Eurocentric standards of comparison, (2) reflecting the social biases of Eurocentric society, (3) formulating policies and practices that have subjugated and done great harm to minority communities, (4) excluding the contributions of minority psychologists in the traditional counseling literature, and (5) formerly benefiting those conducting the research (obtaining research grants and tenure) rather than contributing to the betterment of the groups being studied (Ivey, 1993c; Mio & Iwamasa, 1993; Parham, 1993b; D. W. Sue, 1993; D. W. Sue & D. Sue, 1990; D. W. Sue & S. Sue, 1972).

In April 1993, *The Counseling Psychologist* recognized the importance of these points by devoting nearly a whole issue of the journal to the topic "White American Researchers and Multicultural Counseling." Perhaps the most comprehensive discussion of research issues and new directions needed in the field is found in Ponterotto and Casas's work (1991). In this chapter, we shall focus our analysis on two aspects of multicultural counseling research: new topical research directions and the need to incorporate alternative research paradigms (Goldman, 1989; Helms, 1989; Hoshmand, 1989; Ponterotto & Casas, 1991; D. W. Sue & D. Sue, 1990).

Multicultural Research Focus

A historical analysis of the counseling and mental-health literature indicates that the portrayal of racial/ethnic minorities has often been extremely unfavorable (Mays, 1985; D. W. Sue & S. Sue, 1972; A. Thomas & Sillen, 1972; White & Parham, 1991). These portrayals are partly due to the "cultural encapsulation" of the counseling profession (Wrenn, 1962; 1985), which has operated from research and practice models viewing differences (both physical and cultural) as deviant (D. W. Sue, 1981; D. W. Sue & D. Sue, 1990; White & Parham, 1990). For example, such phrases as *culturally deprived, culturally deficient,* and *culturally disadvantaged* have frequently been used to explain differences between White and minority subjects on measures of intelligence, academic ability, school performance, personality, vocational selection, poverty, unemployment, crime, delinquency and mental illness. Such an ethnocentric perspective fails to take into consideration both cultural and professional biases in research focus and approach. First, the phrase *culturally impoverished* and others like it are conceptually contradictory. They suggest, for example, that African Americans arrived in the United States without a culture or "less of one." Because all groups inherit a culture, such terminology only makes sense if recast into its true ethnocentric meaning: (1) racial/ethnic minority groups lack the "right" culture, and (2) Euro-American culture is more desirable than others (D. W. Sue & D. Sue, 1990). Second, the counseling and mental-health professions relied too much on studying the individual in explaining human behavior (D. W. Sue, 1978) and focusing on problems, disorders, and limitations. The result has been a neglect in the study of wider forces affecting behavior and a disregard of positive attributes and sources of strength in minority populations. To overcome these cultural and professional limitations in research, we advocate the following:

1. Counseling research must start with the premise that culture always influences how one asks and answers questions about the human condition (Atkinson, Morten & Sue, 1993; Pedersen, 1994; D. W. Sue, Arredondo, & McDavis, 1993). One needs to go back and review existing research from a cultural and contextual frame. This metareview will undoubtedly lead to clearer and more precise formulations for MCT theory and will suggest important new directions for the future. Culture is not something tangential or insignificant to the research process. For example, the instruments used to gather data in one cultural context are necessarily biased in a different one (Pedersen, 1994). Attempts at producing fair or culture-free instrumentation suffer from the assumption that such instruments are equally familiar or unfamiliar (an impossible precondition). Ponterotto & Casas (1991), in surveying the studies on counseling, conclude that researchers (1) continue to rely on culturally biased measures, (2) do not apparently attempt to exercise cultural sensitivity in the interpretation of results, and (3) seldom adequately describe the subjects' cultural backgrounds. In a comprehensive study of articles published in the *Journal of Counseling Psychology* from 1976–1986, Ponterotto (1988) found only 5.7% focused on racial/ethnic minority variables. Thus, only a small proportion of studies published in counseling journals include race, ethnicity, or culture, and an even smaller number include them as independent variables.

2. A fundamental change in counseling and therapy research occurs when one moves from examining the individual or self to considering the self-in-relation and people-in-context. MCT theory states that process and outcome research almost uniformly consider the individual or family as the psychosocial unit of study (Ivey et al., 1993). The immense amounts of data

on individual change give minimal attention to how this change relates to other individuals, family members, groups, organizations, and the community. There is a strong need to refocus our research to deal with wider social units (social systems or organizations) in understanding the totality of the human experience (Sue, 1995a). This shift is important not only in understanding the collectivistic attitudes of other cultural groups and the importance of sociopolitical forces in affecting behavior, but also in understanding organizational change in a multicultural society. For example, burgeoning interest in multicultural organizational development (Barr & Strong, 1987; T. L. Cross, Bazron, Dennis, & Isaacs, 1989; Foster, Jackson, Cross, Jackson, & Hardiman, 1988; D. W. Sue, 1991a; 1995a) has provided valuable information about how to manage a diverse work force effectively; increase recruitment, retention, and promotion (graduation) of nontraditionals in the work force and in education; and provide culturally relevant education and training for mental-health professionals.

3. Counseling research would benefit from the study of positive attributes and characteristics of racial/ethnic minority groups that have helped them deal with the stresses of everyday life (Ponterotto & Casas, 1991; D. W. Sue & D. Sue, 1990; D. W. Sue & S. Sue, 1972). Too often, the mental-health literature has focused on the pathological characteristics of minority groups, unwittingly perpetuating stereotypes (Mio & Iwamasa, 1993) and neglecting the adaptive strengths of minority communities. For example, Asian Americans tend to underutilize traditional mental-health facilities and to prematurely terminate counseling when compared with their White counterparts (Sue & Morishima, 1982). Research on these findings has been generally directed at an intrapsychic explanation (Asians tend not to act out their conflicts, somaticize their problems more, feel shame or disgrace at seeking help, etc.) or one that explores how current counseling strategies may discriminate against them (D. W. Sue, 1994). Little attention is given to exploring the natural help-giving networks (such as family reliance) present in almost all culturally different groups, or those adaptive mechanisms developed as a result of experiences in the wider society (Pedersen, 1994; Pedersen & Ivey, 1993; Sue, 1995b). Likewise, some investigators have identified what they label as "cultural strengths" in African-American families (helpful extended relatives, religious worldview, Black pride and culture, training in surviving societal racism, etc.), which should be cultivated in therapy (Stevenson & Renard, 1993). One especially revealing study lends credence to the belief that African-American parents of severely mentally ill offspring handle the stress better and exhibit higher coping mastery than their White counterparts (Pickett, Vraniak, Cook, & Cohler, 1993). The authors attribute these differences to the African-American families' "strength through adversity" experience and to better training in dealing with life's strains.

In addition to these three recommendations, Ponterotto and Casas (1991) outline 12 areas for further multicultural counseling research: (1) Accurate epidemiological data on the incidence and prevalence of psychological problems among the various racial/ethnic groups are needed to formulate culturally sensitive assessment and intervention strategies; (2) Minority identity-development models appear to hold much promise in understanding not only sociopolitical effects on development but also differences within groups; (3) Intensified research is needed to understand the mechanisms and operation of Eurocentric political and educational systems that deny equal access and opportunities for all; (4) Related to the third point is the need to research and develop effective prejudice-prevention programs; (5) Instead of constantly placing minorities under a microscope, researchers need to focus on white racial identity development as well; (6) A balanced perspective is needed to research the assets and strengths of minority communities; (7) Researchers need to place greater importance in studying diversity within groups; (8) Because race seems to be socially defined and often confining, bicultural and biracial identity needs greater study; (9) Studies need to broaden their population base beyond "college students and/or adults"; (10) More research is needed on primary prevention, such as parent-training programs; (11) Researchers need to develop assessment, testing, and general instrumentation applicable to minority populations; and (12) Research needs to balance the study of *emic* (culture-specific) and *etic* (culturally universal) aspects of the helping process.

Alternative Research Methods

Graduate training programs in counseling psychology have traditionally considered objective, quantitative, linear, reductionistic research as the preferred method of investigating the human condition (Goldman, 1976; Hoshmand, 1989; D. W. Sue & D. Sue, 1990). Though the positivistic tradition of reductive experimentation has contributed to an understanding of human behavior, it has also received considerable criticism (Goldman, 1989; Helms, 1989; Hoshmand, 1989; Howard, 1991; Polkinghorne, 1988; Sarbin, 1986). Two of these criticisms appear central to MCT theory.

First, traditional research paradigms make epistemological assumptions that may not be shared by non-Western cultures and societies. For example, Western paradigms assume that one can study phenomena objectively, that the universe operates under linear cause-effect laws, that measurements will remain constant, and that universal statements of truths exist (Hoshmand, 1989). Yet, empirical reality is often influenced by social reality, which in turn reflects one's worldview about the nature of human inquiry (Gergen, 1975; Hesse, 1980).

A comparison of Western and Japanese worldviews and how they affect the nature of inquiry is revealing. The United States has had a history of "rugged individualism," in which values of self-sufficiency and independence have been stressed. As such, differences of experience, ability, and opinion separate individuals and allow them to be unique. The Japanese, however, are less anchored by an internal self-concept (individualism), and much more allied to friends, colleagues, and family (collectivism). While U.S. Americans may fear the loss of self, the Japanese may fear the loss of belonging (Ramsey & Birk, 1983). Thus, research from a Western orientation involves objectivity, by which one tries to remove subjective elements from research design and decision making. The research is thus individualistic, quantitative, and action oriented. The Japanese orientation is more subjective, emphasizing the importance of human relations as indispensable to understanding human behavior. This research tends to be interpersonal, holistic, and interaction oriented. To the Japanese, behavior is the function of interaction and balance—the truth of statements is tied to social bonds and loyalty within the group. Though neither worldview or research approach is better or more accurate than the other, they are clearly different, illustrating how culture impacts philosophies of inquiry.

Second, Goldman (1976; 1977) has long argued that traditional research paradigms are limited given the complexity of counseling questions. Traditional scientific methods require precision in measurement and the operationalization of concepts. Hoshmand (1989) believes that such an approach may narrow the subject matter and restrict the types of questions that one may ask. We would also add that it restricts the range of responses available to the subjects as well. (In an attempt to differentiate elements, traditional research may limit the response of subjects to "yes" or "no," "true" or "false," "right" or "wrong," and "multiple choice.") Given the richness of the human condition and the complexity of culture (Pedersen, 1988), it appears that there is, indeed, a strong need to consider the use of what Hoshmand (1989) calls "alternative research paradigms" and what Ponterotto and Casas (1991) refer to as "qualitative methodology."

Qualitative research methodology possesses four fundamental characteristics: (1) It is primarily inductive, (2) it has a humanistic and holistic perspective, (3) it is flexible in formulating questions and directions as the inquiry proceeds (design and instrumentation are secondary to the content of what is being observed), and (4) the clinical significance or behavioral reality of the given situation is emphasized (Ponterotto & Casas, 1991). Goldman (1989) adds another important dimension: "They are indigenous to the human sciences rather than physical sciences." Helms (1989) believes that these alternative methods will prove a boon to multicultural psychology because they "(a) allow one to account for the reciprocal influences of the researcher and research participants, (b) permit the methodology to shift according to the particular context in which the data were collected even within the same study, (c) value the use of small samples, and (d) encourage usage of nonstandardized measures" (p. 99). Examples of qualitative methodologies include but are not limited to participant observation, in-depth interviewing, life histories, case studies, and narratives (Goncalves, in press; Guidano, 1991; Hoshmand, 1989; Ivey, 1993; Ponterotto & Casas, 1991).

Our position, again, is not that qualitative methods are superior to quantitative ones. Both methods have their strengths and limitations. Indeed, we believe that combining both methods of inquiry would serve the professions. However, it is obvious that researchers need to explore new methods that are culture centered, rather than consider culture as peripheral.

Practice Implications
of MCT Theory

A culture-centered approach to counseling has many implications. Two of these appear crucial to MCT theory. First, within the traditional role of counseling, major changes must occur in (1) broadening the perspective of the helping relationship and (2) expanding the repertoire of culturally appropriate helping responses available to the counselor (Ivey, 1981, 1986; Pedersen & Ivey, 1993; D. W. Sue & D. Sue, 1990). Second, we advocate the development of alternative counseling roles that empower helping professionals to impact the social or environmental forces in their clients' lives (Atkinson, Morten, & Sue, 1993; Pedersen & Ivey, 1993). This involves "out-of-office" activities, in which many counselors are ill prepared to participate.

Changing Conventional Counseling

BALANCING THE FOCUS OF COUNSELING. How would MCT theory affect daily counseling and therapy practice? The most basic question for clinical practice is how to move from a traditional focus on the individual to examining the use of cultural concepts in the sessions. Counselors and therapists therefore need to focus part of their interviews on family and cultural issues. If one is to consider self-in-relation, one needs to consider what "in-relation" means to each client.

Counselors and therapists also need to balance their self-oriented helping approach with a self-in-relation orientation. A simple but useful beginning in this direction is suggested by the microskill of focusing (Ivey, 1993c):

> In this individualistic culture, we are accustomed to making "I" statements and focusing on what an individual can do to help himself or

herself. We have to realize that this may clash with the world views of many minority people whose traditions focus on family. It may be hard for them to sever themselves from others in their family and just think of themselves. Their sense of self is often collective in nature, and their being may be authenticated mainly in terms of others. The counseling significance is that a balanced focus is needed between individual, family, and cultural expectations. (p. 226)

In short, a part of every counseling session needs to attend to significant others and contextual issues. Our previous commentaries on research have pointed out the extreme limitations of our individualistically oriented data. Similarly, counseling and therapy have focused so much on the individual that simply devoting time asking questions, paraphrasing, and interpreting worldviews as they relate to family and cultural issues will make a huge difference in the way the helper and client conceptualize and consider their concerns.

For example, traditional psychology and psychiatry once regarded the ailing Vietnam veteran, now diagnosed as having posttraumatic stress disorder (PTSD), as some sort of malingerer or as suffering from depression. What is now recognized as PTSD was considered an individual problem. It took considerable effort on the part of Vietnam veterans to convince helping professionals that their issues were real and that PTSD is for many a reasonable response to an incredibly stressful environment. Many now would consider it immoral to treat Vietnam veterans as suffering primarily from individual and internal conflicts.

Similarly, women suffering from depression, African-Americans from high blood pressure, and gays from anxiety need to be treated with a focus not only on their individual problems but also on societal sexism, racism, and homophobia, respectively. The microskill of focusing is a simple reminder of how essential it is to broaden one's perspective in the interview. This point is elaborated further in Pedersen and Ivey (1993). MCT theory suggests that it is time to move from a client-centered to a culture-centered focus.

Another way to implement MCT would be to broaden existing counseling theories to include a multicultural focus. The criticism of the honored words *self-actualization, autonomy,* and *independence* by MCT authorities is indeed challenging. MCT theory would also consider additional concepts such as *self-in-relation, connectedness and relationship,* and *interdependence.* At issue is how psychodynamic, cognitive-behavioral, and humanistic theories can still be used in keeping with MCT goals and values. Starting with humanistic theory, for example, we again draw on the microskill of focus. Our clinical experience reveals that most of the traditional Rogerian skills and values can easily survive if one changes the words "You feel..." to "You feel this in relationship to... [family and/or cultural background]." The precise phrasing may vary, but we believe that reflective listening skills and the goals of traditional Rogerian theory can remain useful by adding a focus on relational and cultural issues. Often, clients mention family and cultural issues, but helpers ignore them because of too much focus on the individual.

Though cognitive-behavioral theory works most effectively with many clients, one can consider it a theory of pacification if insufficient attention is paid to environmental determinants. For example, counselors and therapists often attack irrational ideas without first looking for possible rational elements when they view their clients' statements from the perspective of Western culture. Very little is done with rational-emotive or cognitive therapy to inform clients of how family and cultural issues affect their being. Stress-management programs focus on meditation, relaxation, and cognitive issues, giving insufficient attention to how the client is reacting normally to massive environmental stressors, particularly those of racism, sexism, classism, and homophobia.

Assertiveness training needs to be used with cultural sensitivity. What is assertive in one culture may be overly passive or aggressive in another. Furthermore, the cognitive components of assertiveness need cultural attention as well. Cheek (1976) was perhaps the first person to demonstrate how to make assertiveness and cognitive-behavioral interventions culturally sensitive.

EXPANDING THE REPERTOIRE OF HELPING RESPONSES. Related to the assertions that a multicultural focus must be central to any helping approach are the implications regarding the repertoire of helping responses available to the counselor. Traditional counseling/therapy practice has been severely criticized as limited in its helping responses (Ivey, 1981, 1986; D. W. Sue, 1990, 1992). The limitations appear highly correlated to an ethnocentric subscription to Euro-American counseling theories exclusively. Ivey's work (Ivey, 1981, 1986; Nwachuku & Ivey, 1991) presents clear evidence that differing theoretical orientations tend to produce different skill patterns in helping professionals. In other words, the worldview of the counselor (theory of counseling) may dictate how helping (skills and strategies) will be dispensed in the session. These skill patterns may prove antagonistic or inappropriate to the communication or helping styles of culturally different clients. For example, by virtue of their cultural conditioning and training, counselors practicing traditional Euro-American modes may tend to use relatively passive attending and listening skills in counseling (Pedersen & Ivey, 1993; D. W. Sue & D. Sue, 1990). Taboos abound: Counselors should not give advice and suggestions; they should not take a teaching approach; and they should never disclose their own thoughts and feelings. Though many of these culture-bound rules of counseling may possess a good therapeutic rationale, one must reconsider them in light of cultural and sociopolitical factors (Kleinke, 1994).

In so doing, D. W. Sue (1978, 1990) has repeatedly emphasized that one cannot isolate counseling and psychotherapy from the wider societal forces operating on both counselor and client. Race relations or patterns of dominance and subordination are often played out in the counseling situation. Many minority clients seeing White counselors enter a counseling relationship with the following questions: "What makes you any different from other Whites who have oppressed me?" "Are you in touch with your biases, and will they influence how you work with me?" "What makes you immune from inheriting the biases of your forebears?" "How open and honest are you about your own racism, sexism, homophobia, etc.?" "Before I open up to you (trust), I need to know where you're coming from."

In other words, oppressed minority groups are not likely to self-disclose much until the counselor self-discloses. Thus, culturally different clients often initially prefer counselors who use directive, active, and influencing skills. Such clients may, for example, perceive advice and suggestions as direct forms of counselor self-disclosure. Similarly, if the minority client perceives the locus of the problem outside the person (prejudice and discrimination), then an active role on the part of the counselor is more consistent with the helping relationship (Berman, 1979; Nwachuku & Ivey, 1991).

Cultural factors also influence how individuals interpret appropriate helping. For example, among traditional Asian cultures, the following values and characteristics affect what is considered helpful (counseling) behavior: (1) respect for parents and authority figures, (2) subtlety and indirectness in communications, (3) vertical (hierarchical) rather than horizontal communication patterns, and (4) well-defined role relationships within the family (patriarchal) (Ho, 1992; Root, 1985). For many Asian-American clients, the helpful counselor may be one who gives advice and suggestions, avoids confrontation and direct interpretation of motives and actions, indirectly discusses personal issues, does more initial talking than the client, and evidences a formal interactive approach (D. W. Sue, 1994). Many helping professionals would feel uncomfortable or lack experience in these counseling strategies. Yet, these nontraditional approaches will ultimately enhance the perceived credibility and trustworthiness of the helping professional in the eyes of many Asian clients (D. W. Sue & D. Sue, 1990).

Feminist theories of counseling have also shown the importance of cultural flexibility for delivering effective helping services. Though feminism is often thought of as a Western phenomenon, a strong case can be made that women are culturally different from men. Feminist theory thus enters the world of multicultural counseling. According to Ballou and Gabalac (1984), helpful feminist counseling is characterized by (1) an egalitarian relationship that minimizes the counselor-client distinction, (2) an active counseling style that includes information giving and self-disclosure, (3) validation and empowerment of women who suffer from oppression that leads to low self-esteem, and (4) use of community resources by the counselor and client.

Effective multicultural intervention strategies dictate that the helping professional define goals and use methods and strategies consistent with the life experiences and cultural values of the client. No one can successfully apply a single theory or approach equally to all situations, problems, and groups. Counselors need to be able to shift their counseling styles to meet the cultural and sociopolitical dimensions of their diverse clientele (Ivey, 1986; Sue, 1991b).

Alternative Helping Roles

This section is derived primarily from Proposition 5 and its corollaries. Our suggestions for changing the conventional counseling role assume that Euro-American forms of helping can be adequately modified to fit the needs of various cultural groups (D. W. Sue, 1994). Our general approach involves identifying the cultural/contextual forces in the client's life and creating more culturally responsive forms of treatment. Furthermore, some multicultural psychologists believe that research and practice might be better directed at identifying the helping systems indigenous to other cultures first, then at developing new theories, roles, and techniques (Asante, 1987; Atkinson, Thompson, & Grant, 1993; Pedersen & Ivey, 1993; D. W. Sue & D. Sue, 1990; White & Parham, 1990). The move to consider alternative helping roles the counselor may play has also received impetus from the knowledge that much of what affects clients' lives comes from external sources.

IDENTIFYING INDIGENOUS HELPING ROLES. Since the beginning of human existence, all cultures and societies have developed their own explanations of abnormal behaviors and ways of dealing with human problems and distress (Das, 1987; Harner, 1990). In the United States and most Western countries, these forms of helping have been called *counseling* and *psychotherapy*; however, these represent relatively new methods when contrasted with the healing systems that have existed for centuries in other cultures (Kakar, 1982; Lee et al., 1992). While Western forms of treatment are gaining acceptance in these cultures, many ancient indigenous methods continue to exert widespread influence and acceptance among their respective populations.

In a study conducted in 16 countries, Lee et al. (1992) found that these societies relied on three forms of healing: (1) use of communal, group, and family networks such as extended families to shelter the disturbed (Saudi Arabia), community networks such as clans brought together to solve the problem within a group setting (Nigeria), and friendship networks in which a close personal acquaintance is sought in times of distress (Korea); (2) use of spiritualism and religion such as verses of the Koran and religious houses/churches to deal with problems; and (3) use of traditional healers (shamans in Brazil, Senegal, Nigeria, Zambia, and Korea; piris and fakirs in Pakistan and Sudan; black-magic experts and numerous other healers often referred to as *witch doctor, medicine man, sorcerer,* or *wizard* (Lee et al., 1992). Because these traditional healers are all rooted in the spiritual-religious beliefs and assumptions of the culture, these individuals are often viewed with high credibility, enhancing their helping roles.

Understanding these culturally based roles may allow Western helpers to develop new theories of helping and new roles that the counselor may play. The prime example of this new realization is Afrocentric theory and practice. A group of scholars in various settings have put together what amounts to a new theory of helping. Asante's (1987) *The Afrocentric Idea* brings philosophic foundations together, although work by Diop (1981) and others, such as W. E. B. Du Bois precede him. Afrocentric theory presents a major challenge to traditional Western psychotherapy, because its roots lie in ancient African thought, especially from Egypt and Nubia.

Essential to the Afrocentric perspective is the idea that human beings are part of a wholistic fabric and are oriented to collective survival rather than individual accomplishment and achievement. African oral tradition values emotion, emphasizes being rather than doing, and focuses on harmony and cooperation (Asante, 1987; Parham, 1993a; White & Parham, 1990). Reviewing the original cultural identity theories of Cross (1971, 1991), one may see how closely his ideas relate to a black consciousness. Similarly, work by White and Parham (1990) specifies the implementation of a new approach to helping. Cheek's (1976) comments on adapting assertiveness training for African Americans contain important data on specifically applying the theory to practice. Finally, Cheatham (1990) provides useful information and concepts for the African-American family.

Another approach toward applying MCT is represented by Nwachuku (1990) and Nwachuku and Ivey (1991). This model starts with an examination of the culture itself and seeks to determine important personal and interpersonal characteristics. One might call it *applied anthropological counseling and therapy theorizing.* Once a culture is understood, the next task is to identify existing methods of helping. How does the culture go about providing help for its members? Then, specific skills and strategies of that approach are named and tested. In effect, the theory and skills are drawn with intention from the culture. Finally, the new helping theory and role may be tested in action and further feedback obtained from participants.

Nwachuku used this model with the Igbo in Nigeria. After he had made an anthropological study of the Igbo, he videotaped a variety of Igbo helpers in action. From this tape, he could identify skills and strategies.

Among other findings, Nwachuku discerned that decisions among the Igbo are made in relationships and that individual decision making without reference to extended family was likely to be ineffective. These particular findings particularly support MCT theory's major concept of relational being as opposed to individual being.

Naikan and Morita therapies from Japan provide other examples of Nwachuku and Ivey's model. Both widely used methods focus on helping the client become more in tune with others and society, to move away from individualism towards interdependence and connectedness. Japanese psychodrama is particularly interesting, with its many techniques oriented toward harmony with others and the environment, in contrast with the self-expression and acting out often associated with Western psychodrama.

DEVELOPING ALTERNATIVES TO THE CONVENTIONAL COUNSELING ROLE. MCT theory assumes that there are multiple helping roles that complement the conventional counseling/therapy role. We base this assumption on an understanding not only of indigenous healing methods but also of external forces that may either impede or facilitate the healthy functioning of individuals and groups in a society (Atkinson, Morten, & Sue, 1993). These alternative roles have several things in common. First, they are characterized by a more active approach on the part of the counselor. Second, they may demand that the counselor conduct his or her practice outside the office—in the home, community, or organization, whichever impacts the client. Third, counselors in such roles are much more likely to be externally focused and to seek change in environmental conditions—confronting the policies and practices of an organization, enhancing job opportunities, intervening on behalf of the client, etc.—rather than focus on individual (client) change. Fourth, there is less likelihood counselors will see "the problem" (pathology) as residing solely in the client. Fifth, many of these roles evolved through the recognition that prevention was often more economical and had a greater social impact than remediation alone. Last, as a result of these conditions, the counselor shoulders an increased responsibility for determining the course and outcome of her or his part in the helping process.

In addition to the roles of counselor and psychotherapist, Atkinson, Thompson, and Grant (1993) have identified the following helping roles:

1. *Adviser:* Helpers advise clients about how to solve or prevent potential problems, inform them about available options, and may share with them actions they themselves or others have found effective in ameliorating problems. For example, immigrants who have minimal experience with U.S. society may need someone to advise them about potential sources of stress from cultural conflicts.

2. *Advocate:* Helpers represent the best interests of clients to other individuals, groups, or institutional organizations. For example, groups who do not speak English well and therefore do not understand institutional policies or practices nor their own rights may need people who "speak for them," encouraging or demanding appropriate and fair treatment.

3. *Facilitator of Indigenous Support Systems:* Helpers recognize that many clients may respond better to indigenous support systems such as extended family, community elders, and religious support groups in resolving their problems. In essence, the counselor must know what kind of support systems were available in the client's culture and consequently facilitate their use.

4. *Facilitator of Indigenous Healing Systems:* Counselors may take the following actions: (a) referring clients to healers (*currandismo* [Mexican folk healer], T'ai Chi Ch'uan instructor, etc.) knowledgeable about the original culture and/or (b) actually using the indigenous healing methods. This latter role, however, assumes that the counselor is trained and skilled in those healing arts.

5. *Consultant:* Counselors assume a professional but collegial relationship between themselves and the consultee, working to change or impact a third party. The effective consultant should possess knowledge and experience in organizational change.

6. *Change Agent:* Counselors take an action-oriented approach to changing the client's social environment. Like the consultant role in many respects, the change agent goes further than traditional roles in assuming responsibility for making changes that may be oppressing the client or clients.

Atkinson, Thompson, and Grant (1993) provide a very valuable three-dimensional model in which these roles are organized. The selection of an appropriate helping role depends on three major variables. (1) The helper must determine the locus of the problem. Does it reside internally, or is it due to external causes? For example, weak impulse control might be classified as internal, while PTSD, job discrimination, or sexual harassment might be seen as having an external source. (2) Counselors should ascertain the level of acculturation in the clients. *Acculturation* is the process of cultural familiarization and incorporation and the internalization of values, customs, traditions, and language of one culture by another. While cultural conflicts may occur in this process, many racial/ethnic minorities can be bicultural without negative effects. (3) Counseling goals fall on a wide continuum from remediation to prevention. In most cases where the goal is increasingly prevention, a relatively externally oriented approach is considered appropriate.

How these three variables intersect may determine the role taken by the helping professional. For example, if the problem is internal, if the acculturation level is high, and if the goal is remediation, then the traditional psychotherapeutic role may be appropriate. However, if the problem is external, the acculturation level is low, and the goal is prevention, then the adviser role is called for.

Pedersen (1994) proposes another useful organizational framework for determining multiple helping roles. He identifies two variables that affect the type of role played by helpers: context and method of counseling. Each can be formal, nonformal, or informal. These conditions can be arranged three by three, producing nine cells, each representing a different form of helping.

Pedersen (1994) believes that without an adequate framework to organize and classify psychological helping, counselors will rely more on formal and obvious systems and roles defined by the dominant culture, and ignore the less obvious and informal alternatives. Note that the models proposed by Atkinson, Thompson, and Grant (1993) and Pedersen (1994) focus on different dimensions of helper roles, with no one role considered more important than the others.

TRAINING IMPLICATIONS OF MCT THEORY

MCT theory possesses wide-ranging and important implications for counselor education and training. For example, valuable work has been done on multicultural infusion via curriculum models (Copeland, 1982), research instruction (Bernal & Padilla, 1982; Hoshmand, 1989), clinical instruction (Pedersen, 1991; S. Sue & Zane, 1987), practicum and internship experiences (Reynolds, 1995), institutional change (D. W. Sue, 1991b; 1994), and specific cross-cultural training activities (Carney & Kahn, 1984; Corvin & Wiggins, 1989; Sabnani, Ponterotto, & Borodovsky, 1991). Though these are all important directions, we have chosen to concentrate on explicating the implications of MCT theory for multicultural-counseling competencies. For this section, we rely heavily on the work of both the Education and Training Committee of Division 17 (D. W. Sue et al., 1982) and the Professional Standards Committee of the Association of Multicultural Counseling and Development (D. W. Sue et al., 1992).

Objectives and Goals of MCT Training

The culture-centered approach demands a massive change in our counselor-training programs. Whereas cultural issues are now mainly "add-ons" placed at the periphery of such training, in this new framework, all the actions, research, and practice of counselors must be reexamined and reinterpreted through the lens of culture (Ivey et al., 1993; Pedersen & Ivey, 1993; Spindler & Spindler, 1994). The "third presence" of culture (i.e., added to counselor and client) becomes a focal point to view the training of mental-health professionals as well. Multicultural specialists assert that the first step in any effective counselor training is to help would-be mental-health professionals recognize their own culture (Sabnani et al., 1991; Spindler & Spindler, 1994; D. W. Sue, 1991a). For example, Euro-Americans often claim that they "have no culture." Helping people become aware of culture and the "third presence" is one of the most difficult and important tasks facing MCT advocates. Furthermore, African-American, Asian-American, Latin(o)-American, and Native-American counselors and therapists will also benefit from becoming more aware of themselves as cultural beings.

The statement of the Professional Standards Committee (D. W. Sue et al., 1992) serves as a framework for considering training tasks. Table 3.1 presents a summary of these standards for attitudes and beliefs, knowledge, and intervention strategies.

1. GOAL ONE: *Having trainees become more culturally aware of their own values, biases, stereotypes, and assumptions about human behavior.* What are the worldviews they bring to the helping encounter? What value system is inherent in their theory of helping, and which values underlie the strategies and techniques used in counseling? Without such an awareness and understanding, trainees may inadvertently assume that everyone shares their worldview. When this happens, they may become guilty of cultural oppression, imposing values on their culturally different clients. There are a multitude of ways to help trainees become aware of themselves as cultural beings and to acquire knowledge of the culture-bound and class-bound values inherent in the schools of counseling and psychotherapy. While the latter emphasis may be accomplished through didactic instruction, the former is more difficult because it involves a personal integration of concepts. For example, one of the most effective ways to execute the former is to engage trainees in exploring their own ethnic heritage through study of their personal history and genogram (Ivey et al., 1993). Students thus learn that many of their "individual" characteristics are continuations of family and cultural traditions. Many find this type of work personally therapeutic, and the genogram is becoming more and more a standard diagnostic and therapeutic device. Few methods can help a trainee see self-in-context better than the development of a personal genogram.

One of the major objectives of MCT training is multiperspective thought—recognizing that there are many ways to frame a problem other than one's own. The world opens up for students when they realize that

(Text continues on page 50.)

TABLE 3.1
Multicultural Counseling Competencies

Counselor Awareness of Own Cultural Values and Biases

Attitudes/
Beliefs

a. Culturally skilled counselors have moved from being culturally unaware to being aware and sensitive to his/her own cultural heritage and to valuing and respecting differences.
b. Culturally skilled counselors are aware of how their own cultural background/experiences, attitudes, values, and biases influence psychological processes.
c. Culturally skilled counselors are able to recognize the limits of their competencies and expertise.
d. Culturally skilled counselors are comfortable with differences that exist between themselves and clients in terms of race, ethnicity, culture, and beliefs.

Knowledges

a. Culturally skilled counselors have specific knowledge about their own racial/cultural heritage and how it personally and professionally affects their definitions of normality-abnormality and the process of counseling.
b. Culturally skilled counselors possess knowledge and understanding about how oppression, racism, discrimination, and stereotyping affects them personally and in their work. This allows them to acknowledge their own racist attitudes, beliefs, and feelings. While this standard applies to all groups, for white counselors it may seem that they understand how they may have directly or indirectly benefited from individual, institutional, and cultural racism (White Identity Development Models).
c. Culturally skilled counselors possess knowledge about their social impact upon others. They are knowledgeable about communication style differences, how their style may clash or facilitate the counseling process with minority clients, and how to anticipate the impact it may have on others.

Skills

a. Culturally skilled counselors seek out educational, consultative, and training experience to enhance their understanding and effectiveness in working with culturally different populations. Being able to recognize the limits of their competencies, they (a) seek consultation, (b) seek further training or education, and/or (c) refer out to more qualified individuals or resources.
b. Culturally skilled counselors are constantly seeking to understand themselves as racial/cultural beings and are actively seeking a nonracist identity.

Note. From "Multicultural Counseling Competencies and Standards: A Call to the Profession," by D. W. Sue, P. Arredondo, and R. J. McDavis, 1992, *Journal of Counseling and Development, 70,* pp. 484–486. Copyright 1992 by the American Counseling Association. Adapted with permission.

TABLE 3.1 (cont.)
MULTICULTURAL COUNSELING COMPETENCIES

Counselor Awareness of Client's Worldview

Attitudes/
Beliefs

a. Culturally skilled counselors are aware of their negative emotional reactions toward other racial/ethnic groups which may prove detrimental to their clients in counseling. They are willing to contrast their own beliefs and attitudes with those of their culturally different clients in a nonjudgmental fashion.

b. Culturally skilled counselors are aware of their stereotypes and preconceived notions which they may hold toward other racial/ethnic minority groups.

Knowledges

a. Culturally skilled counselors possess specific knowledge and information about the particular group he/she is working with. They are aware of the life experiences, cultural heritage, historical background of their culturally different clients. This particular competency is strongly linked to the "minority identity development models" available in the literature.

b. Culturally skilled counselors understand how race, culture, ethnicity, etc., may affect personality formation, vocational choices, manifestation of psychological disorders, help-seeking behavior, and the appropriateness or inappropriateness of counseling approaches.

c. Culturally skilled counselors understand and have knowledge about sociopolitical influences that impinge upon the life of racial/ethnic minorities. Immigration issues, poverty, racism, stereotyping, and powerlessness all leave major scars which may influence the counseling process.

Skills

a. Culturally skilled counselors familiarize themselves with relevant research and latest findings regarding mental health and mental disorders of various ethnic/racial groups. As in competency 3a, they actively seek out educational experiences which enhance their knowledge, understanding, and cross-cultural skills.

b. Culturally skilled counselors become actively involved with minority individuals outside of the counseling setting (community events, social/political functions, celebrations, friendships, neighborhood groups, etc.) so that their perspective of minorities is more than an academic or helping exercise.

(continues)

TABLE 3.1 (cont.)
MULTICULTURAL COUNSELING COMPETENCIES

Culturally Appropriate Intervention Strategies

Attitudes/
Beliefs

a. Culturally skilled counselors respect clients' religious and/or spiritual beliefs and values, including attributions and taboos, since they affect worldview, psychosocial functioning, and expressions of distress.

b. Culturally skilled counselors respect indigenous helping practices and respect minority community intrinsic help-giving networks.

c. Culturally skilled counselors value bilingualism and do not view another language as an impediment to counseling (monolingualism may be the culprit).

Knowledges

a. Culturally skilled counselors have a clear and explicit knowledge and understanding of the generic characteristics of counseling/therapy (culture-bound, class-bound, and monolingual) and how they may clash with the cultural values of various minority groups.

b. Culturally skilled counselors are aware of institutional barriers which prevent minorities from using mental health services.

c. Culturally skilled counselors have knowledge of the potential bias in assessment instruments and use procedures and interpret findings keeping in mind the cultural and linguistic characteristics of the clients.

d. Culturally skilled counselors have knowledge of minority family structures, hierarchies, values, and beliefs. They are knowledgeable about the community characteristics and the resources in the community as well as the family.

e. Culturally skilled counselors are aware of relevant discriminatory practices at the social and community level that may be affecting the psychological welfare of the population being served.

Skills

a. Culturally skilled counselors are able to engage in a variety of verbal/nonverbal helping responses. They are able to send and receive both verbal and nonverbal messages accurately and appropriately. They are not tied down to only one method or

TABLE 3.1 (cont.)
MULTICULTURAL COUNSELING COMPETENCIES

approach to helping, but recognize that helping styles and approaches may be culture-bound. When they sense that their helping style is limited and potentially inappropriate, they can anticipate and ameliorate its negative impact.

b. Culturally skilled counselors are able to exercise institutional intervention skills on behalf of their clients. They can help clients determine whether a "problem" stems from racism or bias in others (the concept of healthy paranoia) so that clients do not inappropriately personalize problems.

c. Culturally skilled counselors are not averse to seeking consultation with and/or including traditional healers, religious/ spiritual leaders/practitioners in the treatment of culturally different clients when appropriate.

d. Culturally skilled counselors take responsibility for interacting in the language requested by the client and, if not feasible, to make appropriate referral. A serious problem arises when the linguistic skills of a counselor do not match the language of the client. If not possible, counselors should (a) seek a translator with cultural knowledge and appropriate professional background, and (b) refer to a knowledgeable and competent bilingual counselor.

e. Culturally skilled counselors have training and expertise in the use of traditional assessment and testing instruments. They not only understand the technical aspects of the instruments, but are aware of the cultural limitations. This allows them to use test instruments for the welfare of the diverse clients.

f. Culturally skilled counselors attend to, as well as work to eliminate, biases, prejudices, and discriminatory practices. They should be cognizant of sociopolitical contexts in conducting evaluation and providing interventions, and develop sensitivity to issues of oppression, sexism, elitism, and racism.

g. Culturally skilled counselors take responsibility in educating their clients to the processes of psychological intervention, such as goals, expectations, legal rights, and the counselor's orientation.

their own point of view, though valid, is only one of many interpretations of the universe. The concept of worldview is particularly important in this regard. Students and professionals alike need to become accustomed to the idea of a constructed world heavily mediated by cultural forces as well as cognitive issues.

Armed with personal knowledge of multiperspective thought and the validity of alternative worldviews, one can anticipate the development of more flexible therapists not caught up with such concerns as whether cognitive methods are better than psychodynamic or DSM-IV diagnoses must be used in the same way with all clients. Sad to say, psychology is still very much caught in the dualistic Newtonian, Cartesian model of "which is best." The real question, however, is this: "Can psychology move to multiplicity?"

Specific knowledge of oppression and its many manifestations is also essential. Key among these are oppressions related to language, gender, ethnicity/race, religion, sexual preference, age, physical or emotional issues, socioeconomic status, or trauma. Counseling trainees need to be accountable for this understanding of themselves as cultural beings in all these contexts. Again, the issue of multiperspective thought becomes important. It is essential that counselors hold the complex and varied cultural issues in mind while they work with clients. And, ultimately, one of the best things they can do for clients is to help them move to this multidimensional way of viewing the universe.

2. GOAL TWO: *Having trainees acquire knowledge and understanding of the worldview of minority or culturally different clients.* What are the values, biases, and assumptions about human behavior that culturally different clients hold? How similar or dissimilar is the counselor's worldview to the trainee's value system? Can the prospective helping professional understand and accept, for example, the differing worldviews of African Americans, Asian Americans, Latina(o) Americans, Native Americans, and the many other different groups in our society?

Teaching about client worldviews must again deal with attitudes, beliefs, knowledge, and skills. Besides traditional "book learning," experiential training that integrates the cognitive, affective, and behavioral experiences of trainees must be tapped. Examples of this approach include role playing using the triad model (Pedersen, 1986), training in the cultural assimilator model (Triandis, 1983), and a variety of other experiential exercises (Carney & Kahn, 1984; Parker & McDavis, 1979; Sabnani et al., 1991). At a deeper level, experiences of cultural immersion such as the Peace Corps or significant practicum experiences with culturally different groups can be most beneficial.

Cultural identity theories involving many different groups remind one that there is no unitary worldview—each client will construct the issue somewhat differently from the next (Atkinson, Morten, & Sue, 1989; W. E. Cross, 1971; Downing & Roush, 1985; Helms, 1984, 1992; Ivey & Payton, in press; Jackson, 1975; Parham & Helms, 1981; D. W. Sue & S. Sue, 1972). Similarly, white identity-development theories help racial/ ethnic minorities realize that how whites perceive themselves as racial beings differs markedly from their own ways (Helms, 1984, 1992; Rowe, Bennett & Atkinson, 1993; Sabnani, Ponterotto, & Borodovsky, 1991; D. W. Sue & D. Sue, 1990). The level of consciousness or stage of development of group members provide a way for counselors to map how clients consider issues. One can neither expect all African Americans to have the same worldview nor expect Euro-Americans to be unanimous in their ways of thought.

Furthermore, different counseling theories and strategies may be useful for different identity levels. For example, an African-American woman at the reflective-introspective level might respond well to a humanistic listening approach, but the same woman at the integrative level might demand more involvement from the counselor, such as opinions on key social issues and actions in the community. These behaviors, which counselors often do not associate with help giving, may cause them to examine the premises of their limited view of helping strategies. MCT theory is not just about client growth—it is equally about growth for constricted therapists and counselors.

3. GOAL THREE: *Having trainees begin the process of developing culturally appropriate intervention strategies in the counseling process.* This involves developing individual counseling and communication skills as well as systems-intervention skills. It also involves using the indigenous helping approaches of culturally diverse groups. Skills and theories used with white middle-class populations are often inappropriate with culturally different groups. As you have seen, conceptual frameworks for developing culturally appropriate intervention strategies have been proposed by Pedersen (in press), D. W. Sue (1992), and Atkinson, Thompson, & Grant (1993). Furthermore, helping professionals need to consider cultural meaning in every interview, adapt existing theories to become multiculturally relevant, learn new theories and strategies from Africa, Asia, and other parts of the world, and start thinking about counseling and therapy as a liberating process.

The three training goals just described have been derived directly from the multicultural-counseling competencies developed from the Division of Counseling Psychology (D. W. Sue et al., 1982) and the Association of Multicultural Counseling and Development Professional Standards Committee (D. W. Sue et al., 1992). Widely accepted by multicultural specialists, these standards have specific training implications (Pedersen,

(1994). Of particular value is instrumentation based on these competencies, such as the Cross-Cultural Counseling Inventory (LaFromboise, Coleman, & Herdandez, 1991), the Multicultural Awareness-Knowledge-Skills Survey (D'Andrea, Daniels, & Heck, 1991), the Multicultural Counseling Inventory (Sodowsky, Taffe, Gutkin, & Wise, 1994), and the Multicultural Counseling Awareness Scale (Ponterotto, Sanchez, & Magids, 1991). The development of these instruments provides helping professionals with not only ways to measure multicultural counseling competencies but also the opportunity to measure the effectiveness of specialized training models, modules, or programs in mental health or counseling.

Summary

In closing our discussion, we would like to quote some passages taken from *Cultural Therapy* (Spindler & Spindler, 1994) but paraphrased slightly to uphold a counseling framework (our words in boldface):

> Our basic premise is that culture is not simply a "factor," or "an influence," or "a dimension" but that it is a process, in everything that we do, say, or think in or out of **counseling and therapy practice. Regardless of clientele, issues to be discussed, or theoretical persuasion, we** are caught up in cultural processes. With this in mind, we designate **counseling** as a . . . cultural process and the counselor or therapist as a cultural agent. Of course, **the interview** is also a political or a social institution and a lot else. . . .
>
> We can state that cultural therapy is a process of bringing one's own culture, in its manifold forms—assumptions, goals, values, beliefs, and communicative modes—to a level of awareness that permits one to perceive it as a potential bias in social interaction and in the acquisition or transmission of skills and knowledge. . . . At the same time, one's own culture, brought to this level of awareness, is perceived in relation to the "other" culture, so that potential conflicts, misunderstandings, and "blind spots" in the perception and interpretation of behavior may be anticipated. One's own culture as well as the other's culture become a "third presence," removed somewhat from the person, so that one's actions can be taken as "caused" by one's culture and the interactions with "other" and not **just** by one's personality. (pp. 2–4)

Counseling research, practice, and training become radically different when seen through the lens of a liberated cultural perspective. Our theory of MCT represents a beginning step in freeing mental-health professionals from the narrow confines of ethnocentric conditioning. We believe that MCT theory does represent the "fourth force in counseling" and that it holds promise for providing a framework that promotes equal access and opportunities for all clients regardless of race, culture, ethnicity, gender, sexual orientation, religion, etc. We know, however, that MCT theory calls for a major paradigmatic shift, challenging the very foundations on which traditional counseling and therapy rests. How helping professionals meet that challenge will ultimately determine their future.

REFERENCES FOR PART I

Adler, N. J. (1986). Cultural synergy: Managing the impact of cultural diversity. *The 1986 annual: Developing human resources* (pp. 229–238). San Diego, CA: University Associates.

American Psychological Association. (1993). Guidelines for providers of psychological services to ethnic, linguistic, and culturally diverse populations. *American Psychologist, 48*, 45–48.

Asante, M. (1987). *The Afrocentric Idea*. Philadelphia: Temple University Press.

Atkinson, D. R. (1983). Ethnic similarity in counseling psychology: A review of research. *The Counseling Psychologist, 22*, 79–92.

Atkinson, D. R., Maruyama, M., & Matsui, S. (1978). The effects of counselor race and counseling approach on Asian Americans' perceptions of counselor credibility and utility. *Journal of Counseling Psychology, 25*, 76–83.

Atkinson, D. R., Morten, G., & Sue, D. W. (1989). *Counseling American minorities* (3rd ed.). Dubuque, IA: Brown.

Atkinson, D. R., Morten, G., & Sue, D. W. (1993). *Counseling American minorities* (4th ed.). Dubuque, IA: Brown & Benchmark.

Atkinson, D. R., Thompson, C. E., & Grant, S. K. (1993). A three-dimensional model for counseling racial/ethnic minorities. *The Counseling Psychologist, 21*, 257–277.

Attneave, C. (1969). Therapy in tribal settings and urban network interventions. *Family Process, 8*, 192–210.

Ballou, M., & Gabalac. (1984). *A feminist position on mental health*. Springfield, IL: Thomas.

Banks, J. A. (1993). Multicultural education: Characteristics and goals. In J. A. Banks & C. A. McGee Banks (Eds.), *Multicultural education* (2nd ed., pp. 3–28). Boston: Allyn and Bacon.

Barr, D. J., & Strong, L. J. (1987, May). Embracing multiculturalism: The existing contradictions. *ACU-I Bulletin*, pp. 20–23.

Beck, A. (1976). *Cognitive therapy and the emotional disorders*. New York: International Universities Press.

Beck, A. (1985). Cognitive therapy, behavior therapy, psychoanalysis, and pharmacology: A cognitive continuum. In M. Mahoney & A. Freeman (Eds.), *Cognition and psychotherapy* (pp. 226–248). New York: Plenum.

Berman, J. (1979). Counseling skills used by Black and White male and female counselors. *Journal of Counseling Psychology, 26*, 81–84.

Bernal, M., & Padilla, A. (1982). Status of minority curricula and training in clinical psychology. *American Psychologist, 37*, 780–787.

Brammer, L. M., & Shostrom, E. (1984). *Therapeutic psychology.* Englewood Cliffs, NJ: Prentice-Hall.

Bronfenbrenner, U. (1986). The ecology of the family as a context for human development. *Developmental Psychology, 22,* 723–742.

Brown, L., & Ballou, M. (1992). *Theories of personality and psychopathology.* New York: Guilford.

Carney, C. G., & Kahn, K. B. (1984). Building competencies for effective cross-cultural counseling: A developmental view. *The Counseling Psychologist, 12,* 111–119.

Casas, J. M. (1976). Applicability of a behavioral model in serving the mental health needs of the Mexican American. In M. R. Miranda (Ed.), *Psychotherapy with the Spanish speaking: Issues in research and service delivery* (pp. 61–65). Los Angeles: Spanish-Speaking Mental Health Research Center.

Casas, J. M. (1984). Policy, training and research in counseling psychology: The racial/ethnic minority perspective. In S. D. Brown & R. Lent (Eds.), *Handbook of counseling psychology* (pp. 785–831). New York: Wiley.

Casas, J. M. (1985). A reflection on the status of racial/ethnic minority research. *The Counseling Psychologist, 13,* 581–598.

Casas, J. M., & San Miguel, S. (1993). Beyond questions and discussions, there is a need for action: A response to Mio and Iwamasa. *The Counseling Psychologist, 21,* 233–239.

Cheatham, H. (1990). Empowering black families. In H. Cheatham & J. Stewart (Eds.), *Black families* (pp. 373–393). New Brunswick, NJ: Transaction.

Cheek, D. (1976). *Assertive Black . . . Puzzled White.* San Luis Obispo, CA: Impact.

Chomsky, N. (1977). *Language and responsibility.* New York: Pantheon.

Comas-Diaz, L. (1990). Hispanic Latino communities: Psychological implications. *The Journal of Training & Practice in Professional Psychology, 1,* 14–35.

Copeland, E. J. (1982). Minority populations and traditional counseling programs: Some alternatives. *Counselor Education and Supervision, 21,* 187–193.

Corvin, S., & Wiggins, F. (1989). An antiracism training model for White professionals. *Journal of Multicultural Counseling and Development, 17,* 105–114.

Cross, T. L., Bazron, B. J., Dennis, K. W., & Isaacs, M. R. (1989). *Towards a culturally competent system of care.* Washington, DC: Child and Adolescent Service System Program Technical Assistance Center.

Cross, W. E. (1971). The Negro-to-Black conversion experience: Toward a psychology of black liberation. *Black World, 20,* 13–27.

Cross, W. E. (1978). The Cross and Thomas models of psychological nigrescence. *Journal of Black Psychology, 5,* 13–19.

Cross, W. E. (1987). A two-factor theory of Black identity: Implications for the study of identity development in minority children. In J. S. Phinney & M. J. Rotheram (Eds.), *Children's ethnic socialization: Pluralism and development* (pp. 117–133). Newbury Park, CA: Sage.

Cross, W .E. (1989). Nigrescence: A nondiaphanous phenomena. *The Counseling Psychologist, 17,* 273–276.

Cross, W. E. (1991). *Shades of Black: Diversity in African American identity.* Philadelphia: Temple University Press.

D'Andrea, M., Daniels, J., & Heck, R. (1991). Evaluating the impact of multicultural training. *Journal of Counseling and Development, 70,* 143–150.

Das, A. K. (1987). Indigenous models of therapy in traditional Asian societies. *Journal of Multicultural Counseling and Development, 15,* 25–37.

Dauphinais, R., Dauphinais, L., & Rowe, W. (1981). Effects of race and communication style on Indian perceptions of counselor effectiveness. *Counselor Education and Supervision, 21,* 72–80.

Diop, C. (1981). *Civilization or barbarism.* New York: Lawrence Hill.

Dolliver, R. H., Williams, E. L., & Gold, D. C. (1980). The art of Gestalt therapy or: What are you doing with your feet now? *Psychotherapy: Theory, Research & Practice, 17,* 136–142.

Downing, N. E., & Roush, K. L. (1985). From passive acceptance to active commitment: A model of feminist identity development for women. *The Counseling Psychologist, 13,* 195–709.

Edwards, H. P., Boulet, D. B., Mahrer, A. R., Chagnon, G. J., & Mook, B. (1982). Carl Rogers during initial interviews: A moderate and consistent therapist. *Journal of Counseling Psychology, 29,* 14–18.

Egan, G. (1985). *Change agent skills in helping and human service settings.* Pacific Grove, CA: Brooks/Cole.

Ellis, A. (1962). *Reason and emotion in psychotherapy.* New York: Stuart.

Ellis, A. (1989). Rational-Emotive therapy. In R. J. Corsini & D. Wedding (Eds.), *Current psychotherapies* (pp. 197–238). Itasca, IL: F. E. Peacock.

Erikson, E. (1963). *Childhood and society.* New York: Norton.

Foster, B. G., Jackson, G., Cross, W. E., Jackson, B., & Hardiman, R. (1988). Workforce diversity and business. Alexandria, VA: American Society for Training and Development. (Reprinted from *Training and Development Journal,* pp. 1–4, 1988, April).

Frankl, V. E. (1985). Logos, paradox, and the search for meaning. In M. J. Mahoney & A. Freeman (Eds.), *Cognition and psychotherapy* (pp. 259–276). New York: Plenum.

Franklin, J. H. (1988). A historical note on black families. In H. P. McAdoo (Ed.), *Black families* (pp. 44–59). Newbury Park, CA: Sage.

Freire, P. (1972). *Pedagogy of the oppressed.* New York: Herder & Herder.

Garfield, S. L., & Kurtz, R. (1976). Clinical psychologists in the 1970s. *American Psychologist, 31,* 1–9.

Garfield, S. L., & Kurtz, R. (1977). A study of eclectic views. *Journal of Consulting and Clinical Psychology, 45,* 78–83.

Goldfried, M. R., Greenberg, L. S., & Marmar, C. (1990). Individual psychotherapy: Process and outcome. *Annual Review of Psychology, 41,* 659–688.

Goldfried, M. R., & Safran, J. D. (1986). Future directions in psychotherapy integration. In J. C. Norcross (Ed.), *Handbook of eclectic psychotherapy* (pp. 463–483). New York: Brunner/Mazel.

Goldman, L. (1976). A revolution in counseling research. *Journal of Counseling Psychology, 23,* 543–552.

Goldman, L. (1977). Toward more meaningful research. *Personnel and Guidance Journal, 55,* 363–368.

Goldman, L. (1989). Moving counseling research into the 21st century. *The Counseling Psychologist, 17,* 81–85.

Goncalves, O. F. (in press). Cognitive narrative psychotherapy: The hermeneutic construction of alternative meanings. *Journal of Cognitive Psychotherapy.*

Grencavage, L. M., & Norcross, J. C. (1990). Where are the commonalities among the therapeutic common factors? *Professional Psychology: Research and Practice, 21,* 372–378.

Grier, W., & Cobbs, P. (1968). *Black rage.* New York: Basic Books.

Grier, W., & Cobbs, P. (1971). *The Jesus bag.* San Francisco: McGraw-Hill.

Guidano, V. F. (1991). *The self in process: Toward a post-rationalist cognitive therapy.* New York: Guilford.

Halleck, S. (1970). *The politics of therapy.* New York: Science House.

Halleck, S. (1971). Therapy is the handmaiden of the status quo. *Psychology Today, 4,* 30–34, 98–100.

Hardiman, R. (1982). White identity development: A process oriented model for describing the racial consciousness of white Americans. *Dissertation Abstracts International, 43,* 104A. (University Microfilms No. 82-10330).

Harner, M. (1990). *The way of the shaman.* San Francisco: Harper & Row.

Heath, A. E., Neimeyer, G. J., & Pedersen, P. B. (1988). The future of cross-cultural counseling: A Delphi poll. *Journal of Counseling and Development, 67,* 27–30.

Helms, J. E. (1984). Toward a theoretical model of the effects of race on counseling: A black and white model. *The Counseling Psychologist, 12,* 153–165.

Helms, J. E. (1986). Expanding racial identity theory to cover counseling process. *Journal of Counseling Psychology, 33,* 62–64.

Helms, J. E. (1989). At long last—Paradigms for cultural psychology research. *The Counseling Psychologist, 17,* 98–101.

Helms, J. E. (1990). *Black and white racial identity: Theory, research, and practice.* New York: Greenwood Press.

Helms, J. E. (1992). *A race is a nice thing to have: A guide to being a White person or understanding the White persons in your life.* Topeka, KS: Content Communications.

Helms, J. E. (1993). I also said, "White racial identity influences white researchers." *The Counseling Psychologist, 21,* 240–243.

Hesse, M. (1980). *Resolutions and reconstructions in the philosophy of science.* Bloomington: Indiana University Press.

Hills, H. I., & Strozier, A. L. (1993). Multicultural training in APA approved counseling psychology programs: A survey. *Professional Psychology, 23,* 43–51.

Ho, M. K. (1987). *Family therapy with ethnic minorities.* Newbury Park, CA: Sage.

Ho, M. K. (1992). *Family therapy with ethnic minorities* (2nd ed.). Newbury Park, CA: Sage.

Hoshmand, L. S. T. (1989). Alternate research paradigms: A review and teaching proposal. *The Counseling Psychologist, 17,* 3–79.

Howard, G. (1991). Cultural tales: A narrative approach to thinking, cross-cultural psychology, and psychotherapy. *American Psychologist, 46,* 187–197.

Ibrahim, F. A. (1985). Effective cross-cultural counseling and psychotherapy: A framework. *The Counseling Psychologist, 13,* 625–638.

Inclan, J. (1985). Variations in value orientations in mental health work with Puerto Ricans. *Psychotherapy, 22,* 324–334.

Ivey, A. E. (1981). Counseling and psychotherapy: Toward a new perspective. In A. J. Marsella & P. B. Pedersen (Eds.), *Cross-cultural counseling and psychotherapy* (pp. 17–33). New York: Pergamon Press.

Ivey, A. E. (1986). *Developmental therapy.* San Francisco: Jossey-Bass.

Ivey, A. E. (1988). *Intentional interviewing and counseling.* Pacific Grove, CA: Brooks/Cole.

Ivey, A. E. (1993a). *Instructor's manual for counseling and psychotherapy: A multicultural perspective.* Boston: Allyn and Bacon.

Ivey, A. E. (1993b). *Intentional interviewing and counseling facilitating development in a multicultural society.* Pacific Grove, CA: Brooks/Cole.

Ivey, A. E. (1993c). On the need for reconstruction of our present practice of counseling and psychotherapy. *The Counseling Psychologist, 21,* 225–228.

Ivey, A. E., & Authier, J. (1978). *Microcounseling: Innovations in interviewing training.* Springfield, IL: Thomas.

Ivey, A. E., Ivey, M. B., & Simek-Morgan, L. (1993). *Counseling and psychotherapy: A multicultural perspective.* Boston: Allyn and Bacon.

Ivey, A. E., & Payton, P. (in press). *Cornish identity theory: Affirmation or denigration?* Cornwall, England: Cornish Studies.

Jackson, B. (1975). Black identity development. *Journal of Educational Diversity, 2,* 19–25.

Johnston, W. B., & Packer, A. H. (1987). *Workforce 2000: Work and workers for the twenty-first century.* Indianapolis, IN: Hudson Institute.

Jones, J. M. (1972). *Prejudice and racism.* Reading, MA: Addison-Wesley.

Kakar, S. (1982). *Shamans, mystics, and doctors: A psychological inquiry into India and its healing traditions.* New York: Knopf.

Katz, J. (1985). The sociopolitical nature of counseling. *The Counseling Psychologist, 13,* 615–624.

Kelly, G. (1955). *The psychology of personal constructs.* New York: Norton.

Kleinke, C. L. (1994). *Common principles of psychotherapy.* Pacific Grove, CA: Brooks/Cole.

Kluckhohn, F. R., & Strodtbeck, F. L. (1961). *Variations in value orientations.* Evanston, IL: Row, Patterson, & Co.

Korchin, S. J. (1976). *Modern clinical psychology.* New York: Basic Books.

Kuhn, T. S. (1970). *The structure of scientific revolutions* (2nd ed.). Chicago: University of Chicago Press.

LaFromboise, T. D. (1988). American Indian mental health policy. *American Psychologist, 43,* 388–397.

LaFromboise, T. D., Coleman, H., & Hernandez, A. (1991). Development and factor structure of the cross-cultural counseling inventory—revised. *Professional Psychology: Research and Practice, 22,* 380–388.

LaFromboise, T. D., Trimble, J. E., & Mohatt, G. V. (1990). Counseling intervention and American Indian tradition: An integrative approach. *The Counseling Psychologist, 18*(4), 628–654.

Lazarus, A. A. (1967). In support of technical eclecticism. *Psychological Reports, 21,* 415–416.

Lazarus, A. A. (Ed.). (1976). *Multimodal behavior therapy.* New York: Springer-Verlag.

Lazarus, A. A. (1984). Multimodal therapy. In R. J. Corsini (Ed.), *Current psychotherapies.* Itasca, IL: F. E. Peacock.

Lazarus, A. A., & Messer, S. B. (1991). Does chaos prevail? An exchange on technical eclecticism and assimilation integration. *Journal of Psychotherapy Integration, 1,* 143–158.

Lee, C. C., Oh, M. Y., & Mountcastle, A. R. (1992). Indigenous models of helping in nonwestern countries: Implications for multicultural counseling. *Journal of Multicultural Counseling and Development, 20,* 1–10.

Lee, D. Y., & Uhlemann, M. R. (1984). Comparison of verbal responses of Rogers, Shostrom, and Lazarus. *Journal of Counseling Psychology, 32,* 91–94.

Lee, Y. T. (1993). Psychology needs no prejudice but the diversity of cultures. *American Psychologist, 48,* 1090–1091.

Leong, F. T. (1986). Counseling and psychotherapy with Asian-Americans: Review of literature. *Journal of Counseling Psychology, 33,* 196–206.

Locke, D. C. (1992). *Increasing multicultural understanding.* Newbury Park, CA: Sage.

Lum, R. G. (1982). Mental health attitudes and opinions of Chinese. In E. E. Jones and S. J. Korchin (Eds.), *Minority mental health* (pp. 165–189). New York: Praeger.

Marsella, A. (1979). Culture and mental disorders. In A. J. Marsella, R. Tharp, & T. Ciborowski (Eds.), *Perspectives on cross-cultural psychology* (pp. 233–262). New York: Academic Press.

Mays, V. M. (1985). The Black American and psychotherapy: The dilemma. *Psychotherapy, 22,* 379–388.

McGoldrick, M., Pearce, J., & Giordano, J. (Eds.). (1982). *Ethnicity and family therapy.* New York: Guilford Press.

McIntosh, P. (1989, July/August). White privilege: Unpacking the invisible knapsack. *Peace and Freedom,* pp. 8–10.

Meara, N. M., Pepinsky, H. B., Shannon, J. W., & Murray, W. A. (1981). Semantic communication and expectations for counseling across three theoretical orientations. *Journal of Counseling Psychology, 28,* 110–118.

Meichenbaum, D. (1985). *Stress inoculation training.* New York: Pergamon Press.

Mio, J. S., & Iwamasa, G. (1993). To do, or not to do: That is the question for White cross-cultural researchers. *The Counseling Psychologist, 21,* 197–212.

Nishio, K., & Bilmes, M. (1987). Psychotherapy with Southeast Asian American clients. *Professional Psychology: Research and Practice, 18,* 342–346.

Nobles, W. (1986). *African psychology: Toward its reclamation, reascension, and revitalization.* Oakland, CA: Black Family Institute.

Norcross, J. C., & Prochaska, J. O. (1988). A study of eclectic (and integrative) views revisited. *Professional Psychology, 19,* 170–174.

Nwachuku, U. (1990, July). Translating multicultural theory into direct action: Culture-specific counseling. Paper presented at the International Round Table for the Advancement of Counseling, Helsinki, Finland.

Nwachuku, U., & Ivey, A. (1991). Culture specific counseling: An alternative approach. *Journal of Counseling and Development, 70,* 106–111.

Padilla, A. M., Lindholm, K. J., Chen, A., Duran, R., Hakuta, K., Lambert, W., &

Tucker, C. R. (1991). The English-only movement: Myths, reality and implications for psychology. *American Psychologist, 46*, 120–130.

Paniagua, F. (1994). *Assessing and treating culturally diverse clients*. Newbury Park, CA: Sage.

Parham, T. A. (1989). Cycles of psychological nigrescence. *The Counseling Psychologist, 17*, 187–226.

Parham, T. A. (1993a). *Psychological storms: The African American struggle for identity*. Chicago, IL: African American Images.

Parham, T. A. (1993b). White researchers conducting multicultural counseling research: Can their efforts be "mo' betta"? *The Counseling Psychologist, 21*, 250–256.

Parham, T. A., & Helms, J. E. (1981). The influence of Black students' racial attitudes on preferences for counselor's race. *Journal of Counseling Psychology, 28*, 250–257.

Parham, T. A., & McDavis, R. J. (1987). Black men and endangered species: Who's really pulling the trigger? *Journal of Counseling and Development, 66*, 24–27.

Patterson, C. H. (1980). *Theories of counseling and psychotherapy*. New York: Harper & Row.

Pedersen, P. B. (1985). *Handbook of cross-cultural counseling and therapy*. Westport, CT: Greenwood Press.

Pedersen, P. B. (1986a). The cultural role of conceptual and contextual support systems in counseling. *Journal of the American Mental Health Counselor's Association, 8*, 35–42.

Pedersen, P. B. (1986b). Developing interculturally skilled counselors: A training program. In H. Lefley & P. Pedersen (Eds.), *Cross-cultural training of mental health professionals* (pp. 50–62). Springfield, IL: Thomas.

Pedersen, P. B. (1987). Ten frequent assumptions of cultural bias in counseling. *Journal of Multicultural Counseling and Development, 15*, 16–24.

Pedersen, P. B. (1988). *A handbook for developing multicultural awareness*. Alexandria, VA: American Association for Counseling and Development.

Pedersen, P. B. (Ed.). (1991). Multiculturalism as a fourth force in counseling [special issue]. *Journal of Counseling and Development, 70*.

Pedersen, P. B. (1994). *A handbook for developing multicultural awareness* (2nd ed.). Alexandria, VA: American Counseling Association.

Pedersen, P. B. (1994). *Culture-centered counseling: A search for accuracy*. Newbury Park, CA: Sage.

Pedersen, P. B., & Ivey, A. (1993). *Culture-centered counseling and interviewing skills*. New York: Greenwood Press.

Piaget, J. (1965). *The moral judgement of the child*. New York: Macmillan, 1965.

Pickett, S. A., Vraniak, D. A., Cook, J. A., & Cohler, B. J. (1993). Strengths in adversity: Blacks bear burden better than Whites. *Professional Psychology: Research and Practice, 24*(4), 460–467.

Polkinghorne, D. E. (1988). *Narrative knowing and the human sciences*. Albany, NY: SUNY Press.

Ponterotto, J. G. (1988a). Racial consciousness development among White counselor trainees. *Journal of Multicultural Counseling and Development, 16*, 146–156.

Ponterotto, J. G. (1988b). Racial/ethnic minority research in the *Journal of Counseling Psychology:* A content analysis and methodological critique. *Journal of Counseling Psychology, 53,* 410–418.

Ponterotto, J. G. (1993). White racial identity and the counseling professional. *The Counseling Psychologist, 21,* 213–217.

Ponterotto, J. G., & Casas, J. M. (1991). *Handbook of racial/ethnic minority counseling research.* Springfield, IL: Thomas.

Ponterotto, J. G., & Sabnani, H. B. (1989). "Classics" in multicultural counseling: A systematic five-year content analysis. *Journal of Multicultural Counseling and Development, 17,* 23–37.

Ponterotto, J. G., Sanchez, C. M., & Magids, D. M. (1991, August). Initial development and validation of the Multicultural Counseling Awareness Scale (MCAS). Paper presented at the annual meeting of the American Psychological Association, San Francisco.

Ramsey, S., & Birk, J. (1983). Preparation of North Americans for interaction with Japanese: Considerations of language and communication style. In D. Landis & R. Brislin (Eds.), *Handbook of intercultural training: Vol. 3. Area studies in intercultural training* (pp. 227–259). New York: Pergamon Press.

Red Horse, J. (1983). Indian family values and experiences. In G. J. Powell, J. Yamamoto, A. Romero, & K. A. Morales (Eds.), *The psychosocial development of minority group children* (pp. 258–272). New York: Brunner/Mazel.

Reisman, J. (1971). *Toward the integration of psychotherapy.* New York: Wiley.

Reynolds, A. (1995). Challenges and strategies for teaching multicultural counseling courses. In J. G. Ponterotto, J. M. Casas, L. A. Suzuki, & C. M. Alexander (Eds.), *Handbook of multicultural counseling* (pp. 312–330). Newbury Park, CA: Sage.

Ridley, C. R. (1984). Clinical treatment of the nondisclosing Black client. *American Psychologist, 39,* 1234–1244.

Root, M. P. P. (1985). Guidelines for facilitating therapy with Asian American clients. *Psychotherapy, 22,* 349–356.

Rowe, W., Bennett, S., & Atkinson, D. R. (1993). White racial identity consciousness: A social learning analysis. *The Counseling Psychologist, 22*(1), 129–146.

Ruiz, P., & Ruiz, P. P. (1983). Treatment compliance among Hispanics. *Journal of Operational Psychiatry, 14,* 112–114.

Sabnani, H. B., Ponterotto, J. G., & Borodovsky, L. G. (1991). White racial identity development and cross-cultural counselor training. *The Counseling Psychologist, 19,* 76–102.

Sarbin, T. (Ed.). (1986). *Narrative psychology: The storied nature of human conduct.* New York: Praeger.

Schofield, W. (1964). *Psychotherapy: The purchase of friendship.* Englewood Cliffs, NJ: Prentice-Hall.

Shostrom, E. L. (Producer). (1966). *Three approaches to psychotherapy: I* [Film]. Santa Ana, CA: Psychological Films.

Shostrom, E. L. (Producer). (1977). *Three approaches to psychotherapy: II* [Film]. Santa Ana, CA: Psychological Films.

Smith, E. M. J. (1985). Ethnic minorities: Life stress, social support, and mental health issues. *The Counseling Psychologist, 13,* 537–579.

Sodowsky, G. R., Taffe, R. C., Gutkin, T. B., & Wise, S. L. (1994). Development of the multicultural counseling inventory: A self-report measure of multicultural competencies. *Journal of Counseling Psychology, 41*, 137–148.

Spiegel, J., & Papajohn, J. (1983). *Final report: Training program on ethnicity and mental health.* Waltham, MA: The Florence Heller School, Brandeis University.

Spindler, G., & Spindler, L. (1994). *Pathways to cultural awareness: Cultural therapy with teachers and students.* Thousand Oaks, CA: Corwin.

Steenbarger, B. (1991). Contextualism in counseling. *Journal for Counseling and Development, 70*, 288–299.

Stevenson, H. C., & Renard, G. (1993). Trusting Ole' Wise Owls: Therapeutic use of cultural strengths in African American families. *Professional Psychology: Research and Practice, 24*(4), 433–442.

Sue, D. W. (1978). Eliminating cultural oppression in counseling: Toward a general theory. *Journal of Counseling Psychology, 25*, 419–428.

Sue, D. W. (1981). *Counseling the culturally different: Theory and practice.* New York: Wiley.

Sue, D. W. (1990). Culture specific techniques in counseling: A conceptual framework. *Professional Psychology, 21*, 424–433.

Sue, D. W. (1991a). A conceptual model for cultural diversity training. *Journal of Counseling and Development, 70*, 99–105.

Sue, D. W. (1991b). A diversity perspective on contextualism. *Journal of Counseling and Development, 70*, 300–301.

Sue, D. W., (1992). The challenge of multiculturalism: The road less traveled. *American Counselor, 1*, 7–14.

Sue, D. W. (1993). Confronting ourselves: The White and racial/ethnic minority researcher. *The Counseling Psychologist, 21*, 244–249.

Sue, D. W. (1994). Asian American mental health and help-seeking behavior: Comment on Solberg, et al. (1994), Tata & Leong (1994), and Lin (1994). *Journal of Counseling Psychology, 41*, 292–295.

Sue, D. W. (1995a). Multicultural organizational development: Implications for the counseling profession. In J. G. Ponterotto, J. M. Casas, L. A. Suzuki, & C. M. Alexander (Eds.), *Handbook of multicultural counseling* (pp. 474–492). Newbury Park, CA: Sage.

Sue, D. W. (1995b). Toward a theory of multicultural counseling and therapy. In J. A. Banks & C. A. McGee Banks (Eds.), *Handbook of research on multicultural education* (pp. 647–659). New York: Macmillan.

Sue, D. W., Arredondo, P., & McDavis, R. J. (1992). Multicultural competencies/ standards: A pressing need. *Journal of Counseling and Development, 70*(4), 477–486.

Sue, D. W., Bernier, J. B., Durran, M., Feinberg, L., Pedersen, P., Smith, E., & Vasquez-Nuttall, E. (1982). Position paper: Cross-cultural counseling competencies. *The Counseling Psychologist, 10*, 45–52.

Sue, D., Sue, D. W., & Sue, S. (1994). *Understanding abnormal behavior* (4th ed.). Boston: Houghton-Mifflin.

Sue, D. W., & Sue, D. (1977). Barriers to effective cross-cultural counseling. *Journal of Counseling Psychology, 24*, 420–429.

Sue, D. W., & Sue, D. (1990). *Counseling the culturally different: Theory and practice.* New York: Wiley.

Sue, D. W., & Sue, S. (1972). Ethnic minorities: Resistance to being researched. *Professional Psychology, 2,* 11–17.

Sue, S., Allen, D., & Conaway, L. (1975). The responsiveness and equality of mental health care to Chicanos and Native Americans. *American Journal of Community Psychology, 5,* 583–591.

Sue, S., & McKinney, H. (1975). Asian Americans in the community mental health care system. *American Journal of Orthopsychiatry, 45,* 11–118.

Sue, S., McKinney, H., Allen, D., & Hall, J. (1974). Delivery of community health services to Black and White clients. *Journal of Consulting Psychology, 42,* 794–801.

Sue, S., & Morishima, J. (1982). *The mental health of Asian Americans.* San Francisco: Jossey-Bass.

Sue, S., & Zane, N. W. S. (1987). The role of culture and cultural techniques in psychotherapy: A critique and reformulation. *American Psychologist, 42,* 37–45.

Szapocznik, J., & Kurtines, W. M. (1993). Family psychology and cultural diversity. *American Psychologist, 48,* 400–407.

Szasz, T. (1961). *The myth of mental illness.* New York: Dell.

Taub-Bynum, E. B. (1984). *The family unconscious.* Wheaton, IL: Quest.

Taub-Bynum, E. B. (1992). *Family dreams: The intimate web.* Ithaca, NY: Hayworth.

Thomas, A., & Sillen, S. (1972). *Racism and psychiatry.* New York: Brunner/Mazel.

Thomas, M. B., & Dansby, P. G. (1985). Black clients: Family structures, therapeutic issues, and strengths. *Psychotherapy, 22,* 398–407.

U.S. Census Bureau. (1990). *Statistical abstract of the United States: 1990.* Washington, DC: U.S. Government Printing Office.

Weinrach, S. G. (1986). Ellis and Gloria: Positive or negative model? *Psychotherapy, 23,* 642–647.

White, J. L. (1984). *The psychology of Blacks: An Afro-American perspective.* Englewood Cliffs, NJ: Prentice-Hall.

White, J. L., & Parham, T. A. (1990). *The psychology of Blacks.* Englewood Cliffs, NJ: Prentice-Hall.

Wrenn, C. G. (1962). The culturally-encapsulated counselor. *Harvard Educational Review, 32,* 444–449.

Wrenn, C. G. (1985). Afterward: The culturally-encapsulated counselor revisited. In P. B. Pedersen (Ed.), *Handbook of cross-cultural counseling and therapy.* Westport, CT: Greenwood Press.

P A R T   I I

IMPLICATIONS OF MCT THEORY

This part focuses on the broadest implications of MCT theory rather than on specific populations. Contributors discuss MCT theory with respect to traditional theories of counseling, research, practice, training, and organizational development; indigenous models of helping; and ethnocentrism/bias in counseling. Again, authors were given considerable freedom in how they wanted to tackle the subjects. While some chose to focus on specific points and others addressed broader issues, we encouraged all to consider initially (1) general implications of the topic, (2) strengths and limitations of MCT theory with respect to the topic, and (3) future directions and/or recommendations they would make.

As mentioned in the introduction to Part I, we offer a brief "assumption audit" of each contributor's chapter at the beginning of each one. Again, we encourage you to conduct your own analysis of the chapters as well.

CHAPTER 4

MCT Theory and Implications for Organizations/Systems

Pamela Highlen
The Ohio State University

Assumption Audit

- MCT theory embodies social constructionism, allowing people to construct their worlds through social processes.
- MCT theory includes cultural relativism, a sociopolitical stance, an ecological and social-systems approach, and participant-focused methodologies.
- MCT theory extols a relational view of language rather than a representational one.
- MCT theory is contextualist.
- MCT theory offers a both/and rather than an either/or theory.
- MCT theory is pluralistic and addresses multiple oppressions.
- MCT theory defines self-in-relation.
- MCT theory acknowledges the strengths of clients' different backgrounds.
- MCT theory reiterates the importance of multiple counseling roles.
- MCT theory advocates reframing narrowly defined ethical perspectives.
- All theory, including MCT theory, is culture-bound.
- MCT theory combines multiculturalism with transpersonal psychology in its claim to be a "fourth force."
- MCT theory bridges the schism between indigenous/metaphysical and Western healing practices by drawing on parallels with chaos and complexity theory.
- MCT theory focuses on the roles of change agents by combining self with context.
- MCT theory combines internal and external data from multiple cultural viewpoints.

- MCT theory conceptualizes the organization as a living entity: organization-in-relation.
- MCT theory combines metaphysical and Western approaches in assessment and intervention strategies.
- MCT theory serves as a bridge between counseling and the social sciences.

Myers, Echemendia, and Trimble (1991) conclude that "the average new PhD in psychology is only slightly more competent to meet the mental health needs of our culturally diverse population than psychologists who completed their training 20 years ago" (p. 3). Sue, Ivey, and Pedersen's metatheory of MCT (see Chapters 1–3) provides one promising tool for remedying the current state of affairs. Multiculturalism needs a pluralistic and inclusive metatheory as the helping profession moves into the 21st century.

This chapter begins with an overall reaction to MCT theory by highlighting its strengths (1) specifically as a theory within postmodernism and (2) generally as a theory of multiculturalism. Next, I offer the interface between quantum physics and the metaphysical as a bridge between indigenous healing approaches and MCT. Using this expanded framework, I then address the implications of MCT theory for organizational development.

MCT THEORY:
THE VIRTUES ARE MANY

MCT Theory Within the Postmodern Tradition

MCT theory exemplifies many strengths of the postmodern philosophy of science. First, MCT theory embodies *social constructionism*, meaning that people construct their worlds through social processes that contain cultural symbols and metaphors. MCT theory addresses four implications of social constructionism identified by Watts (1992): (1) *cultural relativism*, meaning that each culture is unique and must be understood in reference to itself, not in reference to the dominant (or any other) culture; (2) a *sociopolitical stance*, implying the unfairness of one group imposing its standards on another, and noting the dynamics of dominant-subordinate relationships

Mary Hill's review of this manuscript is gratefully appreciated. Her "student perspective" contributed to the readability of this paper.

among culturally different groups; (3) an *ecological and social-systems approach*, meaning that people are influenced by historical, cultural, and social conditioning when they interact with the environment; and (4) *participant-focused methodologies*, meaning that helping professionals must understand *and* acknowledge the impact of their social conditioning and worldview on their research, theory, and practice (p. 117). Each theorist, researcher, and practitioner has a gender and is multiculturally situated, speaking "from a particular class, racial, cultural, and ethnic community background," who "approaches the world with a set of ideas, a framework (theory, ontology) that specifies a set of questions (epistemology) that are then examined (methodology, analysis) in specific ways" (Denzin & Lincoln, 1994, p. 11).

Second, MCT theory extols a *relational view of language*, as opposed to a representational one. Gergen (1994) notes that the *representational* view of language in the modern tradition of positivist psychology speaks of "objective knowledge" and

> operates as a conversational trump . . . denigrating all hands not dealt in these terms (e.g., evidence, measurement, reliability). Any views not based on scientific tenets—for example, those of sundry religions, political action groups, ethnicities, genders, cultures—can be dismissed as folk beliefs—or more pejoratively, as value-based, superstitious, or despotic. (p. 413)

MCT theory implicitly acknowledges the *relational* view of language of *all* cultures, thereby allowing "realities" and "truths" to exist beyond the Western scientific tradition. This position is critical for MCT theory to be inclusive.

Third, MCT theory is *contextualist*, meaning that behavior must be understood within the context of its occurrence and that context can be embedded within context upon context, and so on (Szapocznik & Kurtines, 1993). As such, MCT theory challenges the notion of "universal psychology" (see Highlen, 1994) by acknowledging that traditional counseling theories are Euro- and androcentric (male-oriented) in origin, which makes them culture-bound. Assumptions regarding their applicability to many cultural groups are erroneous unless supported by systematic inquiry and data using diverse ontologies and epistemologies.

Fourth, MCT theory offers a "both/and" rather than an "either/or" view of theory, research, and practice. For example, all theories are allowed to exist under the MCT umbrella, even if they posit diametrically opposed principles (e.g., reductionism vs. wholism). Like an artistic sculpture, multiculturalism can be viewed and appreciated from all perspectives. Diverse theories and counseling practices provide different perspectives of the same phenomenon. Each perspective captures a different *and* valid view. This "both/and" perspective is reiterated in terms of MCT theory's view of research. Although the qualitative (empirical) paradigm is offered as particularly well suited for MCT investigations, MCT theory validates the quantitative (experimental) paradigm as well. One challenge contemporary helping professionals face is to allow multiple perspectives to coexist, even if they break with conventional and familiar ways of knowing. MCT invites the profession to do that.

A Theory of Multiculturalism

As a theory of multiculturalism, MCT theory exhibits additional strengths. First, this theory is *pluralistic*—that is, it acknowledges all "-isms" by addressing sexism, classism, heterosexism, and "biracialism" as well as racism. This inclusionary approach allows for the direct consideration of *multiple oppressions*, thus acknowledging the reality many people face (for instance, African-American working-class lesbians). Reynolds and Pope (1991) offer a Multidimensional Identity Model (MIM) that may assist helping professionals in working with multiple oppressions. The use of MIM has been extended to vocational counseling as well (Highlen & Sudarsky-Gleiser, 1994). Furthermore, MCT theory implicitly acknowledges that ethnocentrism is not the exclusive domain of Euro-Americans—that, for example, as African, Asian, European, or Latina(o) Americans, we accept and appreciate the richness of *all* diversity (that is, gender, sexual orientation, race/ethnicity, age, religion, physical ability, etc.).

Second, MCT theory reformulates "self" as *"self-in-relation."* In Western psychology, *self* has been defined primarily as the self-contained individual acting with autonomy and a sense of separation from and even opposition to others and the environment (Page & Berkow, 1991). In contrast, African (L. J. Myers, 1988), Asian (Knoblauch, 1985), Latina(o) (Padilla, Ruiz, & Alvarez, 1989) and indigenous (Highwater, 1981) cultures emphasize collectivism; that is, family, community, and ancestors are inherently intertwined with *self*. Nobles (1976) uses the phrase *extended self* to describe the African sense of self that includes all ancestors—those yet to be born and all of nature, as well as the surrounding community. More recently, *extended self* has been defined as "one's sense of self inextricably *intertwined* with one's sense of family, community, culture(s), and cosmos as they reside *within*" (Highlen & Sudarsky-Gleiser, 1994, p. 307). Reframing "self" as "self-in-relation" for *all* people, including Euro-Americans, is important, because one's worldview is not synonymous with one's apparent characteristics (i.e., race/ethnicity, sex).

Third, MCT theory acknowledges the *strengths* clients bring with them from their multiple backgrounds. In an extension of this position, one can assess facilitators *and* the barriers clients have incorporated into their extended self from ethnic culture(s), family, and community, as well as from the dominant social order (Highlen & Sudarsky-Gleiser, 1994). For example, a gay Latino American may internalize the barriers of racism and heterosexism that his family, community, and ethnic culture have espoused, in addition to the barriers he may have introjected from Euro-American culture. Likewise, his sense of *familismo* (that he and his family are inseparable, and each will support the other) may act as a facilitator in his struggle to reclaim his sense of worth.

Fourth, MCT theory reiterates the importance of *multiple counselor roles* beyond those of counselor and psychotherapist. As identified by Atkinson, Thompson, and Grant (1993), the roles of advisor, advocate, facilitator of indigenous support and healing systems, consultant, and change agent are crucial in serving *all* clients. Graduate education has to date excluded nontraditional roles. These new roles thus challenge graduate programs to incorporate these multiple roles in the educational experiences of its students.

Fifth, MCT theory acknowledges the *"culturally narrow perspective" of contemporary ethical principles* and advocates reframing or violating them as necessary to serve clients. When helping professionals work in a homogeneous ethnic environment, avoiding dual relationships is difficult and potentially harmful. Often, members of racial/ethnic groups must get to know helping professionals as members of the community before they will trust them as helpers. For example, working on a Lakota Sioux reservation requires one to honor Lakota Sioux customs. Informal nonprofessional contact may be necessary to establish the counselor's credibility.

A Bridge Between Western and Indigenous Healing Approaches

As Sue, Ivey, and Pedersen note, all theory is culture-centered. They acknowledge that MCT theory is culture-bound in terms of their worldview; that is, they "still often rely on western concepts of theoretical and research validity" (p. 30). It is also culture-bound in its use of English, given that every language carries with it a particular structure and meaning, one that is not universal. Culture-bound conceptualization is reflected in images as well as words. For example, the authors employ three-dimensional cube representations. Other writers (Fukuyama, 1994; Myers et al., 1991) prefer spirals and circles. Diverse images reflect different ways theorists, researchers, and practitioners view the world. One needs an awareness of such differences to recognize the specific culture-bound parameters of any theory. Because of these inescapable culture-bound parameters, Sue et al. welcome ongoing examination and evaluation of MCT theory. Their invitation for diverse input assists a commonly shared quest: the enhancement of MCT. They have also encouraged helping professionals to draw on new and indigenous systems of healing as well as on traditional Western systems of helping. It is in this spirit that I offer the following comments.[1]

The Western Ontology of MCT Theory

A strength and limitation of MCT theory is that its propositions and corollaries are grounded in the *available* multicultural theory and research. That is, this theory is comprehensive in its use of Western literature embedded within a Western ontology, but it is limited by its primary reliance on "mainstream" multicultural literature. Although MCT theory advocates the study of indigenous systems of healing, it does not articulate an ontology that actively embraces indigenous and new healing approaches. This limitation is due primarily to the schism that occurred between religion and science centuries ago. (See Highlen, 1994, and Jecmen, 1993, for an elaboration of the split between science/psychology and religion.) Within contemporary Western psychology, this schism has continued to restrict metaphysical and indigenous approaches from entering "mainstream" professional organizations and journals. For example, transpersonal psychology (TP)[2] has been denied divisional status in the American Psychological Association three times. This exclusionary stance has hampered the exchange of knowledge between Western and metaphysical journals as well. Use of the phrase "fourth force" illustrates this point. Sutich (1969) first used *fourth force* to describe the new movement of transpersonal psychology. Sutich's article and others related to TP have appeared outside of standard Western journals (e.g., the *Journal of Transpersonal Psychology*). More recently, *fourth force* has been used to characterize multiculturalism (Pedersen, 1991). Therefore, multiculturalism is considered the "fourth force" in mainstream psychology.

Transpersonal psychology is not that removed from Western psychology. In fact, it bridges the gap between Western existential and psychodynamic traditions and the world's perennial philosophy, or the mystical tradition that underlies spiritual practices across religions (Wittine, 1989). The word *transpersonal*, derived from Latin, means "beyond and through the mask or personality." Wittine (1989) has identified five postulates of transpersonal psychology:

1. The need for healing/growth on all levels of the spectrum of identity—egoic, existential, and transpersonal

---

[1] This material reflects my worldview and comes from work I have done to bridge the chasm between science and the metaphysical.

[2] Transpersonal psychology "has been defined as referring to states of consciousness extending beyond the customary ego boundaries and the ordinary limitations of time and space" (Grof, 1985; Walsh & Vaughan, 1980; both cited in Wittine, 1989, p. 269).

2. The therapist's unfolding awareness of the Self, or deep center of Being, and his or her spiritual perspective on life as central to the therapeutic process
3. The process of awakening from a lesser to a greater identity
4. The healing, restorative nature of inner awareness and intuition
5. The transformative potential in the therapeutic relationship, not only for the client but also for the therapist. (pp. 269–270).

Although I have followed these tenets in my work as a psychologist for many years, it wasn't until I began reading the transpersonal psychology literature that I realized that my professional work was transpersonal in nature. Because other mainstream helping professionals may share my experience, I have included a case example that illustrates how MCT consultants can apply transpersonal psychology to their work with an organization.

Say, for instance, MCT consultants are hired by a corporate executive officer (CEO) because his company is "failing." The CEO has, in his words, "hit a wall." Sales are down; marketing techniques that worked in the past are no longer effective. In sum, all previously successful business strategies have failed. These strategies are based on a "win-lose" mentality, an authoritarian leadership style, and a reward-punishment philosophy. Because of his "winning record" during the past 10 years, the CEO has *become* his occupational role. He defines his self-worth in terms of his accomplishments. Now that his accomplishments are crumbling, he feels fear, anxiety, and depression. From a transpersonal perspective, the CEO has lost touch with his deep center of Being. The consultants help the CEO examine his fears. For example, what would it mean if his business failed? Would he be worthless as a person? Would his family and friends desert him? Would he desert himself? They also explore the CEO's high need for control and mistrust of himself and of his employees. To move from a lesser to a greater personal and organizational identity, the CEO must recognize that he must accept "death" (letting go) for transformation to occur. In other words, he must let go of beliefs and practices that no longer work.

Concurrently, the consultants provide alternate ways for the CEO to respond to this crisis. Instead of finding people to blame for the company's misfortunes, he is encouraged to redirect his energy to creative and collaborative problem solving. The consultants reframe employees as allies who can assist in this process; a positive, nonjudgmental "we're in this together" atmosphere is fostered. As a result, risk taking is rewarded. Diverse ideas are actively solicited and acknowledged. The "win-lose" mentality is replaced with a "win-win" approach, in which people receive support and respect for who they are. Through this process, the CEO sees that everyone in the organization is interconnected and essential to the system's well-being. All members of the organization begin relating to each other in more authentic and respectful ways. As his faith and trust in himself and others increases, the CEO is encouraged to listen to his inner awareness and to trust his intuition more. Through the spiraling process of change, the CEO becomes increasingly in touch with his deep center of Being. The consultants realize that they, too, have been affected by their work with the CEO. As their consultation comes to a close, the consultants discuss with the CEO the transformative effects this shared experience has had on them. By incorporating transpersonal psychology and metaphysical literature, MCT can thus bridge the schism between indigenous/metaphysical and Western healing practices.

Ontology of Indigenous Worldviews

Indigenous worldviews and healing approaches are holistic and based on knowledge of self rather than context. For example, shamans[3] who journey to other planes of existence in their healing rituals know that their experiences are real. Similarly, people who experience near death experiences (NDEs), do not have to have NDE replicated or experimentally validated to know that during NDE they left their physical bodies, observed what was happening around them, and journeyed to "higher" levels of existence. (See personal accounts by Brinkley, 1994, and Eadie, 1992). In contrast, through the ontology and epistemology of Western counseling and therapy, healing methods are caught in their *reliance on sensory information, defined by the physical plane of existence*. As a result, Western science has been reluctant to examine phenomena that cannot be measured. Hence, ancient healing methods have not been acknowledged as "legitimate" areas of study. This perspective is both shortsighted and unfortunate, because western healing can learn much from that which it has eschewed over the centuries.

Indigenous Healing Approaches
Briefly Noted

The metaphysical tradition acknowledges that an energy field surrounds and penetrates the physical body. This three-dimensional energy field occupies the same space as the physical body and extends beyond it (Talbot, 1991). Ancient methods of healing, such as Chinese acupuncture and Hindu chakra work, acknowledge the existence of *subtle matter* (matter less

---

[3] Walsh (1990) defines *shamanism* as "a family of traditions whose practitioners focus on voluntarily entering altered states of consciousness in which they experience themselves or their spirit(s), traveling to other realms at will, and interacting with other entities in order to serve their community" (p. 11).

dense than the physical). This subtle matter or etheric body is seen as a counterpart of the physical body. According to Talbot (1991), ancient Indian yogic texts refer to special energy centers called *chakras* (Sanskrit for "wheels"), which are connected to endocrine glands and nerve centers. These chakras take in higher energies that the physical body can use. As reported by Gerber (1988), acupuncture identifies a meridian system of microscopic ducts that connect the physical and etheric aspects of the body. These meridians relay ch'i (a subtle form of energy) to parts of the physical body through energetic portals in the skin called *acupuncture points*. Chakra and acupuncture healing practices utilize subtle matter to balance and heal the body and mind on the physical plane. People commonly view acupuncture as a treatment to relieve pain; however, acupuncture as an energetic treatment heals the body of disease.

Ancient indigenous traditions, such as African and Lakota Sioux, also believe in the inseparability of all life as it exists on earth and in the cosmos. This interconnectedness transcends time and space. The microcosm (e.g., the individual) is believed to mirror the macrocosm (the cosmos) (see Myers, 1988, and Neihardt, 1972). "Psi phenomena" are accepted as natural aspects of healing, because space and time have no true meaning. Examples of psi phenomena include clairvoyance (seeing across space and time—retrocognition and precognition) and out-of-body experiences, such as the shaman's "journey" to other worlds.

The Bridge Between the Physical and the Metaphysical

Recent advances in quantum physics and holography, in particular, have made it possible to bridge the chasm between the physical (science) and the metaphysical (spirituality).[4] This bridge can help healers understand and legitimize traditional indigenous and new systems of healing. Quantum physics and the holographic paradigm challenge the following assumptions within traditional counseling and therapy:

1. Reality consists of distinct and separate objects (e.g., counselor and client, observer and observed).
2. Reality consists of what can be observed and measured through the five senses.
3. Space and time are fixed, absolute constructs of reality.

Quantum physics has demonstrated that at the particle level all matter is energy; in other words, matter and energy are dual expressions of the

---

[4]Only simplified and limited coverage of this topic is given here. For those interested in pursuing this topic, I highly recommend Talbot (1991) and Gerber (1988).

same universal substance (Gerber, 1988). Energy and matter possess frequency characteristics. The higher the frequency of matter, the less dense it becomes (Gerber, 1988). Therefore, one can view etheric or subtle energy bodies, recognized by indigenous healers, as matter that vibrates at a higher frequency than the matter of the physical body.

Research in holography has led some scientists to propose a holographic theory of the brain (Pribram, 1977) and of the universe (Bohm, 1980). Holography allows three-dimensional representations to be created when interference patterns of two energy waves ripple through each other.[5] Each interference pattern is a holistic representation of all interference patterns contained in the whole. Therefore, any piece of a hologram can recreate the whole. For example, any portion of a holographic picture of a rose held up to laser light will show an image of the entire rose. Also, increasing the accumulation of interference patterns creates the denser energy/matter associated with physical objects; everything in the universe is composed of sets of interference patterns, varying in density. Gerber (1988) believes that the human energy field is a holographic template, and that thoughts, as manifestations of consciousness, affect physical health. Interference patterns of holograms are translated by the human brain (a complex interference pattern) into familiar objects and images. The implications of the holographic brain suggest that "objective" reality does not exist. Is it possible

> that what the mystics had been saying for centuries was true, reality was *maya*, an illusion, and what was out there was really a vast, resonating symphony of wave forms, a "frequency domain" that was transformed into the world as we know it only after it entered our senses? (Talbot, 1991, p. 31)

Bohm's holographic theory of the universe says that the cosmos consists of energy interference patterns with holographic characteristics. Decoding a small part of the cosmic hologram can provide information about the whole universe. Bohm believes that

> the tangible reality of our everyday lives is really a kind of illusion, like a holographic image. Underlying it is a deeper order of existence, a vast and more primary level of reality that gives birth to all the objects and appearances of our physical world in much the same way that a piece of holographic film gives birth to a hologram. . . . This deeper level of reality [is] the *implicate* (which means "enfolded") order, and . . . our own level of existence [is] the *explicate*, or unfolded, order. (Talbot, 1991, p. 46)

---

[5] This brief description of holographic theory was distilled from Gerber (1988), Jecmen (1993), and Talbot (1991).

Bohm "believes that everything in the universe is part of a continuum. Despite the apparent separateness of things at the explicate level, every-thing is a seamless extension of everything else, and ultimately even the implicate and explicate orders blend into each other" (Talbot, 1991, p. 48). Furthermore, there is unity of manifestation; that is,

> animate and inanimate matter are inseparably interwoven, and life, too, is enfolded throughout the totality of the universe. Even a rock is in some way alive . . . "energy," "space," "time," "the fabric of the entire universe," and everything else we abstract out of the holomovement and mistakenly view as separate things. (Bohm, cited in Talbot, 1991, p. 50)

According to Bohm, consciousness is a nonlocal phenomenon that originates in the implicate order. This suggests that past, present, and future exist simultaneously in the same space; to access the "past" or "future" may simply require a shift in human focus (Talbot, 1991). Bohm characterizes the holographic universe as the *holomovement* because of its dynamic enfoldings and unfoldings. As every part of the holomovement contains the image of the whole, every part of the universe enfolds the whole, which suggests that every cell in the human body enfolds the cosmos (Talbot, 1991, p. 50). The dynamic holographic brain interprets a dynamic holographic universe in an ever-changing continuous enfolding and unfolding process.

The holographic principles of the interpenetration of whole and part, the unity of manifestation (i.e., distributed information), and spaceless-ness/timelessness provide an interpretive framework for understanding the indigenous worldview and healing practices. For example, the Afrocentric worldview of extended self (Nobles, 1976), which includes all ancestors, those yet to be born, all of nature, and the surrounding community, acknowledges the inseparable, interwoven fabric of the cosmos, in which space and time are meaningless. From the holographic paradigm, one may view a shaman's journey to other worlds as his or her consciousness shifting its attention from the explicate to the implicate order of the universe. Because "space" is only a meaningful perception in an "awake" state of con-sciousness, the shaman journeys without his or her body having to "move" on the physical plane. The shaman's consciousness accesses the past-present-future, because everything exists simultaneously. In altered states of con-sciousness, the shaman's energy body resonates at higher frequencies, which allows the part (individual consciousness) to access elements of the whole (universal consciousness).

Vibrational Healing Using the Metaphysical Plane

According to Gerber (1988), just as cells in the human body contain DNA to replicate the entire body, the etheric or subtle energy body serves as a holographic template (interference pattern) that carries information for the growth, development, and repair of the physical body. Gerber's premise is that people comprise a series of interacting multidimensional energy systems that penetrate and surround the body. If these systems become imbalanced, pathological symptoms may occur on the physical, emotional, mental, or spiritual planes. The appropriate frequency of what Gerber calls *vibrational medicine* can heal these disturbances by rebalancing the subtle energy templates. In vibrational medicine, "a hierarchy of subtle energetic systems . . . coordinate[s] electrophysiologic and hormonal function as well as cellular structure within the physical body. It is primarily from these subtle levels that health and illness originate" (p. 43). These energy systems are influenced positively and negatively by a person's emotions and spiritual balance and by environmental factors, such as computers, cellular phones, and electromagnetic power lines.

Given Gerber's view, ancient healing practices can now be better understood. In ancient healing traditions, vibrational medicine was used to manipulate these subtle energy fields by realigning and directing energy into the physical body. In quantum physics, this three-dimensional energy body is conceptualized as a hologram that serves as a template for the physical body. For example, as noted by Talbot (1991), ancient Chinese texts report two smaller acupuncture systems in both ears. A map of these acupuncture points resembles a miniature human inverted like a fetus, which the Chinese called "the little man in the ear." This acupuncture system may thus reflect a holographic image of the mind and body (Oleson, cited in Talbot, 1991), which reflects the holographic principle that every part of the whole contains an image of the whole. According to Leviton (cited in Talbot, 1991), "the ear holograph is logically connected to the brain holograph which itself is connected to the whole body [and] the way we use the ear to affect the rest of the body is by working through the brain holograph" (p. 115). It follows that sound is a potent form of vibrational healing.

SOUND AS A FORM OF VIBRATIONAL HEALING. Sound, as a type of energy wave, affects health in positive and negative ways. Intoning and chanting (for example, Tibetan overtones, Hindu mantras, Christian Gregorian chants) have been used to restore and maintain health. According to Campbell (1989),

> by sounding one's own body, it is possible to give it a tune-up. Singing is a good way to start, but most songs do not sustain a sound for a long enough time to reap its benefits. To tone for ten to fifteen minutes a day can greatly change the way the mind and body work together. When the body is healthy, all the systems and organs are in harmony and without pain. The body's natural function is to grow and to balance

and continually to heal itself. By allowing sound to move into the body through the breath, the life force can activate, vibrate and restore balance within. (pp. 65–66)

Rhythmic drumming, as in the rituals of indigenous and African peoples, has healing properties too. For example, research suggests that rapid drumming (4 to 4.5 beats per second) induces theta brain waves (4 Hz to 8 Hz) and can lead to altered states of consciousness (Maxfield, 1992).

One may explore other metaphysical healing approaches using the holographic paradigm: for example, the use of form, color and sound (Gimbel, 1987), healing through the human energy field (Brennan, 1988), soul retrieval (Ingerman, 1991), and mind/body healing, using imagery, that integrates shamanic practices with modern medicine (Achterberg, 1985). A large literature on indigenous healing practices exists. Perhaps by understanding these practices in terms of holographic theory, Western helping professionals will be more amenable to incorporating these methods into their healing practices.

The Holographic Paradigm Applied to Counseling

Sprinkle (1985) applies holographic principles to the therapeutic relationship, while Stratton (1990) applies them to catharsis. The holographic principle of vibrational resonance has also been applied specifically to dynamics associated with therapeutic change. Levenson (1976) likens the therapeutic interaction to the phenomenon that occurs between two tuning forks with the same pitch: When one is set in motion, the other also begins to vibrate. Levenson suggests that resonance is the key to therapeutic change: Therapeutic techniques are effective only to the extent that they facilitate resonance among therapist, client, and the basic structure of the client's experiencing.

Furthermore, vibrational resonance applies to *nonverbal presence* in the therapeutic encounter. The three-dimensional energy fields of counselor and client are interdependent, interacting to affect both participants, whether or not the participants consciously realize it. However, if counselors resonate too completely with their clients' pain, their own energy fields are adversely affected; continued counselor resonance with client distress may lead to burnout (Jecmen, 1993). Well-balanced, effective counselors, who are unaware of energy resonance, unconsciously emit their higher vibrational frequencies which, in turn, positively affect their clients.

Counselors who consciously work with their energy increase its potency (i.e., higher vibrational resonance). The effect of their "presence" in the therapeutic encounter is therefore enhanced. In groups, the effect of resonance is synergistic (the whole is greater than the sum of its parts).

Anyone who has meditated with others of like mind has experienced the synergistic power of collective energy. One method I have found helpful for building energy potential is recreating in one's imagination a previous experience of heightened awareness. This re-creation brings forward all sensations associated with the previous experience, resulting in higher vibrational resonance in the present. One often experiences this heightened state as "tingling" throughout the body accompanied by increased alertness. Repeated practice makes it possible to heighten states of awareness —that is, increase vibrational resonance—at will. This principle of vibrational resonance challenges the assumption of traditional Western counseling theories that verbal interaction is the most powerful channel for therapeutic change. Walt Whitman's statement, "We convince by our presence," takes on new significance within the holographic paradigm.

MCT AND ORGANIZATIONAL DEVELOPMENT

When applying MCT to organizational development, counselors will use the roles of change agent, consultant, advisor (teacher), advocate, and facilitator of indigenous support and healing systems. These roles are often used simultaneously. MCT consultants must be aware of three things: their own *personal biographies* (speaking from a particular class, race, culture, and ethnic perspective); that they operate from a particular *ontology* and *theory* (Denzin & Lincoln, 1994); and the interaction of their personal biographies and worldviews with those of the organization (client system). The MCT helping professional can (1) act as an *internal* or *external* change agent, working respectively from within the system or outside it; (2) work with organizations espousing a predominantly *monocultural worldview* (e.g., Euro-American, Japanese American) or *bicultural worldview* (e.g., Euro-American–Japanese American); (3) deal with *"generic" concerns* and/or explicitly identified *multicultural concerns*; and (4) use *Western and metaphysical perspectives*.

When MCT consultants deal with multicultural issues, Jackson and Hardiman's Multicultural Organizational Development model (MOD; cited in Jackson & Holvino, 1988) and Sue's Cultural Diversity Training Model (Sue, 1991) are recommended. Although both models deal explicitly with multicultural organizational development, consultants can also use them when their tasks do not directly involve multicultural assessment and intervention. For example, problems identified by the client system may partially arise from multicultural dynamics within the system. Also, a multicultural assessment can help identify the worldview and related underlying dynamics that guide the organization. In the United States, many organizations operate from a Euro-American worldview, making knowledge of such client systems helpful. For instance, Levinson (1994) provides a useful resource for understanding the failure of Euro-American corporations.

Blending Metaphysical and Western Approaches

With the proposed expanded view of MCT, one can conceptualize an organization as a "living entity" that operates simultaneously on the physical and metaphysical planes. This living entity is understood as *organization-in-relation*, comprising diverse elements (such as people) and interlocking networks, which exist primarily to maintain the system and help it thrive. Employees may differ in their personal biographies; worldviews; physical, emotional, mental, and spiritual health; and specific job functions. Furthermore, because organizational dynamics recapitulate the family structure and actions of the culture in which they are embedded (Levinson, 1994), it is important to assess that culture's functional and dysfunctional family dynamics. As with a family, the organization consists of interrelated subsystems. These subsystems may be determined by organizational purpose, power dynamics among groups, commonly held values, and other factors. The atmosphere or cultural climate will be determined primarily by those with the most power (e.g., the CEO). The health and leadership practices of those with most influence will have a potent effect on the organization's atmosphere (collective energy). The predominant emotions of those in power will pervade the individual and collective well-being of the organization. For instance, consistent negative energy (fear, mistrust, disrespect) will result in lower morale, poorer health, lower satisfaction, and decreased productivity. Often, an organization discourages the expression of feelings, disregards the importance of family to its workers, and ignores their spiritual needs. In short, employees are not valued for who they are; instead, they are valued for what they can do for the company.

Positive energy creates the opposite effect. Concern for the *total* well-being of employees, treating them as respected family members who have lives outside the work place, will have positive synergistic effects on both individuals and the collective. The following will create higher morale and greater productivity among workers: flexible working hours and day-care programs support their family home lives; recreational facilities acknowledge the need for physical activity; and activities such as meditation and t'ai chi ch'uan, honor their spiritual well-being.

Physical environment also affects an organization. From a metaphysical perspective, the "noise" of lights, electrical devices such as computers, and other sources of electromagnetic energy have potentially deleterious effects on the moods and well-being of personnel. Exposure to high-density electromagnetic and inaudible low-frequency sounds (e.g., power lines, cellular phones) have been increasingly linked to health problems such as cancer. Although the human brain quickly becomes habituated to audible sounds and disregards them, these other vibrations continue to operate "silently." These frequencies are "so out of harmony with the earth's drone of 7.8 vibrations per second that people between this sound and the earth incur disease" (Campbell, 1989, p. 65). An environmental assessment would identify intense energy sources that may harm workers' health. Potential interventions may include eliminating fluorescent lighting and encouraging frequent, short breaks from computer use.

Sound, color, and form can be utilized to create a more harmonious working environment. Incorporation of natural elements, such as light from skylights and spacious windows, aquariums, indoor waterfalls or ponds, plants, and harmonious sounds such as music or sea sounds enhance personal and collective well-being. The strategic use of colors and art, along with placement of furniture, can also enhance the workplace. For example, openness within the organization may be expressed by having desks positioned against walls rather than placed between employees and the public.

In general an organizational consultant tries to help the collective balance its energy so that it operates in greater harmony and health. MCT consultants use both physical and metaphysical information. For example, a consultant would assess the organization's strengths, weaknesses, and power dynamics by examining leadership styles, communication patterns, and organizational structure.

MCT consultants using a combined metaphysical and Western approach must communicate their assessment and interventions in ways that can be understood from the organization's worldview. For example, consultants working with a Euro-American organization would focus on problem identification at the physical, concrete level, such as linking employee stress and fear to decreased productivity. Management would be reframed as management-in-relation-to-employees. How the health and well-being of all employees affects productivity would also be shown. Suitable interventions from both metaphysical and Western perspectives, couched in terms the organization can understand and accept, would follow.

The organization as "living entity" also exists *in-relation-to-its-external-environment*. This environment may be defined in many ways, such as the organization-in-relation-to- (1) the dominant and subordinate cultures, (2) other organizations, (3) the socio-economic-political-ecological climate, and (4) the cosmos. The organization-in-relation-to-itself (internal) and to-the-environment (external) operate simultaneously. This focus on organization-in-relation-to-environment emphasizes the contextual and interdependent nature of all macrosystems. Through this reframing process, organizations expand their consciousness (MCT Proposition 6) to more fully understand how their actions, no matter how small, impact the whole. Long- and short-term implications for organizational behavior would be considered. For example, criteria for choosing a new building site could be expanded to include long-term effects on the ecological health of the land and socioeconomic systems in the surrounding community.

Bicultural and Non-Western Organizational Consultation

MCT consultants also work with organizations that reflect non-European and bicultural worldviews. A few brief examples may illuminate the importance of understanding and respecting the metaphysical belief systems these organizations may espouse. N. Patel, an Asian-Indian woman, raised biculturally in the United States, has provided the following information concerning consultation with an organization maintaining the Indian Hindu tradition (personal communication, August 14, 1994).

A Hindu business that is not doing well may call on Laxmi, Goddess of wealth and prosperity. They may call in a spiritual consultant to conduct a *puja*, or devotional ritual to invoke Laxmi. The *puja* may consist of creating a ritual fire in which offerings of rice and *ghee* (butter oil) are offered for Laxmi's return to the business. A similar ritual would have occurred when the business first opened. All people invited to the *puja* would be given silver coins with a picture of Laxmi on them. The giving of silver reflects a basic Hindu principle that one must give in order to receive. Gains and losses in the business may be spoken of as "Laxmi has moved in" or "Laxmi has left us."

Asian-Indian businesses often operate biculturally. For example, an Asian-Indian woman who owns a bookstore may know that her grandmother did *pujas* for Laxmi to restore prosperity. As a bicultural business person working within the dominant Euro-American system, this woman may be reluctant to rely on these traditions. She may contact a consultant rather than a spiritual healer. If the consultant asks whether she has tried a *puja* for Laxmi, however, the consultant will validate her cultural traditions, helping her feel comfortable pursuing interventions from both cultures (a "both/and" approach). Multicultural consultants must know diverse ethnic traditions well and allow multiple worldviews to coexist in their assessment and intervention strategies. By going into the Euro-American world (i.e., the consultant's office), the Asian-Indian bookstore owner calls forth the Euro-American part of her bicultural identity, which automatically creates distance between her and the consultant. In other words, she will rely on the rules of behavior operating in the dominant culture. If her Asian-Indian culture is not acknowledged, she will most likely put on a false mask to conform to the consultant's monocultural stance. An imperative for MCT consultants is to acknowledge and validate the indicated cultural interventions. In this case, they would state that they would be honored to attend a *puja* for Laxmi but also offer assessment and intervention from a Western perspective.

Organizational consultants, by definition, go into the client system's world. How they operate within the client system's world, however, can facilitate or hinder their effectiveness. Specifically, MCT consultants must be aware of differences between low- and high-context cultures. As noted by D. N. Jackson and Denise (1993), high-context cultures, such as Asian-Indian, African, Japanese, and Arabian, are characterized by a polychronic, or nonlinear, perception of time. The concept of polychronic time may not be respected by consultants trained within the Western monochronic, or linear, use of time (e.g., allowing only two hours to meet with members of the organization). In the example of the Asian-Indian business, agreeing to eat with members of the organization, even if business isn't directly discussed, will demonstrate a willingness to share and a willingness to follow Asian-Indian cultural rituals.

Communication patterns also vary between low- and high-context cultures. The low-context Euro-American culture depends on the written word (D. N. Jackson & Denise, 1993). Messages are direct and explicit, with words carrying most of the information. In high-context cultures, oral communication and contracts are particularly valued. For example, in Latina(o) cultures, the need for personalized interactions is esteemed (Padilla et al., 1989). Members of some high-context cultures (e.g., Chinese, Japanese) may prefer indirect and deferential communication (Leong, 1993). As Leong (1993) notes, "direct questions may place some . . . Japanese-Americans in a position where they would say 'yes' to a request when they really want to say 'no', but to do so would make the requestor lose face, which is to be avoided" (p. 28). Nonverbal cues will provide information regarding their position in the business. For example, in the Japanese cultural tradition, where employees stand in relation to the CEO reflects their status in the organization. Nonverbal cues are important for consultants to note and respond to in their interactions with members of high-context organizations.

MCT consultants are aware of limitations inherent in certain guidelines established by Euro-American professional organizations (see American Psychological Association [APA], 1992). Being flexible in meeting outside of Western "office hours," in the client's home or cultural environment, may be expected. Refusal to do so may be perceived as an affront to the client system's culture and values. In many cultures, such as Hindu, gift giving is a sign of trust, appreciation, and acknowledgment. At the end of organizational consultation, the consultant's refusal to accept such a gift may be perceived as insensitive, or, more likely, as an insult.

CONCLUSION

Bridges can assist helping professionals in overcoming obstacles that impede their journey. The holographic paradigm has been offered as one vehicle to bridge the gap between indigenous (metaphysical) and Western (scientific) healing approaches. The holographic principles of (1) the inter-penetration of whole and part, (2) the unity of manifestation (i.e., distributed information), and (3) spacelessness/timelessness provide an interpretive framework for understanding indigenous healing practices. With the holographic paradigm, one can more inclusively appreciate MCT from all sides and perspectives. This bridge provides a path for Western helping professionals to explore new directions in theory, research, and practice.

In terms of organizational development, the blending of indigenous and Western approaches creates a multidimensional perspective for working with diverse client systems. Organizational consultation that combines such approaches can provide comprehensive delivery of services to mono-, bi-, and multicultural organizations. Traversing this bridge between indigenous and Western approaches is not easy; journeys into unknown territory never are. And yet,

> to live in an evolutionary spirit means to engage with full ambition and without any reserve in the structure of the present, and yet to let go and flow into a new structure when the right time has come. (Erich Jantsch, in Wheatley, 1992, p. 74)

MCT theory offers a promising new structure for helping professionals as they journey across this bridge into the new millennium.

REFERENCES FOR CHAPTER 4

Achterberg, J. (1985). *Imagery in healing: Shamanism and modern medicine*. Boston: Shambhala.

American Psychological Association. (1992). Ethical principles of psychologists and code of conduct. *American Psychologist, 47*, 1597–1611.

Atkinson, D. R., Thompson, C. E., & Grant, S. K. (1993). A three-dimensional model for counseling racial/ethnic minorities. *The Counseling Psychologist, 22*, 257–277.

Bohm, D. (1980). *Wholeness and the implicate order*. London: Routledge & Kegan Paul.

Brennan, B. A. (1988). *Hands of light: A guide to healing through the human energy field*. New York: Bantam Books.

Brinkley, D. (1994). *Saved by the light*. New York: Villard Books.

Campbell, D. G. (1989). *The roar of silence: Healing powers of breath, tone, and music*. Wheaton, IL: Quest Books.

Denzin, N. K., & Lincoln, Y. S. (1994). Introduction: Entering the field of qualitative research. In N. K. Denzin & Y. S. Lincoln (Eds.), *Handbook of qualitative research* (pp. 1–17). Thousand Oaks, CA: Sage.

Eadie, B. J. (1992). *Embraced by the light.* Carson City, NV: Gold Leaf Press.

Fukuyama, M. (1994). Multicultural training: If not now, when? If not you, who? *The Counseling Psychologist, 22,* 296–299.

Gerber, R. (1988). *Vibrational medicine: New choices for healing ourselves.* Santa Fe, NM: Bear & Company.

Gergen, K. J. (1994). Exploring the postmodern: Perils or potentials? *American Psychologist, 49,* 412–416.

Gimbel, T. (1987). *Form, sound, colour, and healing.* Essex, England: Saffron Walden.

Highlen, P. S. (1994). Racial/ethnic diversity in doctoral programs of psychology: Challenges for the twenty-first century. *Applied & Preventive Psychology, 3,* 91–108.

Highlen, P. S., & Sudarsky-Gleiser, C. (1994). Co-Essence Model of Vocational Assessment for Racial/Ethnic Minorities (CEMVA-REM): An existential approach. *Journal of Career Assessment, 2,* 304–329.

Highwater, J. (1981). *The primal mind: Vision and reality in Indian America.* New York: New American Library.

Ingerman, S. (1991). *Soul retrieval: Mending the fragmented self.* San Francisco: HarperCollins.

Jackson, B. W., & Holvino, E. (1988). Developing multicultural organizations. *Journal of Religion and the Applied Behavioral Sciences, 9*(2), 14–19.

Jackson, D. N., & Denise, H. H. (1993). Multicultural issues in consultation. *Journal of Counseling and Development, 72,* 144–147.

Jecmen, D. J. (1993). Toward an integration of spirituality and psychology: A contribution from metaphysical tradition. *Dissertation Abstracts International, 54,* 4371B. (University Microfilms No. 94-01282)

Knoblauch, D. L. (1985). Applying Taoist thought to counseling and psychotherapy. *American Mental Health Counselors Association Journal, 1,* 52–63.

Leong, F. T. L. (1993). The career counseling process with racial-ethnic minorities: The case of Asian Americans. *The Career Development Quarterly, 42,* 26–40.

Levenson, E. A. (1976). A holographic model of psychoanalytic change. *Contemporary Psychoanalysis, 12,* 1–20.

Levinson, H. (1994). Why the behemoths fell: Psychological roots of corporate failure. *American Psychologist, 49,* 428–436.

Maxfield, M. C. (1992). The journey of the drum. In D. Campbell (Ed.), *Music and miracles* (pp. 137–155). Wheaton, IL: Quest Books.

Myers, H. F., Echemendia, R. J., & Trimble, J. E. (1991). The need for training ethnic minority psychologists. In H. F. Myers, P. Wohlford, L. P. Guzman, & R. J. Echemendia (Eds.), *Ethnic minority perspectives on clinical training and services in psychology* (pp. 1–12). Washington, DC: American Psychological Association.

Myers, L. J. (1988). *Understanding an Afrocentric worldview: Introduction to optimal psychology.* Dubuque, IA: Kendall/Hunt Publishers.

Myers, L. J., Speight, S. L., Highlen, P. S., Cox, C. I., Reynolds, A. L., Adams, E. M., & Hanley, C. P. (1991). Identity development and worldview: Toward an optimal conceptualization. *Journal of Counseling and Development, 70,* 54–63.

Neihardt, J. G. (1972). *Black Elk speaks.* New York: Pocket Books.

Nobles, W. (1976). Extended self: Rethinking the so-called Negro self-concept. *Journal of Black Psychology, 2,* 15–24.

Padilla, A. M., Ruiz, R. A., & Alvarez, R. (1989). Community mental health services for the Spanish-speaking/surnamed population. In D. R. Atkinson, G. Morten, & D. W. Sue (Eds.), *Counseling American minorities: A cross cultural perspective* (3rd ed., pp. 219–241). Dubuque, IA: Brown.

Page, R. C., & Berkow, D. N. (1991). Concepts of the self: Western and Eastern perspectives. *Journal of Multicultural Counseling and Development, 19,* 83–93.

Pedersen, P. B. (Ed.). (1991). Multiculturalism as a fourth force in counseling [Special issue]. *Journal of Counseling and Development, 70.*

Pribram, K. (1977). *Languages of the brain.* Monterey, CA: Wadsworth.

Reynolds, A. L., & Pope, R. L. (1991). The complexities of diversity: Exploring multiple oppressions. *Journal of Counseling and Development, 70,* 174–180.

Sprinkle, R. L. (1985). Psychological resonance: A holographic model of counseling. *Journal of Counseling and Development, 64,* 206–208.

Stratton, D. (1990). Catharsis reconsidered. *Australian and New Zealand Journal of Psychiatry, 24,* 543–551.

Sue, D. W. (1991). A model for cultural diversity training. *Journal of Counseling and Development, 70,* 99–105.

Sutich, A. J. (1969). Some considerations regarding transpersonal psychology. *Journal of Transpersonal Psychology, 1,* 11–20.

Szapocznik, J., & Kurtines, W. M. (1993). Family psychology and cultural diversity: Opportunities for theory, research, and application. *American Psychologist, 48,* 400–407.

Talbot, M. (1991). *The holographic universe.* New York: HarperColllins.

Walsh, R. N. (1990). *The spirit of shamanism.* Los Angeles: Jeremy P. Tarcher.

Watts, R. J. (1992). Elements of a psychology of human diversity. *Journal of Community Psychology, 20,* 116–131.

Wheatley, M. J. (1992). *Leadership and the law.* San Francisco: Berett-Kohler.

Wittine, B. (1989). Basic postulates for a transpersonal psychology. In R. S. Valle & S. Halling (Eds.), *Existential-phenomenological perspectives in psychology* (pp. 269–287). New York: Plenum Press.

CHAPTER 5

MCT Theory and Implications for Indigenous Healing

Courtland C. Lee
University of Virginia, Charlottesville

Assumption Audit

- Indigenous counseling/helping approaches emphasized by MCT theory are vital.
- Psychological helping must be based on the principle of cultural relativism.
- MCT theory values historical and prehistorical values or perspectives.
- There is an increased need for indigenous models of helping used by healers and traditional figures in non-Western societies.
- There is more emphasis on spirituality and cosmology in MCT than in traditional counseling.
- Indigenous theories embrace a more multifaceted human existence.
- MCT theory is more holistic in its perspective.
- MCT theory lends itself to case analysis.
- MCT theory stresses the importance of qualitative subjective truth.
- The scientific method has been used to disguise culturally biased assumptions.
- MCT theory defines modalities and goals from client perspectives.
- MCT theory encourages training approaches for indigenous helping with a psychospiritual perspective.
- MCT theory provides the context for a paradigm shift in counseling.
- MCT theory points out that culturally responsive counselors are modern-day shamans, and counseling is the manifestation of historical traditions.

The six propositions of the MCT theory proposed by Sue, Ivey, and Pedersen expand the notion of helping beyond a culture-bound perspective. MCT theory allows for an examination and validation of key aspects of counseling and therapeutic intervention inherent in those helping traditions outside a European/Euro-American cultural context.

As suggested in Corollary 5C of MCT theory (p. 21), counseling has developed as a formal, 20th century, primarily Euro-American, profession designed to help individuals resolve both situational and developmental problems in various aspects of their lives. However, in non-Western cultures, which predate that of the United States and Europe, people have for centuries found sources of help for resolving educational, career, or personal problems (Das, 1987; Harner, 1990; Kakar, 1982; Lee, Oh, & Mountcastle, 1992; Lee & Armstrong, 1995; Vontress, 1991). These sources of help occur naturally within the traditions of many non-Western cultures and have evolved into what one may consider as psychoeducational intervention models.

Recent studies of indigenous models of helping have revealed examples of healing practices in many parts of the non-Western world (Kakar, 1982; Lee et al., 1992; Vontress, 1991). For example, in many parts of West Africa, healing specialists known variously as herbalists, fetish men, mediums, healers, or sorcerers, employ spiritual forces to help address a variety of physical and emotional issues. In many Islamic countries, *piris* and *fakirs* are religious leaders within the Moslem faith who use verses from the Koran to treat illness. *Sufis* are secular traditional healers in these same regions who use music to treat psychological distress. In Mexico, *curranderas* (female) or *curranderos* (male) traditional healers use herbalism and massage to alleviate mental and physical suffering.

When considered from a Eurocentric psychoeducational perspective, these sources of help are often seen as primitive, unsophisticated, superstitious, unscientific, and potentially harmful to people in need of help. In short, a prevailing sentiment suggests one should discount them (Pedersen, 1987). However, the first proposition of MCT theory (p. 13) underscores the crucial notion that one must base psychological helping on cultural relativism. Significantly, Eurocentric theories of counseling and psychotherapy and non-Western notions of helping are truly neither "right and wrong" nor "good and bad." Each model of helping actually is merely different, representing a unique view of the world. For example, people in many non-Western cultures view the world from a pervasive religious/spiritual perspective. Religious and spiritual dimensions define what one considers "normal." Behavioral deviance or psychological distress are therefore generally explained within this context, in terms of spiritual possession or violation of religious principles, for instance.

Such thinking about counseling and psychotherapy lends credence to non-Western notions about sickness and health that have developed over centuries of practice. For example, many cultures believe that family dynamics can cause illness. Similarly, fate may also cause sickness; that is, one experiences health problems because one is predestined to do so. Additionally, illness may result from possession by malevolent spirits. These assumptions imply that many societies consider ill health of the mind and body as interrelated and even the punishment imposed by the spirits of ancestors for breaking laws or customs. Behavior such as neglecting family duties or treating the land and its resources carelessly may be punished with sickness. Therefore, healers are consulted for problems of the body and mind as well as the spirit (Das, 1987; Lee et al., 1992; Lee & Armstrong, 1995; Vontress, 1991). MCT theory advances the important concept that these ancient notions are as valid as Eurocentric concepts found in counseling and psychotherapy.

According to Proposition 6 of MCT theory (p. 22), as counseling professionals steeped in Eurocentric notions of helping attempt to become more culturally responsive, they should adapt techniques and theories in a manner consistent with each client's cultural background and special needs. They may find it helpful to draw on traditional methods of helping indigenous to specific cultures.

The remainder of this chapter provides, within the context of the basic assumptions of MCT theory, an examination of indigenous models of helping in non-Western cultures. In addition, I shall make a philosophical comparison between indigenous helping and Western counseling and shall also explore implications for multicultural counseling practice and training that promote an appreciation of indigenous models of helping.

INDIGENOUS MODELS OF HELPING:
A NON-WESTERN PERSPECTIVE

In recent years, interest has grown in the status of psychology, counseling, and related mental-health practices in countries outside of North America and western Europe. Much of this interest has been motivated by the increasing number of clients from non-Western cultural backgrounds who have sought counseling. This interest has also led to a number of investigations into indigenous models of helping in Africa, Asia, and the Middle East (Das, 1987; Idowu, 1992; Kakar, 1982; Lee et al., 1992; Lin, 1983; Makinde, 1974; Vontress, 1991). Data from this research suggest that activity akin to counseling has taken place for thousands of years under a variety of names in different cultures. In addition, this activity has usually been conducted by individuals acknowledged in their communities as possessing special insight and helping skills. Long recognized as "healers," these individuals are believed to possess awareness, knowledge, and skills that grow out of a timeless wisdom. As keepers of this wisdom, they enlist it to help people experiencing psychological distress or behavioral deviance (Lee & Armstrong, 1995). From a Eurocentric perspective, though, this ancient wisdom often appears at best as superstition, primarily because such wisdom often does not lend itself to scientific inquiry, an important cornerstone of Western psychotherapeutic intervention. Instead, the wisdom of the healers rests on notions of intuition and spiritual belief.

In reviewing these non-Western indigenous helping methods, I have found some basic principles that seem to form the foundation of the credibility and effectiveness of the healers who practice them. One can summarize these principles within the context of the *Universal Shamanic Tradition (UST)* (Lee & Armstrong, 1995). Originally from the language of the Tungus people of Siberia, *shaman* is a term adopted by anthropologists to refer to people often called "witch," "witch doctor," "medicine man/woman," "sorcerer," wizard," or "magic man/woman" (Eliade, 1964; Harner, 1990; Some, 1994). It is from this term that the UST draws its focus.

While substantive cultural distinctions exist in the UST, three salient characteristics define the traditions of indigenous helping methodologies (Lee & Armstrong, 1995). First, most of these helping traditions are deeply rooted in religion and spiritualism. Unlike Western counseling and psychotherapy, which draw their focus from rationality and the scientific method, indigenous helping methods generally draw their emphasis from cosmological perspectives imbedded in cultural worldviews. Although religion and spirituality are important forces in most cultures, many cultural groups make little distinction between the religious/spiritual and secular life. Therefore, the philosophical tenets inherent in religious or spiritual beliefs influence all aspects of human development and interaction.

As you have seen, psychological distress and behavioral deviance are often explained in a religious or spiritual framework (Das, 1987; Lee et al., 1992).

Traditional healers in this helping tradition are often religious or spiritual leaders. Their helping activities usually focus on what one may refer to as the *psychospiritual* domain of personality, or the realm of personality that goes beyond the mind and body into a spiritual domain of consciousness (Lee & Armstrong, 1995). Helping or healing, therefore, often involves religious or spiritual rituals that invoke higher powers or forces to assist in resolving problems.

Second, in many indigenous helping systems, healers believe in many levels of human experience, which often include a spirit world where it is believed that answers to human destiny can be discerned. In many cultures, healers will "journey" to these other levels of reality on behalf of people to find answers to their problems (Harner, 1990). Some cultures induce this journey with drugs, while others use a monotonous percussion sound.

In many Native-American cultures, for example, the shaman or "medicine man" will journey to the spirit world by entering a trancelike state induced by the steady beat of a drum. A Native-American healer is said to be journeying to the "lower world" through this method. While in this lower world, the shaman consults with spirits on behalf of people who are having problems. Similarly, among the traditional healers of Australian aborigines, such a journey may be induced by the steady drone of a didgeridoo, which is a musical pipe 4 to 5 feet long made of hollowed bamboo.

Third, most indigenous systems of healing take a holistic approach to helping, making little distinction between physical and mental well-being. Many indigenous healers perceive human distress as an indication that people have fallen out of harmony with both their internal and external environments. Therefore, healers are often consulted for a wide range of both physical and emotional issues. Such issues are often treated in a holistic manner.

CASE STUDY: THE POWER OF INDIGENOUS HELPING

The following is an example of an indigenous helping intervention, related by a Korean-American graduate student in a multicultural counseling class.

The student's mother was born in a village in rural Korea. When she was about 8 years old, she developed an eating problem. She had a ravenous appetite and could not stop eating. Her parents became worried because her constant eating was making her sick. Because there was no medical doctor in the village, the girl's grandparents took her to see the village healer, an elderly woman known as a Mudang. Having practiced her craft for many years, she had a great reputation in the village for her healing powers.

When the student's mother was brought before the Mudang, she easily diagnosed the girl's problem. According to the woman, the girl had been possessed by the spirit of hunger and, because of this, had developed the uncontrollable eating behavior.

The Mudang put herself into a trancelike state in which she made contact with the spirit of hunger and performed an exorcism to remove its presence from the young girl. She apparently directed the spirit's energy into a cow in a nearby field.

When the Mudang returned from her altered state, she proclaimed the student's mother to be free of the spirit. Significantly, when the young girl was taken home, her eating habits returned to normal.

This case study illustrates the essence of the UST, which forms the basis of many indigenous models of helping in non-Western cultures. *Mudangs*, often called *mansin*, are part of an ancient shamanic tradition in Korea (Harvey, 1976, 1979; Kendall, 1985, 1988). Primarily women, these traditional healers have used sorcery to chase out evil spirits believed to possess individuals.

This case points out a basic principle of the UST, and ultimately all helping interventions. Any successful helping practice rests on the assumption that the person in need of assistance believes in the power of the helper. As Frank (1961) notes, "clients" must have an inherent faith that the helping process will benefit them. A primary reason that the young girl's parents went to the Mudang for help was that they believed the Mudang could help their daughter. In large measure, the Mudang's success in solving the problem may have depended on the family's worldview and their belief in her healing ability.

The preceding case also points out that indigenous methods of helping generally exist and are used in places where Eurocentric methods of physical or psychological helping do not exist, are very limited, or are viewed with skepticism. For example, Vontress (1991) reports that in many places in Africa, people seek out healers because there are few Western-trained helping professionals available.

As research suggests, indigenous models of helping continue to exist throughout the non-Western world, despite the growing influence of Eurocentric medical and psychological practices (Lee et al., 1992). The UST forms the basis for important mental and physical health intervention for large numbers of people.

The UST Versus Western Counseling and Therapy

Counselors and psychotherapists with formal Eurocentric training would generally view with considerable skepticism a case study such as the one just presented. Indeed, because formal Eurocentric counseling and therapy rest on a philosophical basis much different from that of the UST, many Western mental-health professionals would tend to dismiss the UST entirely.

Western mental-health practice is defined philosophically by scientific notions of human behavior and personality (Freud, 1920/1955; Hall & Lindsey, 1970; Hilgard, 1948; Skinner, 1953). The helping principles found in Eurocentric counseling and therapy primarily follow the scientific method and are characterized by objectivity, rationality, and empiricism. Issues that interfere with human development are objectively analyzed, often quantitatively, with deductive reasoning used to explain the issues.

Conversely, the helping practices found within the UST can generally be conceptualized within a philosophical framework that goes beyond objectivity and deductive reasoning. This tradition extends into a subjective realm characterized by intuitive reasoning and qualitative understanding.

This fundamental difference between the two helping traditions largely accounts for the traditional skepticism about indigenous methods of helping within the Western psychotherapeutic community. According to the Eurocentric worldview of counseling and therapy, because traditional healing practices usually do not lend themselves to empirical investigation, they provide no scientific basis for therapeutic effectiveness. From a Western perspective, therefore, helping practices based on spiritual intuition have little relevance in the "modern" world of rational thinking and objective empiricism.

As Pedersen (1987) has suggested, the scientific tradition inherent in Western counseling and psychotherapy has fostered a cultural bias against the intuitive and psychospiritual orientation of indigenous helping methods. Furthermore, cultural relativism is often not considered in Western counseling and psychotherapy. However, if one accepts MCT theory's emphasis on such relativism, one sees the scientific approach as merely one culture-bound approach to attributing meaning to the world. Because they also attempt to attribute meaning to the world, helping traditions based on intuition must therefore be considered as valid as those based on logic. Significantly, helping interventions based on intuition often predate scientifically based helping practices by many millennia in most parts of the world.

Implications for Counseling

MCT theory proposes that culturally responsive counselors draw on traditional methods of healing from many cultures. The theory stresses that such counselors use both traditional Eurocentric systems of helping and indigenous non-Western healing interventions. This use suggests that an appreciation of the principles and practices inherent in the UST are crucial to culturally responsive counseling. Indigenous forms of helping and individuals identified as healers must move beyond the realm of non-Western anthropological curiosities to a place of therapeutic legitimacy.

This move is crucial, because one can find the UST and indigenous models of helping not only in non-Western parts of the world, but also throughout the contemporary Western world. For example, some form of indigenous helping or folk healing exists in most North American communities. In fact, they often have as much or more credibility than traditional medical or mental-health practices.

Religious institutions offer an obvious example of indigenous helping in the Western world. They have long served as important sources of psychological support in the United States among all cultural groups, predating counseling and psychotherapy by many generations (Richardson, 1991; Switzer, 1986). People have expected religious leaders of all denominations not only to provide for spiritual needs, but also to offer guidance for physical and emotional challenges. For generations, people have turned to ministers, priests, and rabbis for "counseling." In many instances, one important aspect of this help has involved helping people in psychological distress to enter an altered state of consciousness called *prayer*. Because it is a way to invoke spiritual powers for help, praying is actually part of the UST. Worship similarly offers important psychotherapeutic benefits; religious leaders have long used religious celebrations and services as counseling tools (Frazier, 1963; Lovinger, 1984; Switzer, 1986).

With the growth of cultural diversity in the United States, a variety of indigenous helping methodologies are receiving increasing attention. For example, folk medicine, fortune telling, acupuncture, herbal medicine, and massage have joined religious practices as important physical and psychological interventions. These methodologies often have the greatest credibility among those with identities based on non-Western cultural frameworks. For example, as Chung and Okazaki (1991) point out, common beliefs and practices among many Southeast-Asian Americans, especially recent immigrants, foster a reliance on indigenous healers and folk medicine.

For many individuals, the choice of an indigenous helping methodology over traditional counseling and therapy may be influenced by a number of factors, each underscored by the idea that cultural traditions and worldviews dictate human behavior. For example, cultural differences obviously exist in help-seeking behaviors and preferences for sources of help (Fischer & Cohen, 1972; McKinley, 1973; Neighbors & Jackson, 1984; Van Deusen, 1982; Veroff, Kulka, & Douvan, 1981; Yuen & Tinsley, 1981). Such differences stem from traditional cultural beliefs about the nature of health and well-being.

Often, one can explain a preference for indigenous helping methods as a lack of trust in or ignorance of Eurocentric mental-health services. Research has long suggested that people of color in the United States tend to underutilize traditional mental-health services (Sue, Allen, & Conway, 1975; Sue, McKinney, Allen, & Hall, 1974) or terminate counseling or psychotherapy after one session in far greater numbers than Euro-Americans do.

One may infer, therefore, that many people find cultural comfort and validation with a traditional healer in an indigenous helping system. This, in concert with a basic belief in the effectiveness of the healer, can make an indigenous model far more appealing than traditional counseling and psychotherapy.

FUTURE DIRECTIONS AND RECOMMENDATIONS

Counseling Practice

If traditional healing practices continue to exert a significant influence over the lives of many people, then as Proposition 4 of MCT theory suggests (p. 19), counseling professionals must search for ways to use modalities and define helping goals consistent with the life experiences and cultural values of clients. This means finding ways to accommodate indigenous helping practices into counseling and therapy when necessary and appropriate.

Hickson and Mokhobo (1992) offer options for integrating indigenous models of helping and traditional counseling and therapy. First, they suggest introducing indigenous helpers into existing therapeutic interventions. Because of these helpers' influence among large sectors of certain communities, they could help individuals wary of or unfamiliar with Western counseling services. Concerning interventions with Cambodian refugee clients, Chan (1987) reports a mental-health agency that has a Buddhist monk on the counseling staff, which validates the Cambodian belief system and gives credibility to the counselors because they acknowledge the monk's healing powers.

Second, Hickson and Mokhobo (1992) offer a model of cooperation and collaboration. Though the counselor and the indigenous helper work independently of each other, they refer clients to each other when appropriate. Richardson (1991), for example, suggests ways that counseling professionals can form collaborative relationships with ministers in the African-American church for the benefit of Black clients. First, counseling professionals must earn acceptance within the African-American church by insuring that ministers perceive them as sincere, trustworthy, and genuinely interested in the betterment of African Americans. Second, counselors must work to develop personal relationships with African-American ministers. This should include attempts to demonstrate counseling effectiveness by offering workshops on mental-health issues for ministers and members of their congregation. Finally, counseling professionals must become familiar with the diverse religious traditions of African-American churches. In so doing, counselors should pay attention to and develop respect for the attitudes, values, and traditions that form the cosmology of various African-American denominations.

A third option presented by Hickson and Mokhobo (1992) is the combination of counseling with indigenous helping models to create a new therapeutic system. Such systems have arisen in both rural and urban areas of the midwest and Pacific northwest among health professionals in their efforts to treat substance abuse among Native Americans (McAllister, 1991; Rauch, 1992). In many cases, counselors and related health professionals incorporate traditional Native-American healing practices, such as ceremonies, rituals, and prayers, into their substance-abuse treatment interventions.

For example, in the rite of purification, Native-American clients facing substance abuse sit together in small groups in tents or tepees heated by burning wild sage. As they begin to perspire they chant traditional songs and invoke the help of the "Great Spirit." Often with the help of a traditional healer or indigenous spiritual advisor, who works in conjunction with Western-trained professionals, the clients sweat away impurities and return to their cultural roots. It is believed that this rite of purification can purge an individual's past and reunite him or her with the earth and its goodness.

In many places the "sweat lodge" is often incorporated into the 12 steps of the Alcoholics Anonymous program. This spiritual connection to the past greatly enhances substance-abuse recovery efforts.

A traditional practice such as the "sweat lodge" adds a cultural and spiritual dimension to Eurocentric medical and psychological treatment initiatives. It also gives credence to the Native-American cultural value that the old ways are the best, because they have been proved (Richardson, 1981).

Counselor Training

When one considers recommendations for the development of an adequate theory of MCT as it relates to indigenous healing systems, the issue of training counselors to be culturally responsive is crucial. Counselor training must be tailored to address the validity of indigenous helping models. Educators need to develop training approaches that reflect those propositions of MCT theory that advocate the incorporation of indigenous helping practices into culturally responsive counseling and therapy.

Because most indigenous helping practices focus on the psychospiritual domain of personality, counselor training should therefore also focus on it. Specifically, counseling students should have the opportunity to develop an understanding of spiritual concepts from a transpersonal perspective (Lee & Sirch, 1994). In counseling theory courses, for example, more emphasis should be given to existential and transpersonal approaches to psychotherapy. In addition, counseling methods courses should incorporate training in holistic approaches to healing. As Brown (1986) suggests, counselors need to develop the awareness, knowledge, and skill to empower clients to view their lives from a higher point of view; to clarify their values; to strengthen, regenerate, and renew themselves at the deepest levels; to touch and empower the human spirit; and to experience a sense of the unity that underlies all creation.

Additionally, consulting courses should emphasize the importance of indigenous methods of helping. Students should learn how to develop strategies for establishing consultative relationships with traditional healers and other practitioners of indigenous helping methods in culturally diverse communities.

As part of the personal growth process that distinguishes all counselor training, students should receive the opportunity to explore their own sense of spirituality and be encouraged toward holistic self-awareness. That is, through their own counseling, both individual and group, students should be prepared to explore their personal issues from a transpersonal perspective that includes body, mind, *and* spirit.

Such training should also present ways for students to experience indigenous helping practices firsthand. Whenever possible, practicums and internships should provide chances for students to observe traditional healers or indigenous helping practices in culturally diverse communities. As appropriate, training experiences should offer students the opportunity to practice counseling skills in concert with the work of indigenous helpers or healers.

Such training would capture the essence of the UST and help students develop an appreciation for diverse ways of approaching psychological intervention. This training would thus help to instill in students an appreciation for the importance and power of indigenous helping models.

CONCLUSION

As multicultural counseling continues to emerge as the primary mode of practice, a paradigm shift in the theory of mental health intervention is needed. MCT provides the context for such a shift. As the UST makes clear, counselors must deliver services with a genuine respect for diverse worldviews and an appreciation for resources indigenous to specific cultures. Culturally responsive counseling and therapy is therefore predicated on finding ways to incorporate indigenous sources of helping into strategies for individual and group empowerment.

The propositions of MCT theory make clear that culturally responsive counselors must understand themselves as modern-day shamans. They must come to see counseling and psychotherapy as merely contemporary manifestations of an age-old universal helping tradition. MCT theory suggests that culturally responsive counselors should respect all interpretations of the global wisdom of the healing arts.

REFERENCES FOR CHAPTER 5

Brown, M. H. (1986, August). *Transpersonal psychology: Exploring the frontiers in human resource development*. Paper presented at the annual meeting of the American Psychological Association, Atlanta, GA.

Chan, F. (1987, April). *Survivors of the Killing Fields*. Paper presented at the Western Psychological Association Convention, Long Beach, CA.

Chung, R. C. Y., & Okazaki, S. (1991). Counseling Americans of Southeast Asian descent: The impact of the refugee experience. In C. C. Lee & B. L. Richardson (Eds.), *Multicultural issues in counseling: New approaches to diversity* (pp. 107–126). Alexandria, VA: American Counseling Association.

Das, A. K. (1987). Indigenous models of therapy in traditional Asian societies. *Journal of Multicultural Counseling and Development, 15*, 25–37.

Eliade, M. (1964). *Shamanism: Archaic techniques of ecstasy*. New York: Pantheon.

Fischer, E. H., & Cohen, S. L. (1972). Demographic correlates of attitude toward seeking professional psychological help. *Journal of Consulting and Clinical Psychology, 39*, 70–74.

Frank, J. D. (1961). *Persuasion and healing*. Baltimore: Johns Hopkins.

Frazier, E. F. (1963). *The Negro church in America*. New York: Schocken.

Freud, S. (1955). Beyond the pleasure principle. In J. Strachey (Ed.), *The standard edition of the complete works of Sigmund Freud* (Vol. 18, pp. 73–104). London: Hogarth Press. (Original work published in 1920.)

Hall, C. S., & Lindzey, G. (1970). *Theories of personality* (2nd ed.). New York: Wiley.

Harner, M. (1990). *The way of the shaman*. San Francisco: Harper & Row.

Harvey, Y. S. (1976). The Korean *mudang* as a household therapist. In Lebra, W. P. (Ed.), *Culture-bound syndromes, ethnopsychiatry, and alternative therapies* (pp. 191–198). Honolulu: University of Hawaii Press.

Harvey, Y. S. (1979). *Six Korean women: The socialization of shamans*. St. Paul, MN: West.

Hickson, J., & Mokhobo, D. (1992). Combatting AIDS in Africa: Cultural barriers to effective prevention and treatment. *Journal of Multicultural Counseling and Development, 20*, 11–22.

Hilgard, E. R. (1948). *Theories of learning*. Englewood Cliffs, NJ: Prentice-Hall.

Idowu, A. I. (1992). The Oshun festival: An African traditional religious healing process. *Counseling and Values, 36*, 192–200.

Kakar, S. (1982). *Shamans, mystics, and doctors: A psychological inquiry into India and its healing traditions*. New York: Knopf.

Kendall, L. (1985). *Shamans, housewives, and other restless spirits: Women in Korean ritual life*. Honolulu: University of Hawaii Press.

Kendall, L. (1988). *The life and hard times of a Korean shaman*. Honolulu: University of Hawaii Press, 441–456.

Lee, C. C., & Armstrong, K. L. (1995). Indigenous models of mental health intervention: Lessons from traditional healers. In J. Ponterotto, J. M. Casas, L. A. Suzuki, & C. M. Alexander (Eds.), *Handbook of multicultural counseling*. Beverly Hills, CA: Sage.

Lee, C. C., Oh, M. Y., & Mountcastle, A. R. (1992). Indigenous models of helping in nonwestern countries: Implications for multicultural counseling. *Journal of Multicultural Counseling and Development, 20*, 3–10.

Lee, C. C., & Sirch, M. L. (1994). Counseling in an enlightened society: Values for a new millennium. *Counseling and Values, 38*, 90–97.

Lin, T. (1983). Mental health in the third world. *Journal of Nervous and Mental Disease, 171*, 71–78.

Lovinger, R. J. (1984). *Working with religious issues in therapy*. New York: Aronson.

Makinde, O. (1974). The indigenous Yoruba Babalawo model: Implications for counseling in West Africa. *West African Journal of Education, 18*, 319–327.

McAllister, B. (1991, June 9). At VA hospital, "Medicine Man" helps Indians try to beat an old nemesis. *The Washington Post*, pp. 25–26.

McKinley, J. (1973). Social networks, lay consultation and help-seeking behavior. *Social Forces, 51*, 275–292.

Neighbors, H. W., & Jackson, J. S. (1984). The use of informal and formal help: Four patterns of illness behavior in the Black community. *American Journal of Community Psychology, 12*, 629–644.

Pedersen, P. (1987). Ten frequent assumptions of cultural bias in counseling. *Journal of Multicultural Counseling and Development, 15*, 16–24.

Rauch, K. D. (1992, March 10). How Indian youths defeat addictions. *The Washington Post*, pp. 10–11.

Richardson, B. L. (1991). Utilizing the resources of the African American church: Strategies for counseling professionals. In C. C. Lee & B. L. Richardson (Eds.), *Multicultural issues in counseling: New approaches to diversity*. Alexandria, VA: American Counseling Association.

Richardson, E. H. (1981). Cultural and historical perspectives in counseling American Indians. In D. W. Sue (Ed.), *Counseling the culturally different*. New York: Wiley.

Skinner, B. F. (1953). *Science and human behavior*. New York: Macmillan.

Some, M. P. (1994). *Of water and the spirit: Ritual, magic, and initiation in the life of an African shaman*. New York: Putnam.

Sue, S., Allen, D., & Conway, L. (1975). The responsiveness and equality of mental health care to Chicanos and Native Americans. *American Journal of Community Psychology, 45*, 111–118.

Sue, S., McKinney, H., Allen, D., & Hall, J. (1974). Delivery of community mental health services to Black and White clients. *Journal of Consulting Psychology, 42*, 794–801.

Switzer, D. K. (1986). *The minister as crisis counselor*. Nashville, TN: Abingdon Press.

Van Deusen, J. (1982). Health/mental health studies of Indochinese refugees: A critical overview (Part 3). *Medical Anthropology, 6*, 213–252.

Veroff, J. Kulka, R., & Douvan, E. (1981). *Mental health in America: Patterns of help seeking from 1957–1976*. New York: Basic Books.

Vontress, C. E. (1991). Traditional healing in Africa: Implications for cross-cultural counseling. *Journal of Counseling and Development, 70*, 242–249.

Yuen, R. K., & Tinsley, H. E. A. (1981). International and American students' expectancies about counseling. *Journal of Counseling Psychology, 28*, 66–69.

CHAPTER 6

THEORETICAL IMPLICATIONS OF MCT THEORY

Gerald Corey
California State University, Fullerton

Assumption Audit

- With sufficient adaptations, the traditional limitations of current theories may be transcended.
- Theories may be outmoded and restrictive if they do not allow for cultural diversity.
- Theories are always changing and developing.
- Helping professionals need to include non-Western theories.
- Individualistic perspectives limit counseling effectiveness.
- An adequate theory of counseling must deal with social and cultural aspects of the client's problems.
- No one helping approach or intervention strategy works with equal effectiveness across all populations or life situations.
- Though using eclectic or integrative approaches to deal with diversity has its problems, "technical eclecticism" is preferred.
- An MCT metatheory depends on a broad definition of culture.
- There is a psychoeducational component to MCT.
- Changes needed are not merely theoretical but applied as well.
- Awareness, knowledge, and skill offer an important developmental framework.

Sue, Ivey, and Pedersen have made some excellent points in calling for a new perspective that addresses the needs of culturally diverse client populations. From my vantage point, many of their challenges to theory development, practice, and research are long overdue. The most valuable theme they offer is that counselors and therapists must infuse multiculturalism into their theory and practice to be relevant to a wide range of clients. Practitioners can no longer afford to ignore the issue of culture. Nor can they apply assumptions that fit a monocultural society to a multicultural society.

In Chapters 1–3, Sue, Ivey, and Pedersen minimize the traditional foundations of counseling theory and practice, claiming that they are inadequate for work with a culturally diverse population. As such, the authors take a more radical stance than I do concerning the revamping of traditional counseling theories. Although I grant that traditional theories need to be expanded to include a focus on multicultural, gender, and systemic issues, I neither am ready to admit that these theories are outmoded nor think that their basic limitations cannot be overcome. However, I agree that to the extent that traditional theories disregard culture, they are outmoded and restrictive.

Ivey, Ivey, and Simek-Morgan (1993) claim that although at one time MCT theory seemed opposed to traditional theory, it now appears that MCT theory offers bridges to connect Western and indigenous therapeutic traditions. MCT can draw on many ideas from existing theory. I think multicultural counseling is more than merely a method, for there are some clear propositions and key concepts that have implications for counseling practice. Rather than a separate multicultural theory, I favor developing a multicultural perspective, which is an approach one can incorporate into the fabric of most contemporary theories.

COMMENTARY ON THE MCT PERSPECTIVE

Are Current Theories Relics?

Some writers allege that current theories of counseling and psychotherapy are inadequate to describe, explain, predict, and deal with the richness and complexity of a culturally diverse population (Ivey et al., 1993; Pedersen, 1994). Some have also asserted that because one cannot easily adapt contemporary theories to a wide range of cultures, the helping professions need a theory of MCT (Pedersen, 1991).

I agree, but only to a point, for I believe that current theories can be expanded to include a multicultural perspective. If current theories are not modified, they might well have limited applicability in dealing with the complexity of a culturally diverse population. However, contemporary theories have the capacity to be broadened to encompass a social, spiritual, and political perspective. They can also be expanded to include a focus on gender issues, cultural differences, and family/systemic concerns. Indeed, in their previous writings, Ivey and Pedersen agree that MCT can draw on concepts from existing theories; that is, one need not discard current theories in the search for alternative perspectives. MCT theory adds to the effectiveness and accuracy of traditional theory by recognizing that behaviors are culturally learned.

Ivey et al. (1993) also take the position that MCT theory is a unifying force, in that it seeks to respect multiple perspectives. They believe that although MCT draws heavily on traditional theories, in actual practice helping professionals must adapt these theories to meet the diverse needs of clients. According to Ivey and his colleagues, MCT theory recognizes the value of traditional approaches even as it generates new ways of making theory come to life and increasing its relevance.

In a similar vein, Pedersen (1994) asserts that there is a multicultural dimension in all counseling relationships. I agree with Pedersen's contention that it is essential to adapt and accommodate theory and practice to culturally different clients. He does not call for a separate field of "multicultural counseling," but would like to see cultural dimensions become a vital component of all counseling orientations. A central point that Sue, Ivey, and Pedersen make is that the MCT practitioner draws on both Western and non-European systems of helping (Chapter 1). The practitioner constantly attempts to adapt techniques and theories, respectfully and sensitively, to the client's cultural background and special needs.

From my perspective, contemporary theories have the potential for being expanded and adapted to working with a wide range of cultures. My stance would be termed the "least radical position" by Ridley, Mendoza, and Kanitz (1994), who hold that traditional counseling theories may be valid if one adapts their concepts and techniques to reflect the cultural values of the clients being served. One must realize, however, that Western theories of counseling evolved in the context of a particular time and in response to specific needs. For example, Freud created his theory within the cultural context of the Victorian era and with a particular patient population. Certainly, if one used his concepts and practices in their original form, they would have limited value in dealing with many contemporary problems. Psychoanalytic theory and practice are not static, for in both realms significant developments have taken place. However, I will agree that many of the psychodynamic theories have not adequately focused on the roles of family, gender, and culture in the practice of therapy, thus indicating their limitations from a multicultural perspective.

With respect to many of the traditional theories, assumptions made about mental health, optimum human development, the nature of psychopathology, and the nature of effective treatment are often not relevant to culturally diverse clients. For traditional theories to be relevant in a multicultural society, they need to be expanded to incorporate a person-in-the-environment focus and to account for salient cultural variables. Therapists must create therapeutic strategies congruent with the values and behaviors characteristic of a culturally pluralistic society. Practitioners must also be flexible by demonstrating a willingness to modify strategies to fit the needs and the situations of the individual client.

Are Counseling and Therapy Culture-Bound?

Multicultural specialists have criticized traditional counseling as culture-bound because it arises from a predominantly Eurocentric perspective. Some of the values implicit in contemporary counseling theories include emphases on individualism, the separate existence of the self, individuation as the foundation for maturity, and decision making and responsibility as resting on the individual rather than the group. By contrast, an Asian perspective would focus on interdependence, play down individuality, and emphasize the loss of self in the totality of the cosmos. It would also reflect the life values associated with a focus on inner experience and acceptance of one's environment.

Multicultural psychologists have noted that theories of counseling and psychotherapy represent different worldviews, each with its own values, biases, and assumptions about human behavior. The authors state that counselors bring their own cultural background to the session, and the worldviews associated with that background deeply affect the way they conduct therapy. That is, counselors do not leave their values and cultural backgrounds out of their work. Regardless of which theory they operate from, it behooves them to be aware of their cultural values and how they impact intervention. They also need to be aware of the salient factors operating in the client's culture and how these impact therapy. As Pedersen (1994) notes, effective counselors can no longer ignore their own cultures or the cultures of their clients and still practice ethically.

Wrenn (1962, 1985) believes that when counselors become "encapsulated," or caught in one way of thinking and viewing the world, they tend to resist adaptation and reject alternative ways of practicing. Ivey (1993) calls for a reconstruction of the present practice of counseling and psychotherapy. He suggests that the values and beliefs of African Americans, Asian Americans, Latina(o)s, Native Americans, and women can transform practice and offer an alternative view on it. Rather than focusing on a single dimension of human experience, counseling theory needs to be aimed at the total human condition (Sue, 1992). I think that Sue, Ivey, and Pedersen have made a major contribution by challenging the culture-bound assumptions inherent in contemporary theory and practice; they have also provided a useful direction toward transcending a narrow perspective on counseling.

One cannot deny that theories such as psychoanalytic, behavioral, cognitive-behavioral, and existential originated from Euro-American culture and have a core set of values. I think it is a myth that these approaches are value neutral and applicable to all human beings. There is a danger of imposing these values as the only right ones. Mental-health practitioners must be aware of the underlying philosophy of their theoretical orientation and need to realize that alternative sets of values may be appropriate in working with culturally different clients. This may be the best prevention against encapsulation.

The relationship-oriented therapies, such as person-centered theory, existential therapy, and Gestalt therapy, emphasize individualism, autonomy, freedom of choice, and self-actualization. Practitioners with this orientation tend to focus on the individual's responsibility for making internal changes as a way to cope with problems; they also view individuation as the foundation for healthy functioning. In some cultures, however, the key values center on a collectivism. Rather than emphasizing the development of the individual, these cultures focus on what benefits the collective. Certainly, therapists who assume that all clients should embrace individualism are in error. Regardless of their orientation, therapists must listen to their clients to determine why each one is seeking help and how best to deliver the kind of help appropriate for each. Thus, I agree with Sue, Ivey, and Pedersen's contention that the helping profession needs an approach to counseling that views "individualism" as culture-specific and representative of only one cultural group.

In my view, effective counselors consider the degree to which their general goals and methods fit the cultural background and values of their clients. Both therapist and client must recognize their differences in goal orientation. For example, it can be a therapeutic mistake to encourage some clients to tell their parents assertively and directly all they are thinking and feeling. Some clients believe that it is rude to confront their parents and inappropriate to identify and discuss conflicts. The therapist who would push such clients toward independence and dealing with conflicts within the family will most likely alienate these clients. Interdependence, thinking about what is best for the social group, and striving for harmony are often the clients' most important values, rather than autonomy. Therefore, therapists must carefully listen to their clients and enter their perceptual world. The therapeutic process is best guided by the particular goals and values of each client, not by what the therapist thinks is best. By focusing on what clients want, therapists can reduce the chance of imposing their values and goals on their clients.

Ideally, a theoretical orientation provides practitioners with a map to guide them in a productive direction with their clients. A psychoanalytic practitioner focuses on the past as a way to understand and work with the client's current condition and future. An existential therapist seeks to understand the client's world and trusts that the therapeutic relationship will enable the client to discover a creative and positive direction. The cognitive-behavioral therapist tends to be action oriented, applying short-term interventions to help clients modify their dysfunctional thoughts, because this shift generally leads to emotional and behavioral changes. The systemic therapist views clients' problems in the context of the family and tries to promote change within this system. Because these orientations have definite implications for the practice of therapy, therapists must recognize the underlying assumptions of their approach. To their credit, multicultural therapists view individuals in the context of the family and the culture, with the aim of facilitating social action that will lead to change within the client's community, rather than merely increasing the individual's insight.

According to Sue, Ivey, and Pedersen (Chapter 1), culturally different clients who see problems residing in sociocultural variables (oppression, racism, and sexism) may find the assumptions surrounding the intrapsychic approach antagonistic to their worldviews. Some multicultural experts maintain that therapeutic practice will be effective only to the extent that therapists intervene with some form of social action to change those factors that have created the client's problem, rather than see the client as responsible for his or her condition.

An adequate theory of counseling does deal with the social and cultural factors of an individual's problems. However, counselors might not know where to begin to bring about social change for clients in pain from social injustice. Though focusing on the client's internal dynamics exclusively has some basic limitations, there is something to be said for helping clients deal with their response to environmental realities. By using techniques from many of the traditional therapies, counselors can at least help clients increase their awareness of their options in dealing with barriers and struggles. For example, cognitive-behavior therapists would be interested in developing a collaborative relationship with their clients toward helping them turn what they learn about themselves and their environment into a practical plan of action. There are many ways that one could use a cognitive-behavioral approach as a form of culture-centered counseling that offers strategies for both individual and environmental change. Rather than focus strictly on an individual's intrapsychic dynamics, therapists can help clients clarify how external conditions have personally affected them and challenge them to make decisions about what they can do to change themselves if they cannot directly change external conditions. One must focus on both individual and social factors for change to occur. Indeed, the person-in-the-environment perspective acknowledges this.

As the authors make clear, MCT theory focuses on the importance of viewing the individual-in-context, considers the cultural background of the client, and finds culturally appropriate solutions that may vastly change the way that therapy is conducted. The person-environment relationship is consistent with Herr's (1991) suggestion that counseling be viewed as a sociopolitical instrument designed to bridge the gap between individuals and their environment. Herr believes that one of the challenges of the counseling profession consists of developing future strategies that can help people involved in dramatic environmental flux lead more sane, effective, and fulfilling lives.

Does an Integrative Approach Offer Promise in Dealing with Diversity?

I fully endorse the authors' assertion that no one helping approach or intervention strategy is equally effective across all populations and life situations. One rationale for an integrative perspective is the fact that no single therapeutic approach has all the answers, especially when one considers a pluralistic society. In writing about the future of technical eclecticism, Lazarus, Beutler, and Norcross (1992) acknowledge that many practitioners recognize that there is not a singular true path to conceptualizing and dealing with all human problems; no one orientation has all the answers. Counselors thus need to be able to shift their counseling styles to meet the diverse cultural and sociopolitical dimensions of their clientele. Furthermore, the inherent limitations embodied in any practice directed by a single theory explain the trend toward an integrative approach. The thinking dimensions are emphasized by cognitive-behavioral therapies; the feeling dimensions are highlighted by experiential approaches; the behaving dimensions are emphasized by both behavioral and cognitive-behavioral theories; the social dimensions are emphasized by family systems perspectives. I agree with Sue (1992) that all these aspects of the human condition are essential and need to be considered in therapeutic practice. Because humans are biological, cultural, spiritual, and political beings, a comprehensive theory must address these dimensions of existence. A monocultural approach simply does not make sense. It is time to devise approaches that will integrate the best features of existing theories, to expand the boundaries of current theory development, and to design alternative perspectives and strategies that will fit the needs of diverse client groups.

As Sue, Ivey, and Pedersen note (Chapter 1), there are some difficulties in using eclectic and integrative approaches to address diversity. Depending on what is meant by *eclectic* and *integrative*, I agree. Some eclectics grab for techniques from a bag in an attempt to find something that will work. If they do not have a theoretical rationale for using techniques, their therapeutic efforts will likely lack direction. Practitioners cannot address the needs of diverse client populations unless they develop a basic respect for and employ strategies consistent with the goals and values of their clients. Using techniques randomly in the hope that clients will be reached is not effective.

I like the notion of *technical eclecticism* (Lazarus, 1992). In agreement with Lazarus, I think there are some major problems in attempting to combine certain theories that have incompatible underlying assumptions. However, one can use a wide range of techniques in a systematic way to work with diverse client groups. With a framework of technical eclecticism, procedures are drawn from various approaches without necessarily subscribing to the theories that spawned them. These techniques are tailored to what each particular client needs. There are rich possibilities in integrating techniques from the three traditional therapeutic forces: the first force, including the psychodynamic approaches (psychoanalytic therapy and its derivatives); the second force, involving the behavioral and cognitive-behavioral therapies (behavior therapy, rational-emotive behavior therapy, cognitive therapy, and reality therapy); and the third force, encompassing the existential and humanistic approaches (existential therapy, person-centered therapy, and Gestalt therapy).

Ivey et al. (1993, p. 361) make an excellent point in their discussion of multicultural counseling and therapy as the fourth force. They state that MCT theory does not dismiss traditional approaches but recognizes their value when used in a culturally meaningful and culturally sensitive way. The challenge lies in therapists working collaboratively with clients to discover theories and techniques that will answer the unique needs of each client without coming up with a strict mold or prescription for all clients. Thus, as mentioned earlier, MCT theory does not mean abandoning contemporary theories but challenging therapists to integrate a cultural perspective into existing approaches so that all facets of culture are addressed, including gender issues, lifestyle orientation issues, and issues relating to culture and family.

Is a Multicultural Metatheory a Direction for the Future?

There is a need for a culture-centered metatheory—one that allows each theory to be considered from its cultural perspective. MCT theory is such a metatheory, offering an organizational framework for understanding helping approaches. The idea of the need for a metaframework that focuses on cultural factors is exciting; however, MCT theory is not yet defined enough to unify the diverse theoretical approaches to counseling. Breunlin, Schwartz, and MacKune-Karrer (1992) contend that in the realm of family therapy, a multicultural perspective has yet to impact the field. They propose a multicultural metaframework, consisting of a set of propositions about the importance of a multicultural perspective in treating families. If one considers culture broadly, as Pedersen (1994) calls for, then I believe that a multicultural metaframework has implications for the practice of individual, family, group, and community approaches. Breunlin, Schwartz, and MacKune-Karrer (1992) propose a metaframework based on a broad definition of culture, encompassing the following dimensions: history and generational sequences, immigration and acculturation, economics, education, ethnicity, religion, gender, age, race, minority/majority status, and regional background. By considering culture in this broad way, there is a basis of incorporating cultural dimensions in all theoretical orientations. If culture is not a vital part of counseling practice, then such practice can be considered encapsulated.

As a part of the trend toward the integration of existing approaches, I see promise in building cultural concerns into any integrative framework. A metaframework would provide a blueprint for gender- and culture-sensitive therapeutic practice on a variety of levels: individual, family, group, community, and institutional. Each approach to helping would incorporate ways of addressing salient cultural variables as a way to most effectively reach a wide range of client groups.

What Is the Challenge for Creating New Roles for Counselors?

Sue, Ivey, and Pedersen believe that MCT theory calls for a major paradigmatic shift, because it challenges the very foundations on which traditional counseling and therapy rests (Chapters 1 and 2). The kind of metatheory described in the previous section calls for a major shift in the thinking of most practitioners, not only with respect to theory but also in challenging them to expand their roles as helpers. MCT theory rests on the assumption that multiple helping roles exist that do not antagonize but complement conventional therapy. These alternative roles involve the following: a more active approach, a willingness to conduct practice outside the office, a focus on changing environmental conditions, refusing to see the locus of the problem within the client, a focus on prevention, and the counselor's assumption of increased responsibility for determining the course of the helping process. In short, many of these roles are ones on which social work practice is based. Counselors thus might well add to their approaches functions typical of social work practice.

For mental-health professionals who work in community agency settings, the time has come to devise alternatives to restricting their practice to individual counseling within the confines of an office. The focus needs to

shift from remediation of individual problems to dealing with the individ-
ual-in-community and also on changing conditions within the community.
Education and prevention offer key alternatives to conventional roles. To
its credit, MCT theory stresses the importance of multiple helping roles
developed by many culturally different groups and societies. The role of the
counselor often includes teaching the client about the underlying cultural
dimensions of present concerns. Thus, there is a psychoeducational dimension to MCT. There is room for most counseling theories to include an educational focus that will empower clients by making them a collaborator in
the therapeutic relationship.

What Are Some of the
Ethical Dimensions of MCT?

Although my primary task is to comment on the implications of MCT for
theory development, this cannot be done without considering the ethical
context of practice in a multicultural society. Ethical practice dictates a
respect for diversity and has implications for training programs. The proposed revision of the American Counseling Association's (ACA, 1994)
Code of Ethics and Standards of Practice contains the following guideline:
"Counselors who counsel clients from backgrounds different from their own
respect these differences; gain knowledge, personal awareness, and sensitivity pertinent to the clients; and incorporate culturally relevant practices
into their work" (p. 14). It is neither ethical or clinically sound for counselors to use techniques based on a monocultural model without attempting
to develop strategies that will reflect awareness of and sensitivity to concerns of culture and gender.

Because contemporary ethical guidelines are based on a culturally narrow perspective of counseling, the multicultural counselor might need to
reframe particular ethical guidelines in order to counsel in an ethically
appropriate manner. According to Pedersen (1994), multicultural counselors
often face an ethical dilemma: choosing between "being ethical" in a multicultural context or "following the ethical guidelines" of their professional
associations. He critically evaluates the American Psychological Association's (APA, 1992) Ethical Principles of Psychologists and Code of Conduct
and the ACA's (1988) Ethical Standards on the ground that they do not sufficiently address the values and best interests of minority as well as majority
groups. Although the present ethical codes of the ACA and APA may be
lacking from a multicultural perspective, APA has developed a separate set
of guidelines for providers of psychological services to ethnic, linguistic, and
culturally diverse populations (see APA, 1993). Ethical practice implies
that counselors have the education and training that will allow them to
practice as effective multicultural counselors, a subject to which I now turn.

SOME RECOMMENDATIONS

In my opinion, changing the focus and direction of counseling theory and practice as advocated by Sue, Ivey, and Pedersen rests not exclusively on theoretical grounds, but also on producing counselors who have self-awareness and are open to responding to the challenge of providing relevant services to a range of clients. It is essential that counselor-education programs focus on the counselor as a person and not stop with teaching students an array of intervention strategies. Counselors must first know themselves before they can employ any counseling technique successfully. Sue, Ivey, and Pedersen (Chapter 3) underline the critical importance of trainees acquiring knowledge and understanding of the worldview of culturally different clients. They add that trainees need to learn culturally appropriate intervention strategies and make them basic to their counseling process. I fully support the authors' contention that trainees must become aware of their own values, cultural biases, stereotypes, and assumptions about human behavior. As a part of this broadening of awareness, trainees also need to acquire knowledge and skills that will enable them to become effective multicultural helpers. Both Pedersen (1994) and Pedersen and Ivey (1993) offer some excellent thoughts that could be incorporated into training programs. They propose a culture-centered model of counseling focused on developing the awareness, knowledge, and skills essential to becoming an effective multicultural counselor.

Some trainees are encapsulated in a cultural cocoon in which they escape reality by depending entirely on their own assumptions about what is good for people. In such encapsulation, counselors (1) rely on stereotypes in making decisions about people from different cultural groups, (2) ignore cultural differences among clients, and (3) define reality according to one set of cultural assumptions (Pedersen, 1994; Wrenn, 1962, 1985). To avoid this narrowness, trainees and counselors must challenge their beliefs and reorganize old knowledge when it no longer fits. By increasing one's personal awareness and with training, one can avoid cultural encapsulation.

Most of those writing about the role of culture in the helping process agree that effective helpers do not impose their values and expectations on their clients, they avoid stereotyping clients, they are aware of and challenge their biases and assumptions, and they do not force their clients to fit in one approach to helping. To become a culturally skilled helper, one must (1) be aware of one's own cultural heritage and of biases, values, and preconceived notions that can intrude in helping relationships, (2) acquire knowledge of culturally diverse groups that will pave the way for grasping the worldviews of culturally different clients, and (3) develop a range of intervention strategies and skills that are appropriate, relevant, and sensitive to diverse groups (Sue, Arredondo, & McDavis, 1992; Sue et al.,

1982). Sue and his colleagues have developed and refined what I consider to be the best available conceptual framework for multicultural counseling competencies and standards that describes the necessary ingredients for becoming a culturally skilled counselor or therapist.

From my vantage point, the best way to mobilize the efforts toward providing culturally competent counselors in the future is to integrate a multicultural perspective in counseling and clinical training programs. As I have emphasized elsewhere (Corey, 1991), the intervention strategies of the future need to address the changing social times, and they need to address the reality of cultural diversity. For counselors to deliver these services effectively, they must be aware of their cultural assumptions and how those assumptions affect practice, and they must have multicultural knowledge and skills.

Although the title of this chapter refers to theory, I have constantly referred to both theory and practice, because I view them as intertwined. Theory without a discussion of implications for practice becomes an abstract and dry project; practice not anchored to theory becomes a superficial discussion of technique. A multicultural perspective is an essential foundation of counseling theory and practice. Clearly, I do not believe that the traditional theories are a relic of the past. Training should focus on producing effective counseling practitioners, who must possess multicultural counseling skills and the capacity for flexibility in adapting counseling techniques to meet the needs of a diverse range of client populations. In my view, a multicultural theme can be intertwined within the integrative approaches that are currently being developed.

REFERENCES FOR CHAPTER 6

American Counseling Association. (1988). *Ethical standards* (Rev. ed.). Alexandria, VA: Author.

American Counseling Association. (1994). *Proposed revision of American Counseling Association Code of Ethics and Standards of Practice*. Alexandria, VA: Author.

American Psychological Association. (1992). Ethical principles of psychologists and code of conduct. *American Psychologist, 47*(12), 1597-1611.

American Psychological Association. (1993). Guidelines for providers of psychological services to ethnic, linguistic, and culturally diverse populations. *American Psychologist, 48*(1), 45–48.

Breunlin, D. C., Schwartz, R. C., & MacKune-Karrer, B. (1992). Metaframeworks: Transcending the Models of Family Therapy. San Francisco: Jossey-Bass.

Corey, G. (1991). Invited Commentary on Macrostrategies for Delivery of Mental Health Counseling Services. *Journal of Mental Health Counseling, 13*(1), 51–57.

Herr, E. L. (1991). Challenges to Mental Health Counselors in a Dynamic Society: Macrostrategies in the Profession. *Journal of Mental Health Counseling, 13*(1), 6–20.

Ivey, A. E. (1993). On the need for reconstruction of our present practice of counseling and psychotherapy. *The Counseling Psychologist, 21*(2), 225–228.

Ivey, A. E., Ivey, M. B., & Simek–Morgan, L. (1993). *Counseling and psychotherapy: A multicultural perspective*. Boston: Allyn and Bacon.

Lazarus, A. A. (1992). Multimodal therapy: Technical eclecticism with minimal integration. In J. C. Norcross & M. R. Goldfried (Eds.), *Handbook of psychotherapy integration* (pp. 231–263). New York: Basic Books.

Lazarus, A. A., Beutler, L. E., & Norcross, J. C. (1992). The future of technical eclecticism. *Psychotherapy, 29*(1), 11–20.

Pedersen, P. (1991). Multiculturalism as a generic approach to counseling. *Journal of Counseling and Development, 70*(1), 6–12.

Pedersen, P. (1994). *A handbook for developing multicultural awareness* (2nd ed.). Alexandria, VA: American Counseling Association.

Pedersen, P., & Ivey, A. (1993). *Culture-centered counseling and interviewing skills: A practical guide*. Westport, CT: Praeger.

Ridley, C. R., Mendoza, D. W., & Kanitz, B. E. (1994). Multicultural training: Reexamination, operationalization, and integration. *The Counseling Psychologist, 22*(2), 227–289.

Sue, D. W. (1992). The challenge of multiculturalism: The road less traveled. *American Counselor, 1*(1), 6–14.

Sue, D. W., Arredondo, P., & McDavis, R. J. (1992). Multicultural counseling competencies and standards: A call to the profession. *Journal of Counseling and Development, 70*(4), 477–486.

Sue, D. W., Bernier, Y., Durran, A., Feinberg, L., Pedersen, P., Smith, E. J., & Nuttall, E. V. (1982). Position paper: Cross-cultural counseling competencies. *The Counseling Psychologist, 10*(2), 45–52.

Wrenn, C. G. (1962). The culturally encapsulated counselor. *Harvard Educational Review, 32*, 444–449.

Wrenn, C. G. (1985). Afterward: The culturally encapsulated counselor revisited. In P. Pedersen (Ed.), *Handbook of cross-cultural counseling and therapy* (pp. 323–329). Westport, CT: Greenwood Press.

CHAPTER 7

MCT THEORY AND
IMPLICATIONS FOR PRACTICE

Donald B. Pope-Davis

University of Maryland, College Park

Madonna G. Constantine

Temple University, Philadelphia

Assumption Audit

- MCT theory does not attempt to replace traditional/historical theories.
- Theories have been derived in different cultural contexts.
- MCT theory moves away from dichotomous good/bad judgments to a more integrative perspective.
- MCT reduces the tendency to stereotype clients.
- By expanding the envelope of acceptable counselor behaviors, MCT emphasizes a reciprocity with clients.
- MCT is directive and action oriented.
- One can use MCT with all cultural groups.
- MCT theory parallels social constructionism.
- MCT is interdisciplinary in focus.
- MCT theory has implications for changing society beyond counseling.
- MCT theory lends itself to analysis of case examples.
- MCT theory enlarges the potentially salient perspective beyond the traditional Euro-American categories.

Sue, Ivey, and Pedersen's theory of MCT is thorough, well articulated, and inclusive, with significant implications for the mental-health profession, particularly for those in practice. It represents a comprehensive discussion of much of the previous research on multicultural issues in counseling. The consolidation of this information into one book will likely serve as an often-used tool for counselors who wish to engage in MCT with clients who have a broad range of cultural identities. MCT theory provides "food for thought" for a variety of mental-health personnel and includes specific conceptual guidelines for helping such individuals interpret potential client issues, dynamics, behaviors, and attitudes in a sociocultural context. This type of contribution is critical to their moving beyond frameworks that unnecessarily or inappropriately pathologize clients with diverse backgrounds. By allowing counselors to collect information about multiple identities, MCT potentially works for all individuals. It will ultimately help counselors become more culturally competent.

One of the many strengths of MCT theory is that it does not strive to replace the numerous theories that have historically served the counseling profession. Instead, it attempts to help counselors understand that they can best use these theories in the specific cultural contexts in which they were developed. Furthermore, the culture-specific nature of such theories may be biased against groups who do not share their cultural assumptions.

MCT theory moves counselors from viewing client behavior as dichotomous (e.g., good or bad), to seeing it on a continuum within a cultural context. Similarly, MCT requires counselors to use integrative approaches, which potentially minimize the practice of a "one size fits all" theory of counseling and therapy. It may also decrease the likelihood that counselors will succumb to cultural encapsulation or promote other culture-bound phenomena (Ponterotto & Casas, 1991; Sue & Sue, 1990).

MCT theory also reduces the tendency to stereotype clients because of demographic or cultural characteristics, while it helps mental-health professionals develop a "cultural quilt," or comprehensive understanding of clients' multifaceted identities. MCT theory suggests that counselors use an emic (linguistic) approach in treating clients, a perspective that potentially provides a "cultural thesaurus" in dealing with the various culturally diverse clients (Cheatham, 1994).

In addition, this theory indicates that members of different cultural groups may feel personally empowered in counseling relationships. Counselors are no longer perceived as the "experts" regarding the cultural identities of their clients but are encouraged to learn from them, even remaining open to "instruction" about their clients' cultural identities (Ridley, Mendoza, & Kanitz, 1994; see also Chapter 3). MCT theory expands the idea of the "helping professional" by encouraging counselors to consider a range of roles or helping behaviors that may have been viewed historically as either inappropriate or nontherapeutic. Examples of these behaviors include the following:

1. Encouraging clients to invite family members or partners to engage in a variety of treatment alternatives (such as family therapy, couples therapy, community group activities) as adjuncts to traditional individual therapy.
2. Meeting in a less-structured or informal setting (a church hall, community center, park, etc.) to explore clients' issues and concerns.
3. Using less-formal methods of working with clients. For example, traditional "talk therapy" may not be warranted for members of those cultural groups either accustomed to relatively informal helping relationships and/or to nonverbal aspects of communication rather than direct, verbal feedback or communication.
4. Being more directive and action oriented, rather than process oriented, within the context of a therapeutic relationship if clients request such direction.

One important advantage of MCT theory is that one can apply it to most if not all cultural groups. Its utility extends not only to ethnic and racial minorities, but also to other marginalized cultural populations, such as women, gays, the physically disabled, etc. As such, MCT theory also challenges counselors to expand their theoretical and conceptual perspectives in working with clients. These perspectives have vital implications for building therapeutic relationships, assessing the presenting problem(s), developing counseling goals, therapeutic intervention, termination, and evaluation. The inclusive nature of MCT theory invariably assures the implementation of true multicultural counseling and psychotherapy, which will enhance clinical and ethical standards for practice and, consequently, improve treatment for all clients.

As a general theory, MCT widely applies not only to a number of cultural groups, but also to a variety of social contexts. Many of the concepts of MCT theory parallel principles of social constructionism. Social constructionists advocate that individuals' "realities" are based largely on who they are, what they value, and their biases, personal philosophies, and social status (Flax, 1987; Morawski, 1990; Richardson, 1993). Multiple realities and truths may exist (Bordo, 1990) and may in turn explain differing perceptions of socially constructed realities on the part of several different individuals. MCT counselors are receptive to diverse, even conflictual, conceptualizations of reality. An MCT counselor takes into consideration the components of individuals' realities, then integrates these constructs into a mosaic comprising a plurality of identities.

Furthermore, because individuals are multidimensional and their identities intertwined with each other's, they cannot isolate and analyze any singular aspect of their cultural identity (Pope-Davis & Constantine, 1994; Richardson, 1993). For example, a person cannot be known solely as a woman—apart from her other identities—because one cannot isolate variables such as gender, race, ethnicity, social class, and sexual orientation in understanding an individual. This idea is one of the most crucial underpinnings of MCT, which points to the multiple variables and factors comprising individuals, each of which counselors must consider and understand, particularly in working with culturally different clients.

It appears as though much of MCT theory represents a relationship among various disciplines in the social sciences and humanities, including sociology, anthropology, education, and linguistics. MCT theory challenges the long-standing practice of focusing primarily on individual human behavior and differences, supporting instead the idea of individual-in-context. The experiences and contexts of clients should be the primary means for counselors to understand and interpret their behavior. MCT theory will have significant utility for counselors for a long time. Long overdue, it will likely represent a major paradigm shift in the thinking, attitudes, behaviors, and relationships of many mental-health providers in ways that will benefit both clients and counselors. The impact of MCT theory on the counseling profession will almost certainly be generalized to situations outside the mental-health profession and will contribute to an acknowledgment of cultural differences and similarities in this society.

CASE STUDY: MCT IN ACTION

You can better understand MCT theory by examining the following case study, which illustrates the theory in action. While this case does not address all the propositions and corollaries of MCT theory, it does show how one can integrate MCT theory in practice.

The Case of Denise

Denise (a pseudonym)—a 20-year-old, African-American, lesbian college junior—was majoring in sociology at a large, predominantly White university in the southwestern United States. She lived in one of the campus residence halls with an African-American female roommate whom Denise initially claimed was her "best friend from high school." Denise came to the university counseling center to address feelings of depression and loneliness related to chronic difficulties with interpersonal relationships, particularly with her peers and family members, surrounding her sexual orientation.

During her intake session, Denise appeared somewhat anxious,

fidgeting in her seat. She also verbalized her ambivalence about exploring her presenting issues in counseling, because she had received
numerous messages from her parents and other family members about
the taboo of going to mental-health counselors to address "personal
things." Denise claimed she had "trust issues" and, in general, tended to
feel more comfortable talking about herself after hearing some personal
information about the person(s) with whom she would be interacting.
She then asked her African-American female counselor about her cre-
dentials and whether or not she was "a liberal person." After her counselor responded honestly to these questions, Denise appeared to relax.
Denise also discussed some initial and ongoing adjustment difficulties
she had experienced at the university, related to feeling like she was
"too different from any of these people here": "I just don't know what I
could do to make myself fit in better. I must be doing something wrong
in my relationships."

Specifically, Denise believed that many of her interpersonal difficulties were related to her inability to deal effectively with the homophobic attitudes of many students. She also shared that others' negative
treatment of her in this regard had affected her self-esteem. Denise
claimed that though her family had always fostered a sense of pride
about her racial identity, they had also been "intolerant" of nonheterosexual orientations. "Out" only to her immediate family and college
peers, Denise had been dating her current partner for almost three
years, but she felt that her family did not affirm her lesbianism or
approve of her relationship with her partner. She claimed they frequently told her that she was "going to burn in hell" because of her
sexual orientation. She stated that the African-American students
on campus were also judgmental and "unaccepting" about her sexual
identity. She spoke of feeling "fragmented" because she had to "play
down" her lesbian identity with people who would not accept her or
her voicing pride in being a lesbian with her lesbian and gay friends.
Toward the latter part of the intake session, Denise disclosed that her
roommate was actually her romantic partner. She also shared that she
would be willing to give counseling a try for a minimum of three
sessions, after which time she would evaluate whether or not to
remain in counseling.

During the first few sessions of counseling, Denise explored her relatively unacknowledged feelings of sadness and anger related to feeling
unsupported and oppressed by several individuals and groups in her
social and familial environments because of her sexual orientation.
Denise claimed she felt emotionally supported by her partner, by other
lesbians who were a part of her social circles, and by "some really cool
straight people," but also spoke of feeling powerless in changing some
of the negative attitudes and feelings that others harbored about people
who were gay, lesbian, or bisexual. She also explored issues related to

her own internalized homophobia, heterosexism, racism, and sexism, and began to emerge with a greater awareness of how these issues affected the ways she saw herself and the ways she expected other people to treat her. As her counselor helped her identify various cultural identities and validated her struggles to consolidate them, Denise claimed she was feeling increasingly comfortable with the idea of working to synthesize her multiple identities to formulate a more integrated sense of her being. She also claimed that she was beginning to feel less depressed.

By the end of her third scheduled session, Denise and her counselor had contracted with each other to continue addressing her presenting concerns for the remaining sessions. During that time, Denise continued to explore the impact of her various cultural identities, particularly her sexual orientation, on her presenting issues, and she began to take some responsibility for difficulties in interpersonal interactions. She came to recognize that her difficulties with trust, while warranted on many occasions because of homophobia, sometimes contributed to her feelings of isolation and sadness. Denise traced some of her "trust issues" to relationships with girls in junior high who had ultimately betrayed her "secret" of being a lesbian. She discussed at great length her feelings of disappointment and anger related to not feeling "unconditionally loved" by her family of origin and was beginning to accept the possibility that her family members "may never be okay with my being gay." Over the course of the counseling sessions, Denise and her counselor spent some time exploring their relationship with regard to their cultural differences, issues of trust, and issues of power and mutuality, because they both felt these issues were important. Denise spoke of feeling empowered by her experiences of feeling supported, validated, and challenged in counseling, and she expressed an interest in joining a lesbian support group on campus so she could obtain support and continue struggling with her issues in a deliberative fashion.

Toward the end of counseling, she could speak about her initial fears of being "rejected" by her counselor, an African-American woman. Much of these fears were related to her past experiences of feeling rejected because of her sexual orientation. Denise also realized that much of her initial depression was related to unresolved issues and pent-up feelings she harbored because of her difficulty in being assertive in relationships. When she terminated individual counseling, she rated her counseling experience as highly satisfactory.

This particular case study nicely illustrates how one can use some of the basic principles of MCT theory to aid in the assessment, understanding, and treatment of a culturally different client. Here are a few of these, briefly discussed.

The Case of Multicultural Identities

Denise's case exemplifies how one can conceptualize and apply MCT theory to a client with a variety of cultural group identities. In this case, many identities represented historically marginalized populations. The MCT counselor chose to help Denise identify the interrelationships among her various cultural identities and helped her embrace them with feelings of pride and empowerment. Denise's lesbian identity was the primary issue she chose to explore in the context of her counseling relationship. If the counselor in this case had assumed that Denise's main "cultural" issue was related to her racial identity affiliation, her ability to form an effective working relationship would have been seriously jeopardized.

MCT theory stresses that all people possess multiple identities, though not all necessarily equally salient at a given time. In this case, while Denise's African-American identity might have been the most visible, her lesbian one was most salient. Effective multicultural counselors can free themselves of stereotypes and keep an open approach in relating to culturally different clients. Denise's multiple roles (identities) as a lesbian, woman, African American, and student represent parts of her total being.

MCT theory implies several important principles related to cultural identities. First, the context may often determine which aspect of a cultural identity will emerge more strongly than others. At the university, when among predominantly White students, Denise's identity as an African-American woman came to the forefront. Among predominantly African-American students, her identity as a lesbian was strongest.

Second, like Denise, clients experience identity at several levels. For example, Proposition 2 of MCT theory (p. 15) implies that the counselor/therapist must not only lose sight of reference group identities, but must also recognize clients' uniqueness as well as features common to the universal human experience. To avoid, deny, negate, or lose sight of the totality of these experiences is to miss the "total person."

Sociopolitical Interplay in the Counseling Relationship

Denise initially came to the counseling center with grave concerns about whether or not counseling could even help her and about whether or not she could trust her counselor. She may have viewed her counselor as a representative of "the system," which Denise had experienced as unsupportive and even oppressive. Many culturally different clients have experienced discrimination, prejudice, and oppression; prior experiences with institutions and individuals (teachers, employers, administrators, and counselors) may have been tinged by bias and stereotyping.

Rather than an "inability to trust," "pathological suspiciousness," or "paranoia," Denise's mistrust of counseling should be understood as a possible reflection of the sociopolitical context in which she has been raised. Indeed, one should view her cautious approach to counseling as the operation of healthy, functioning coping mechanisms developed to survive in an intolerant and oppressive society.

Expanding the Repertoire of Helping Responses

That Denise's counselor was an African-American woman might lead one to expect them to form a rapport easily because of similar group membership. Such an assumption, however, may prove quite erroneous. For example, coming from the same racial group is no guarantee that the client will favorably view the counselor. Indeed, some minorities may view a minority helping professional less favorably because of the notion that "they've sold out." Similarly, Denise's African-American counselor may have initially represented those racially similar and important individuals in her life who rejected her because of her sexual identity. These two factors often operate to (1) impede client self-disclosure and (2) encourage clients to test counselors. For example, the initial time limit Denise placed on counseling to "check it out" seemed appropriate in several ways, particularly because Black clients often tend initially to distrust mental-health professionals and may be less likely to view them as helpful (Grier & Cobb, 1968; Thomas & Dansby, 1985).

Though clients usually check out mental-health professionals, the type of testing in multicultural situations often differs qualitatively from that in other counseling circumstances. For example, Denise may have approached the counseling situation with the following: "Before I open up to you, before I can trust you [self-disclosure] . . . I want to know where you're coming from [counselor self-disclosure]." This approach often creates theoretical and practical dilemmas for helping professionals. First, many theories of counseling and therapy claim that therapist self-disclosure is taboo. Fears of "crossing boundaries," "fostering dependencies," "unduly influencing clients," "losing objectivity," etc., are often raised. Second, helping professionals are usually very deficient in the repertoire of appropriate self-disclosure responses. Most counselors are well taught in "attending skills" but have minimal experience in the use of "influencing skills."

In this chapter, there is not enough space to discuss the theoretical issues related to "counselor self-disclosure." Suffice it to say that counselors who find it difficult to engage in traditionally taboo helping responses may be seriously disadvantaged in their ability to form a helpful relationship with a culturally different client. In any case, MCT Proposition 4 (p. 19) makes it quite clear that MCT theory (1) challenges the applicability of one theoretical model to a diverse clientele, (2) encourages cultural flexibility in the helping process, and (3) asks helping professionals to expand their repertoire of clinical skills, even traditionally taboo responses.

In summary, Denise profited from counseling because of the counselor's ability to implement certain MCT principles. Being able to tap the salient and multiple identities of Denise, understanding the sociopolitical influences in her life (including the counseling session), being open and flexible in the use of counselor self-disclosure, and using interpersonal connection were all techniques the counselor used. Denise moved to a place where she could begin to trust her counselor and to do some intensive work on her presenting issues. Because at times some individuals may err in the direction of consistently viewing themselves as "problematic" versus an "individual-in-context," MCT theory proposes that clients and counselors consider the society at large and the ways in which it may impact or shape the perceptions, beliefs, attitudes, and behaviors of individuals. For instance, Denise initially thought her chronic interpersonal difficulties stemmed from her own identity and actions. As she explored this issue in her therapy, she was able to identify her own struggles with self-acceptance and accept partial responsibility for those elements of interpersonal interactions she felt comfortable "owning." Denise also emerged with a greater awareness of her impact on relationships, and an increased understanding of the role of person-environment interactions on her behavior. For example, she could acknowledge through counseling her anger and frustration about the lack of support created by the society at large for nonheterosexual individuals; she also realized she did not have to "change my homosexual behavior or who I am as a person" to gain acceptance or affirmation in an often "oppressive" society.

FUTURE DIRECTIONS

Sue, Pedersen, and Ivey clearly indicate that counselors should consider their clients' diverse characteristics and how they represent multiple cultural group affiliations and identities. Importantly, this perspective implies that counselors need to thoroughly examine their cultural assumptions, biases, and values about cultural groups before attempting to integrate MCT theory into their clinical work. However, it is unclear how they can do this to the point of ensuring appropriate multicultural counseling for all client populations. This issue should be explored in greater depth to help counselors become more culturally competent. Historically, much of counseling theory has encouraged the valuing of such concepts as individuality, autonomy, and independence. Though it does not negate the importance of these attributes, MCT theory clearly moves counselors toward considering individuals in their cultural contexts, where other attributes such as dependence and self-in-relation-to-others are more highly valued. However, while MCT theory may be an important consideration in counseling multicultural populations, little research has examined individuals and their relationships within the framework of this approach. MCT can therefore potentially influence the future of research greatly, and may contribute to a more comprehensive understanding of related issues. There is also a paucity of research that focuses on the assessment of MCT competencies for various cultural populations (Pope-Davis & Ottavi, 1994). An important direction for the ongoing enhancement of MCT is developing measures that can assess whether "true" MCT is being practiced. Such assessment tools will be important in clarifying, expanding, and enhancing MCT propositions and corollaries. While counselors have begun to deliberately and systematically integrate elements of MCT theory into their clinical work, the need remains to make cognitive and emotional shifts in how counselors define the provision of mental health to multicultural populations. For example, many counselors tend to perceive the delivery of counseling services in traditional ways, such as direct service through individual and group psychotherapy. MCT theory challenges counselors to consider alternate ways of providing services (e.g., outreach programs, self-help groups) that may appeal more to many multicultural populations. However, many graduate training programs have not traditionally focused on the development and integration of the knowledge, skills, and behaviors needed to do such work. For MCT to become integrated in the profession, both counselors-in-training and established practitioners may need to receive new and nontraditional ways of delivering services so that they can appropriately meet the needs of an emerging multicultural society.

REFERENCES FOR CHAPTER 7

Bordo, S. (1990). Feminism, postmodernism, and gender-scepticism. In L. J. Nicholson (Ed.), *Feminism/postmodernism* (pp. 133–156). London: Routledge, Chapman & Hall.

Cheatham, H. E. (1994). A response. *The Counseling Psychologist, 22*, 290–295.

Flax, J. (1987). Postmodernism and gender relations in feminist theory. *Signs, 12*, 621–643.

Grier, W. H., & Cobb, P. M. (1968). *Black rage*. New York: Basic Books.

Morawski, J. G. (1990). Toward the unimagined: Feminism and epistemology in psychology. In R. T. Hare-Mustin & J. Maracek (Eds.), *Making a difference: Psychology and the construction of gender* (pp. 150–183). New Haven, CT: Yale University Press.

Ponterotto, J. G., & Casas, J. M. (1991). *Handbook of racial/ethnic minority counseling research*. Springfield, IL: Thomas.

Pope-Davis, D. B., & Constantine, M. G. (1994). *Multicultural identity development: A needed perspective*. Unpublished manuscript, University of Maryland, College Park.

Pope-Davis, D. B., and Ottavi, T. M. (1994). Examining the association between self-reported multicultural counseling competencies and demographic variables among counselors. *Journal of Counseling and Development, 72*, 651–654.

Richardson, M. S. (1993). Work in people's lives: A location for counseling psychologists. *Journal of Counseling Psychology, 40*, 425–433.

Ridley, C. R., Mendoza, D. W., & Kanitz, B. E. (1994). Multicultural training: Reexamination, operationalization, and integration. *The Counseling Psychologist, 22*, 227–289.

Sue D. W., & Sue, D. (1990). *Counseling the culturally different: Theory and practice*. New York: Wiley.

Thomas, M. B., & Dansby, P. G. (1985). Black clients: Family structures, therapeutic issues, and strengths. *Psychotherapy, 22*, 398–407.

CHAPTER 8

MCT Theory and Implications for Training

Ena Vazquez Nuttall
William Sanchez
Jennifer Joyce Webber
Northeastern University, Boston, Massachusetts

Assumption Audit

- MCT theory is a critical milestone in transforming counseling psychology into a culturally competent profession.
- Culturally appropriate treatment will help provide ethnically, linguistically, and culturally diverse clients with satisfactory services.
- MCT theory draws on exciting new developments in cross-cultural counseling —i.e., White and minority racial identity development, worldview, liberation, and sociopolitical oppression—and cross-cultural counseling competencies.
- MCT theory defines *culture* too broadly, overlapping with "diversity," "minority," "race," and "ethnicity," which it also needs to clarify.
- In its quest to redress the absence of cultural emphasis in current theories, MCT theory may overplay the role of cultural influences.
- Good MCT training consists of a sound curriculum, integrative field experiences, knowledgeable and culturally diverse faculty and supervisors, the presence of culturally diverse students, and an evaluation system that measures the outcomes and basic tenets of the theoretical system.
- MCT training should begin with a cross-cultural counseling curriculum using the revised multicultural competencies developed by Sue, Arredondo, & McDavis (1992).
- MCT competencies lack coverage of several important counseling roles, such as research; child, family, and group counseling; assessment; organizational development; prevention; and consultation.

- MCT theory is silent regarding the role of a second language in competency.
- MCT theory must develop a comprehensive evaluation system to ascertain its efficiency and effectiveness for training purposes.
- The main hurdle in the implementation of MCT training is convincing faculty members of the importance of focusing their counseling program in this direction.

If multiculturalism is not limited to exotic populations but provides a fourth force perspective in all counseling theory and practice, then where does that construct fit into the textbooks, the courses, the field experiences, and the preparation of counselors to work in a multicultural world? (P. B. Pedersen, 1991, p. 77)

Sue, Ivey, and Pedersen's theory of MCT is a critical milestone on the long road of transforming counseling and clinical psychology into a culturally competent profession. The "internationalization" and "multiculturalization" of business, the increasing advances in communication that are making the world smaller, the increase in immigration, and the higher birth rates of some minority groups (Atkinson, Morten, & Sue, 1993; Ponterotto & Casas, 1987) have changed the types of clients served by many professionals in the United States, including counseling psychologists.

In business, education, health care, and other professions, typical clients have changed from White, middle-class, English-speaking individuals to a variety of clients, who speak different languages and come from different socioeconomic and widely different cultural backgrounds. With its emphasis on measuring clients' needs and preferences, evaluating delivery of services, and designing and constantly improving services to satisfy and delight customers, the "Total Quality" movement has greatly impacted all segments of the service professions (American Association of School Administrators, 1993). Culturally appropriate treatment is a major ingredient in providing ethnically, linguistically, and culturally diverse clients with satisfactory services. However, most professional groups retain the idea that their new clients can be served in the same way as the old clients. Many still believe that a good psychologist, business manager, or teacher possesses universal skills that can serve all clients. Thus, students in these professions do not receive training to serve these new clients sensitively. Treatment facilities lose clients, companies lose customers, and schools lose students.

Counseling psychologists in training must prepare themselves to meet the needs of multicultural clients. Students who select a program that contains a substantial focus on serving multicultural clients and who also learn a second language will find themselves rewarded by greater and more lucrative employment opportunities than those who do not pursue this kind of education. The "Help Wanted" sections of newspapers in many large cities bulge with advertisements for bilingual/bicultural mental-health professionals. Given the fact that approximately 5% of health-care providers are persons of color (Hickey & Solis, 1990; Kavanaugh & Kennedy, 1992), mainstream students are greatly needed in this area. Clearly, the myth of needing to train only minorities to work with cultural, ethnic, and linguistic minorities does not stand up to the serious need for services among these populations. In addition, noninvolvement by majority groups may condone and perpetuate social inequity (Kavanaugh & Kennedy, 1992).

This chapter presents first a general evaluation of MCT theory, pointing out strengths and areas in need of further development. Next, the implications of MCT theory for training are discussed. Finally, the elements of excellence in multicultural training and the difficulties in convincing program faculty to implement them are presented.

GENERAL EVALUATION

The MCT theory of Sue, Ivey, and Pedersen is an exciting new development that draws on the most promising concepts in cross-cultural counseling. Such important concepts as stages of White and minority racial-identity development (Atkinson, Morten & Sue, 1993; Hardiman, 1982; Helms, 1990; Jackson, 1975), worldview (D. W. Sue & D. Sue, 1990), liberation and sociopolitical oppression (Freire, 1972), and cross-cultural counseling competencies (D. W. Sue, 1981; D. W. Sue, Arredondo, & McDavis, 1992) have been developed in the last 20 years or so. Sue, Ivey, and Pedersen have done an excellent job of organizing these principles into a coherent system. Their theory of theories is an open, systemic, dynamic, and flexible conceptualization designed to be constantly updated.

Problems of Definition

As in any theory in its formative stage, some areas need reformulation and/or development. One difficulty this theoretical scheme presents is the broad way the concept of culture is defined. Sue, Ivey, & Pedersen (Chapter 2) define culture as any group that shares a common issue or theme. This definition would include any social group as a cultural group. It seems that one should consider a more specific definition of culture, such as that of Linton (1945): "the configuration of learned behavior and results of behavior whose components and elements are shared and transmitted by members of a particular society" (p. 32). Further, Betancourt & Lopez

(1993) present a thorough discussion of the definition of culture. They posit that the distinction Triandis et al. (1980) make between the objective and subjective aspects of culture is important to the formulation of research on culture. Triandis et al. refer to roads, buildings, and tools as the objective aspects of culture, while social norms, roles, beliefs, and values constitute subjective culture. Betancourt and Lopez assert that subjective culture includes a wide range of elements such as family roles, communication patterns, affective styles, and values regarding personal control, individualism, collectivism, spirituality, and religiosity.

The difficulty with applying the concept of culture to human services is that it overlaps with "diversity," "minority," "race," and "ethnicity." The MCT theory's concept of culture is most consistent with the relatively new concept of *diversity*, though some scholars would have difficulty including survivors of trauma or any other group with a common theme as representatives of diversity. In truth, the concept of diversity has attained popularity because of the conceptual difficulties of explaining the many groups who experience discrimination. Certainly all the other groups mentioned by Sue and associates—culture/language, gender, age, sexual orientation, and disability—would be considered diverse.

The definition of *minority* must also be clarified because MCT theory refers mostly to people considered minorities. Wirth (1945) defines *minorities* as groups who "because of physical or cultural characteristics, are singled out from the others in the society in which they live for differential and unequal treatment" (p. 347). Dworkin and Dworkin (1976) postulate that a minority group is characterized by four qualities: identifiability, differential power, differential and pejorative treatment, and group awareness. Thus it seems that women; gays and lesbians; the aged; the disabled; people from certain linguistic, ethnic, or cultural groups such as Asians, Hispanics, African Americans, and Native Americans; and any other groups singled out for unequal and differential treatment should be considered cultural minorities.

Because of socialization and/or physical differences, all these groups have generated distinctive cultures—ways of living and behaving in family, work, and other social contexts. For instance, lesbian women develop their own social and work support groups, go through unique identity life cycles, establish different dating and family patterns, and frequent those community and educational institutions where they feel most comfortable. These cultural groups have long histories, and their norms cover many areas of behavior passed from one generation to another.

Race is generally defined in terms of physical characteristics, such as skin color, facial features, and hair type, which are common to inbred, geographically isolated people (Betancourt & Lopez, 1993). However, the use of the concept of race is increasingly being questioned because racial groups are more alike than different, even in genetic and physical characteristics. Nonetheless, some people tend to think that members of minority groups are alike for genetic reasons alone rather than any social and cultural variables such as poverty or inadequate education.

Often used interchangeably with *culture* and *race*, *ethnicity* has been defined broadly and narrowly. The broad definition posits that ethnicity is determined by physical and cultural characteristics (Atkinson et al., 1993). Because physical characteristics are linked with race, ethnicity can become confused with race. However, this is misleading. For example, Latina(o) Americans belong to all different racial groups and mixtures: African, Asian, Native-American, and European, depending on geographic location. The narrow definition of *ethnicity* is based on national or cultural characteristics. For example, Jewish Americans would be considered an ethnic group different from other Jewish peoples. In any case, that this and the rest of the concepts just discussed have evolved from social movements and scientific advances and continue to change creates difficult intellectual challenges.

Overplaying Cultural Influences

Another difficulty with MCT theory is that in its quest to redress the absence of cultural emphasis in prevalent theories, it tends to overplay the role of cultural influences. Not all psychological problems stem from cultural issues; personality and individual differences also play an important part in social adjustment. For instance, an extroverted Asian child may have an easier time adjusting to an American classroom than an introverted one with the same cultural background. In addition, this theory does not address the important interplay among ethnicity, race, culture, and social class. A culturally different client who is middle class will tend to experience less difficulty adjusting to a predominantly middle-class society such as the United States than a client of low socioeconomic status.

In any event, practitioners need to understand the implications of culture for it to influence their assessment, diagnosis, and treatment. Many of the errors in treating multicultural clients occur because clinicians fail to distinguish between those difficulties stemming from cultural influences, social class, or ethnicity and those unique to the person (Porter, 1994).

For example, say a Puerto Rican psychologist begins treatment with a middle-aged, working-class Puerto Rican woman with significant depressive features. After the first session, the client brings the therapist a carafe of hot coffee. The client notes how hard the counselor works and hopes the coffee might help him through the afternoon. The client herself does not drink any of the coffee. The counselor politely accepts the coffee from the client, who then brings coffee in for the following counseling sessions.

When the psychologist presents this incident to his Euro-American supervisor, she has a significantly different reaction. The supervisor, who supports a traditional individual counseling and transference model, discusses how inappropriate it is for the counselor to accept the coffee and how the client is attempting to "manipulate" the counseling situation. She stresses the need to examine the "internal causes" of this client's need to bring coffee to the session and that a counselor must "strictly refuse" any "gift" or "offering" presented by a client, at the risk of "boundary difficulties." The supervisor fails to see that refusal of the coffee would have been a severe negation of this woman's cultural, social, and personal values of providing and repaying directly for something that one receives from another. Cultural, social, and individual considerations are critical and necessary in an increasingly multicultural society.

Other Problems

The MCT theory presented by Sue et al. presents further problems. It focuses primarily on adult individual counseling, fails to address issues of bilingualism, and barely touches on prevention, consultation, and assessment. Family, child, group, and organizational interventions are scarcely developed. The lack of attention to children's services is a serious omission, considering the multiplicity of problems faced by children in general and minority children in particular (Nuttall, Romero, & Kalesnik, 1992). Child-oriented psychologists have expended considerable energy to develop programs to promote sensitivity and effective services for multicultural children (Esquivel & Keitel, 1990; Herring, 1989; Locke, 1989; Parker, 1989; Nuttall, De Leon, & Valle, 1990). Specifically, "cuento therapy," or story-telling therapy, has been used with Puerto Rican children (Rogler & Prodicano, 1986) and with preadolescents and adolescents (Constantino, Malgady, & Rogler, 1988). Through the reading of traditional Puerto Rican folktales, therapists reach cultural values and reinstate cultural pride and identity in such clients. Cuento therapy has helped stimulate growth in children and adolescents who feel "caught" between two different cultures.

MCT theory justifiably concentrates on training mainstream students, because most multicultural clients will be served by them. However, though people assume that one develops specific multicultural counseling skills naturally by merely belonging to a particular culture, many multicultural students are in as great need of appropriate training as their majority counterparts. For example, a Latina student whose parents came from Mexico as youngsters may not speak Spanish, identify with mainstream American culture, or be aware of the culture and predicaments of recent low-income Puerto Rican immigrants.

TRAINING IMPLICATIONS OF
MCT THEORY

This section presents the main elements in the effective implementation of MCT theory. The basic components of good training in multicultural counseling consist of a sound curriculum, integrative field experiences, knowledgeable and culturally diverse faculty and supervisors, the presence of culturally diverse students, and a system of evaluation that measures the outcomes and basic tenets of MCT theory. Some of these components were highlighted by Sue, Ivey, and Pedersen in Chapters 2 and 3; others are presented here as areas in need of further development.

Besides incorporating these basic components, one must consider how to change the prevailing low priority given to multicultural issues, making MCT theory a central curriculum component that will transform the counseling profession. Issues pertinent to the undertaking of this major organizational change are discussed.

The Curriculum

How to teach cross-cultural counseling has received widespread attention (Anderson & Cranston-Gingras, 1991; D'Andrea & Daniels, 1991; Garcia, Wright, & Corey, 1991; Ivey, Ivey, & Simek-Morgan, 1993; Kiselica, 1991; Leong & Kim, 1991; Lewis & Hayes, 1991; McRae & Johnson, 1991; Midgette & Meggert, 1991; Nwachuku & Ivey, 1991; T. Pedersen & Carey, 1987; Ridley, Mendoza & Kanitz, 1994; D.W. Sue, 1991). MCT theory proposes the use of one of the best contributions to cross-cultural counseling curriculum—the revised multicultural competencies developed by Sue and associates (D. W. Sue et al., 1992). These competencies have influenced the development of several assessment measures, including the Cross-Cultural Inventory–Revised (CCCI-R) (LaFromboise & Foster, 1989), the Multicultural Awareness–Knowledge-Skills Survey (MAKSS) (D'Andrea, Daniels, & Heck, 1991), the Multicultural Counseling Awareness Scale–Form B (MCAS–Form B) (Ponterotto, Sanchez, & Magids, 1991), and the Multicultural Counseling Inventory (MCI) (Sodowsky, Taffe, Gutkin, & Wise, 1994). The work of Sodowsky and associates (1994) reveals that the MCI contains four factors: multicultural counseling skills, multicultural awareness, multicultural counseling relationships, and multicultural counseling knowledge. Because of the great interest in such testing, one soon will be able to determine how competent a student or potential employee is in multicultural counseling and human relations skills. These instruments will thus make it possible to individualize courses according to the level of expertise of students and to make more informed decisions when hiring a professional who is to serve a multicultural population.

The Office of Ethnic Minority Affairs of the American Psychological Association (APA, 1991) has also developed relatively broad guidelines for providing services to multicultural populations. These guidelines cover many areas, including therapy, research, assessment, and broad systemic interventions. Though not presented as competencies, they have been widely disseminated. The Massachusetts Board of Registration of Psychologists has taken the lead in incorporating these guidelines into the documents consulted in judging ethical violations.

The competencies prepared by Sue et al. (1992) compose the major training model proposed for MCT theory and focus on three areas of counselor expertise: (1) being aware of their own assumptions, values, and biases; (2) understanding the worldviews of culturally different clients; and (3) developing appropriate interventions and strategies. Competencies are arranged by attitudes, knowledge, and skills (see Table 3.1).

Overall, the competencies approach presented in MCT theory, coupled with outcome measures, is the most currently accepted approach to training. To measure excellence, higher education in the United States is moving from the quality of the faculty and number of grants obtained to what students learn and their competencies at graduation (Angelo & Cross, 1993). The competencies approach that Sue et al. propose is based on this new paradigm of educational evaluation.

The competencies proposed, however, fail to cover several important professional roles such as research; child, family, and group counseling; assessment; organizational development; prevention; and consultation. Surprisingly, the competencies do not include learning a second language, even though it is a major need, especially when one works with recently arrived immigrants. The role of a second language and its impact on assessment and psychotherapy, as well as the effective use of interpreters, are not discussed.

Given the premise that the competencies approach offers a sound teaching methodology, a crucial issue arises: How does one accomplish all these competencies in the single cross-cultural counseling course that constitutes the typical curricular offering (Hills & Strozier, 1993)? Even model programs (Ponterotto & Casas, 1987) do not address all the competencies; some specialize in research (Santa Barbara), others in practice (Syracuse). In addition, most programs help develop awareness and provide knowledge but tend not to develop professional skills (McRae & Johnson, 1991). None of the programs contains provisions for learning or improving a second language.

Integrative Field Experiences

It seems that the only way to produce culturally competent counselors is to integrate multicultural issues in as many aspects of academic training and fieldwork as possible (Atkinson, 1994). In addition to a strong academic curriculum, appropriate fieldwork placement is vital to multicultural training (Kiselica, 1991; Porter, 1994).

To learn how to work successfully with minority clients, students need to interact directly with them (LaFromboise & Foster, 1992; McRae & Johnson, 1991). Methods such as triad simulations, encounters with students from different ethnic groups, intercultural sensitizers, or role playing do not sufficiently prepare students to be culturally sensitive service providers. On the other hand, working with a supervisor of a particular ethnic group in conjunction with helping clients from that group, an approach used at Boston City Hospital Multicultural Training Program, is extremely effective. Rotating supervisors of different ethnic groups with concomitant clients, though difficult to engineer, is a superior hands-on way to teach specific counseling skills.

A Culturally Knowledgeable and Diverse Faculty

A key ingredient to delivering a superb program in multicultural counseling is the degree of knowledge and expertise of the faculty. Most departments offering strong multicultural programs have one or two people who truly understand multicultural counseling training; occasionally, a school will also have institutes and other resources with a multicultural focus (Ponterotto & Casas, 1987). If a department lacks appropriately trained personnel, which is often the case (Clark, 1993; Midgette & Meggert, 1991), then it needs to provide multicultural in-service training or sabbatical leaves for faculty and staff to become competent. The quality of the education in MCT depends on the competence, knowledge, and enthusiasm of the faculty members offering the courses.

In addition to having trained faculty members, departments need multicultural faculty members to serve as role models for mainstream and minority students. Unfortunately, the number of minority faculty members available for academic jobs is limited (Vetter, 1991). Recruiting these faculty members and helping them obtain tenure are major challenges in maintaining a vibrant multicultural program. Many minority professionals shy away from teaching because of the difficulties of obtaining tenure. Stories of other minority members experiencing limited acceptance of their work, receiving little support or mentoring, and feeling ethnically and culturally isolated abound. Because minority professors are underrepresented, they tend to be assigned to more committees than equivalent mainstream professors. Support for minority faculty members in publishing and research is sorely needed.

The Presence of Culturally Different Students

Any program that seeks to enhance multicultural training has to consider the pivotal role minority students can play in the delivery of programs. The recruitment of students of color is critical to transforming programs to fit an MCT framework. The potential for support along common issues is derived from increasing diversity. The minority student's expertise and knowledge are useful to mainstream students. Because their presence enriches learning, they constitute a hidden curriculum.

However, attracting minority students to a program requires considerable effort. Very few students of color can negotiate the complex maze of survival through high school, college, graduate school, and postgraduate training (Hickey & Solis, 1990). Although MCT as presently conceptualized does not focus on culturally different students, the theory clearly applies to them. Often these students must work in an educational environment that is sometimes hostile to either their own cultural diversity or those initiatives directed to enhance services to cultural and ethnic minorities.

Many "nightmare" stories have been told by students at all levels who have had to face issues of discrimination, stereotyping, and hostility because of their views regarding multiculturalism. The mainstream training "culture" is very quick to label and "victim blame" these students as well. At faculty/staff meetings, comments such as the following are typical of cultural encapsulation and narrow training culture biases exhibited by many programs (D'Andrea & Daniels, 1991; D. W. Sue & D. Sue, 1990): "This student is a trouble maker," "He is not a team player," "These students cannot cut it intellectually," "She is a manipulator." Similar to the complexities that clients face in negotiating a culturally oppressive health and mental-health-care system, many minority students do not escape the traditional "victim blaming" ideology (Ryan, 1971).

This atmosphere can occur in many settings, such as interactions with advisors during individual courses, discussions with professors, and relationships with supervisors and specialists at practicum and internship placements. Many minority students have described the process of "playing the game"—that is, going along with the dominant ideology, no matter how culturally oppressive the atmosphere may be.

Furthermore, the careers of such students may hinge on the evaluation of culturally oppressive supervisors. As Kavanaugh and Kennedy (1992) point out, "Power is the crucial variable in minority-majority relations and affects the ability of individuals or groups to realize their goals and interests, even in the face of resistance to the power" (p. 17). The concept described by D. W. Sue and D. Sue (1990) as "fronting," by both faculty and students, takes on significance in this context. The very act of challenging cultural stereotypes, racism, and cultural oppression becomes a "threat to professional survival" for these young professionals. Support for minority students thus proves critically important and needs to be addressed by all training initiatives.

Programs have also sought to increase the numbers of minority students without determining the types of supports these students may need. The prevailing attitude is that one training model will fit all situations. Typically, departments have merely increased the number of minority students and offer only one or two faculty members who represent and truly integrate issues of diversity and multiculturalism. Culturally different mentors are needed to enhance students' professional careers and to help them confront issues of racism and cultural oppression within these programs. Offering mentors, however, does not answer the more critical question of wider system supports for students and multiculturalism and diversity as integral parts of all college and training curriculums.

Measuring Outcomes and Basic Tenets

For MCT theory to be efficiently and effectively implemented, it needs a comprehensive evaluation system incorporated into its design. Although some reseach addresses some of the basic concepts of the theory, such as racial identity and acculturation scales (Sabnani & Ponterotto, 1992), the evaluation of the impact of MCT training has barely begun (D'Andrea et al., 1991; Ridley et al., 1994). Instruments to measure the outcomes of the different dimensions of training (skills, knowledge, attitudes) must continue to be developed and tested. The impact of both academic and field-work experience must also be assessed. It would be premature to settle on a specific number of competencies or approaches without continually testing the effectiveness of the training. Both qualitative and quantitative approaches should be used. Follow-up studies of students who have completed programs should be conducted to assess their level of satisfaction with their training and their self-perceptions of competence. The supervisors' and clients' evaluations should also be obtained. Because MCT theory and its implementation is a new and controversial paradigm, having strong empirical data to support its adoption will be helpful.

GETTING FACULTY TO BECOME COMMITTED TO MCT

The main hurdle in the implementation of MCT theory is convincing faculty members of its importance. So Sue (1991) has pointed out some of the difficulties of encouraging faculty and other professional training staff to look at how their own attitudes and biases affect the course work, training, and supervision they provide. He postulates a wider "training and research culture" with its own rules, values, biases, myths, and worldview, which affects multicultural training. In some instances, significant "clashes" arise even within the "training culture" of a particular graduate program or internship site. These conflicts are transmitted to students. How the business of professional education is handled, and under whose rules, again becomes a complex and at times hostile political issue, which in many settings remains "closed to discussion."

Many psychologists who have worked in hospital settings, for example, have clearly run into a "wall" in attempting to confront the traditional psychiatric and even more traditional medical model to address issues of diversity and cultural oppression within these settings.

An example of how power can truly decide whether an MCT model can be integrated within these types of settings follows: A hospital in Florida makes this statement about privileges for psychologists: "Psychologists and Neuropsychologists shall hold NO admitting privileges. Appropriately credentialed psychologists/neuropsychologists may provide testing to inpatient per direct order of the attending physician. The provision of psychotherapy for hospitalized patients must be in conjunction with a psychiatrist who holds clinical privileges." Psychologists and trainees working in these types of settings are clearly under pressure to accept this definition, basic to the medical model. Given such power hierarchies, one finds it difficult to imagine clients and professionals alike advocating for practices that mirror MCT theory.

As D. W. Sue et al. (1992) point out, issues of diversity and multiculturalism have traditionally been addressed in graduate training programs and practicum/internship sites by merely adding a course or lecture to fulfill the requirement that the program be sensitive to cultural issues. D. W. Sue et al. (1992) clearly spell out the inadequacies of this approach in addressing a true "curriculum transformation" and confronting the fact that this has not occurred in most training programs. Frequently, faculties respond to this "transformation" with openly hostile attitudes or by raising issues of academic freedom. Concerns with "watered-down" programs are cited (S. Sue, 1991). Openly biased and culturally oppressive attitudes are exhibited with further "splits" in departments and staff.

Students are very sensitive to these issues and to whether or not a faculty or internship training staff truly embrace a model similar to that proposed by MCT theory. The following case demonstrates the complexities of convincing students to address these issues without the training system having "its own act together":

> A minority staff member is scheduled to present a series of lectures on addressing cultural issues in working with Latino clients to an internship class of 16. This "required" series of presentations is chaired by another minority staff member (the second of only 4 minority professionals in a department of 40 professionals). The afternoon of the scheduled lecture, 4 of the 16 interns arrive for the 90-minute presentation. Further exploration by the seminar leader of this and other incidents of nonattendance reveals the students' attitudes regarding issues of diversity and culture: "Why do you ask us to accept and use these concepts when your own staff does not practice what you preach?"

Graduate programs and internships sites have a long way to go in examining their own culturally oppressive and racist attitudes, the most painful and dramatic aspect of "rethinking" that many faculty programs need to accomplish.

Process issues become critical in any "transformation" initiative. The attitudes of graduate programs (as well as faculties and work sites) need to be integrated in any initiative that embodies MCT theory. The paradigm shift that must occur is critical if this initiative is not to become just another "add-on."

MCT theory needs to be applied to senior staff and faculty—in many settings, the most difficult to change. Here, the commitment needs to be launched on a much wider professional practice scale. The authors agree with D. W. Sue et al. (1992), who specifically charge the following major policy-making and accreditation bodies to address these issues: American Psychological Association, American Counseling Association, American Association of State Psychology Boards, state psychological associations, state departments of education personnel, and others. The development of competencies needs to be of primary ethical and professional importance, at both state and national levels. Policy change is critical as evidenced by other client-oriented movements, such as consumerism and client-developed services, the Americans with Disabilities Act, and educational inclusion models. MCT theory will assist in conceptualizing at both macro- and microsystems levels. Without these changes, MCT theory will be just another theory, albeit a "theory of theories," and left to an intellectual death by those in positions of power. If, as Pedersen states, multiculturalism is to "provide a fourth force perspective," then these system changes need to take place.

REFERENCES FOR CHAPTER 8

American Association of School Administrators. (1993). *Quality goes to school: Readings on quality management in education.* Washington, DC: Author.

American Psychological Association. (1991). *Guidelines for providers of psychological services to ethnic, linguistic, and culturally diverse populations.* Washington, DC: Author.

Anderson, D. J., & Cranston-Gingras, A. (1991). Sensitizing counselors and educators to multicultural issues: An interactive approach. *Journal of Counseling and Development, 70*(5), 91–98.

Angelo, T. A., & Cross, K. P. (1993). *Classroom assessment techniques: A handbook for college teachers* (2nd ed.). San Francisco: Jossey-Bass.

Atkinson, D. R. (1994). Multicultural training: A call to standards. *The Counseling Psychologist, 22*(2), 300–307.

Atkinson, D. R., Morten, G., & Sue, D. W. (Eds.). (1993). *Counseling American minorities: A cross-cultural perspective.* Dubuque, IA: Brown.

Betancourt, H., & Lopez, S. R. (1993). The study of culture, ethnicity, and race in American psychology. *American Psychologist, 48*(6), 629–637.

Clark, L. W. (Ed.). (1993). *Faculty and student challenges in facing cultural and linguistic diversity.* Springfield, IL: Thomas.

Constantino, G. Malgady, R. G., & Rogler, L. H. (1988). *Cuento therapy: Folktales as a culturally sensitive psychotherapy for Puerto Rican children* (Monograph 12). New York: Fordham University, Hispanic Research Center.

Coyne, R. K. (1987). *Primary preventive counseling: Empowering people and systems.* Muncie, IN: Accelerated Development, Inc.

D'Andrea, M., & Daniels, J. (1991). Exloring the different levels of multicultural counseling training in counselor education. *Journal of Counseling and Development, 70*(5), 78–85.

D'Andrea, M., Daniels, J., & Heck, R. (1991). Evaluating the impact of multicultural counseling training. *Journal of Counseling and Development, 70*(5), 143–150.

The discreet charm of the multicultural multinational. (1994). *The Economist, 332*(7874), 57–62.

Dworkin, A. G., & Dworkin, R. J. (1976). *The minority report.* New York: Praeger.

Esquivel, G. B., & Keitel, M. A. (1990). Counseling immigrant children in the schools. *Elementary School Guidance and Counseling, 24*(2), 213–221.

Freire, P. (1972). *Pedagogy of the oppressed.* New York: Herder & Herder.

Garcia, M. H., Wright, J. W., & Corey, G. (1991). A multicultural perspective in an undergraduate human services program. *Journal of Counseling and Development, 70*(5), 86–90.

Hardiman, R. (1982). *White identity development theory.* Unpublished doctoral dissertation, University of Massachusetts, Amherst.

Helms, J. E. (1990). *Black and White racial identity: Theory, research and practice.* Westport, CT: Greenwood Press.

Hernandez, A. Z., & LaFromboise, T. D. (1985). *The development of the Cross-Cultural Counseling Inventory.* Paper presented at the 93rd Annual Convention of the American Psychological Association, Los Angeles, CA.

Herring, R. D. (1989). Counseling Native-American children: Implications for elementary school counselors. *Elementary School Guidance and Counseling, 23*(4), 272–281.

Hickey, C. A., & Solis, D. (1990). *The recruitment and retention of minority trainees in university affiliated programs—Hispanics* (M. L. Kuehn, Ed.). Madison: University of Wisconsin.

Hills, H. I., & Strozier, A. L. (1993). Multicultural training in APA-approved counseling psychology programs: A survey. *Professional Psychology: Research and Practice, 23*(1), 3–12.

Ivey, A. E., Ivey, M. B., & Simek-Morgan, L. (1993). *Counseling and psychotherapy: A multicultural perspective.* Boston: Allyn and Bacon.

Jackson, B. (1975). Black identity development. In L. Golobschick & B. Persky (Eds.), *Urban social educational issues.* Dubuque, IA: Kendall-Hunt.

Kavanaugh, K. H., & Kennedy, P. H. (1992). *Promoting cultural diversity: Strategies for health care professionals.* Newbury Park, CA: Sage.

Kiselica, M. S. (1991). Reflections on a multicultural internship experience. *Journal of Counseling and Development, 70*(5), 126–135.

LaFromboise, T. P., & Foster, S. L. (1991). Ethics in multicultural counseling. In P. B. Pedersen, W. J. Lonner, & J. E. Trimble (Eds.), *Counseling across cultures* (3rd ed.). Honolulu: University of Hawaii Press.

Leong, F. T. L., & Kim, H. H. (1991). Going beyond cultural sensitivity on the road to multiculturalism: Using the Intercultural Sensitizer as a counselor training tool. *Journal of Counseling and Development, 70*(5), 112–118.

Lewis, A. C., & Hayes, S. (1991). Multiculturalism and the school counseling curriculum. *Journal of Counseling and Development, 70*(5), 119–125.

Linton, R. (Ed.). (1945). *The science of man in the world crisis.* New York: Columbia University Press.

Locke, D. C. (1989). Fostering the self-esteem of African-American children. *Elementary School Guidance and Counseling, 23*(4), 254–259.

McRae, M. B., & Johnson, S. D. (1991). Towards training for competence in multicultural counselor education. *Journal of Counseling and Development, 70*(5), 131–135.

Midgette, T. E., & Meggert, S. S. (1991). Multicultural counseling instruction: A challenge for faculties in the 21st century. *Journal of Counseling and Development, 70*(5), 136–141.

Nuttall, E., De Leon, B., & Valle, M. (1990). Best practices in considering cultural factors. In *Best practices in school psychology II* (pp. 219–233). Washington, DC: National Association of School Psychologists.

Nuttall, E., Romero, I., & Kalesnik, J. (1992). *Assessing and screening preschoolers: Psychological and educational dimensions.* Boston: Allyn and Bacon.

Nwachuku, U. T., & Ivey, A. E. (1991). Culture-specific counseling: An alternative training model. *Journal of Counseling and Development, 70*(5), 106–111.

Parker, L. D. (1989). An annotated bibliography in cross-cultural counseling for elementary and middle school counselors. *Elementary School Guidance and Counseling, 23*(4), 313–321.

Pedersen, P. B. (1991). Multiculturalism as a generic approach to counseling. *Journal of Counseling and Development, 70*(5), 6–12.

Pedersen, T., & Carey, J. C. (1987). *Multicultural counseling in schools: A practical handbook*. Boston: Allyn and Bacon.

Ponterotto, J. G. (1988). Racial/ethnic minority research in the *Journal of Counseling Psychology. Journal of Counseling Psychology, 35*, 410–418.

Ponterotto, J. G., & Casas, J. M. (1987). In search of multicultural competence within counselor education programs. *Journal of Counseling and Development, 65*(4), 430–434.

Ponterotto, J. G., Sanchez, C. M., & Magids, D. M. (1991). *Initial development and validation of the Multicultural Counseling Awareness Scale (MCAS)*. Paper presented at the Annual Convention of the American Psychological Association, San Francisco, CA.

Porter, N. (1994). Empowering supervisees to empower others: A culturally responsive supervision model. *Hispanic Journal of Behavioral Sciences, 16*(1), 43–56.

Ridley, C. R., Mendoza, D. W., & Kanitz, B. E. (1994). Multicultural training: reexamination, operationalization, and integration. *The Counseling Psychologist, 22*(2), 227–289.

Rogler, L. H., & Prodicano, M. (1986). The effect of social networks on marital roles: A test of the Bott hypothesis in an international context. *Journal of Marriage and the Family, 48*, 693–701.

Ryan, W. (1971). *Blaming the victim*. New York: Vantage Books.

Sabnani, H. B., & Ponterotto, J. G. (1992). Racial/ethnic minortiy-specific instrumentation in counseling research: A review, critique, and recommendations. *Measurement and Evaluation in Counseling and Development, 24*, 161–187.

Sodowsky, G. R., Taffe, R. C., Gutkin, T. B., & Wise, S. L. (1994). Development of the multicultural counseling inventory: A self-report measure of multicultural competencies. *Journal of Counseling Psychology, 41*, 137–148.

Sue, D. W. (1981). *Counseling the culturally different*. New York: Wiley.

Sue, D. W. (1991). A model for cultural diversity training. *Journal of Counseling and Development, 70*(5), 99–105.

Sue, D. W., Arredondo, P., & McDavis, R. J. (1992). Multicultural counseling competencies and standards: A call to the profession. *Journal of Counseling and Development, 70*(2), 477–486.

Sue, D. W., & Sue, D. (1990). *Counseling the culturally different: Theory and practice* (2nd ed.). New York: Wiley.

Sue, S. (1991). Ethnicity and culture in psychological research and practice. In J. D. Goodchilds (Ed.), *Psychological perspectives on human diversity in America*. Washington, DC: American Psychological Association.

Triandis, H., Lambert, W., Berry, J., Lonner, W., Heron, A., Brislin, R., & Draguns, J. (Eds.). (1980). *Handbook of cross-cultural psychology* (Vols. 1–6). Boston: Allyn and Bacon.

Vetter, B. M. (1991). *Professional women and minorities: A manpower data resource service*. Washington, DC: Commission on Professionals in Science and Technology.

Wirth, L. (1945). The problem of minority groups. In R. Linton (Ed.), *The science of man in the world crisis* (pp. 342–363). New York: Columbia University Press.

CHAPTER 9

MCT THEORY AND IMPLICATIONS FOR RESEARCH

J. Manuel Casas
David Mann
*University of California
Santa Barbara*

Assumption Audit

- Western cultural influences are pervasive.
- MCT theory sometimes claims to be a metatheory and sometimes a theory of counseling.
- Assumptions should be related to empirical definitions.
- MCT theory does not explicitly define culture.
- Racism is not explicitly defined in MCT theory.
- Underlying assumptions seem superficial, with no philosophical basis.
- The terms and variables of MCT theory are not defined well enough to be as useful as they could be.
- MCT theory has great heuristic value.
- MCT theory needs to suggest predictive hypotheses for research.
- MCT interacts with communication styles in different cultures.
- There is too much analogue data and not enough empirical research to support MCT theory.
- MCT research needs to accommodate within-group differences.
- MCT research needs to move outside the ivory tower of academia.
- MCT theory requires developing new measures for assessment.
- More qualitative research is needed to supplement quantitative data.

Over the years, a number of researchers in multicultural counseling (e.g., Casas, 1984, 1985b; Ponterotto & Benesch, 1988; D. W. Sue, 1978) have consistently expressed a concern that the majority of research in the field is not solidly grounded in counseling theory. That is, most studies have essentially been conducted without the benefit of a conceptual framework to guide important research questions and hypotheses effectively. Seeking to validate this concern empirically, Ponterotto and Casas (1991) have conducted a systematic review of the counseling psychology literature and found that, out of the 80 multicultural studies published over 6 years in five of the counseling profession's most prestigious national journals, only 28 (35%) of these studies were well grounded in counseling/psychological theory. Such validation has encouraged researchers to extend initial efforts toward the identification and/or formulation of theories that one can use to underscore and guide future multicultural research and clinical endeavors (e.g., Ramirez, 1992). Such an effort is well exemplified in the proposed MCT theory in this book.

Chapter Objectives

As with all initial efforts to formulate, refine, and eventually test the substance and validity of a theory, critical input and direction from those with related interests or specializations are absolutely necessary. To this end, this chapter has three major objectives. First, it will critically examine in a nonexhaustive manner some of the philosophical and theoretical precepts that underlie the proposed MCT theory as well as its terminology. Unless the precepts and terminology that underlie a theory are precisely explained and defined, it is very difficult to design and conduct programmatic research to examine both the utility and the validity of a theory. The examination undertaken in this chapter is based on the generic criteria traditionally used to evaluate theories (see Hall & Lindzey, 1957).

Second, specific attention is directed to a selective critical review of recent multicultural research. The intent of this review is to alert MCT theorists of steps they need to take to ensure the highest quality of research required to validate MCT theory. This review will include suggestions on topics that merit immediate research attention.

Finally, to ensure the maximum utility of such research, the chapter presents the need to conduct future studies based on a variety of methodological approaches. You should note from the onset that the critical assessment of the proposed MCT theory is not culture-free. As will become evident, the major points made in this chapter are very strongly tied to the scientific philosophy, originally proposed by Comte, called *logical positivism* (Kendler, 1987).

A CRITICAL EXAMINATION OF PRECEPTS AND TERMS IN MCT THEORY

Theoretical Consistency

This critical examination of MCT theory relies selectively on the definitional criteria of a theory used by Hall and Lindzey (1957), even though these are based on a Western worldview that emphasizes the value of precision and empirical definitions. Given that psychology as a field has been rooted in these same values since its beginnings in the late 1800s (Kendler, 1987), it may be impossible to avoid theoretical analysis and research methodology also based on this cultural view. Furthermore, as you will see later, MCT theory itself subscribes to some of these values, especially regarding multiculturalism. It seems, then, that Western cultural influences pervade both MCT theory and its analysis. However, this discussion of the various research methodologies that one may use to validate and develop MCT theory will attempt to move beyond the traditional quantitative perspective of modern psychology. Looking to other approaches (such as ethnographic ones) will offer a broader perspective on MCT theory's theoretical and applied bases.

One criterion suggested by Hall and Lindzey (1957) stipulates that a theory should contain a cluster of relevant assumptions systematically related to each other and to a set of empirical definitions. MCT theory contains two such clusters, which seem to be associated with two unrelated topics. The theory claims at various points to be a "theory of theories" or metatheory on the one hand, and a theory of counseling on the other. The propositions either concern ways in which various counseling theories can be accommodated under one counseling metatheory or deal with specific methods of making counseling more useful and sensitive to individuals from a wide range of cultures. Both areas offer rich research opportunities. With both included, though, MCT theory seems to be two theories presented as one. For MCT theory to fulfill Hall and Lindzey's criterion, a decision must be made as to which of these two foci will be the subject of this theory, or if indeed two theories are needed to truly fulfill the authors' original purpose. Furthermore, until this is done, it will be difficult to know which avenues of research are needed to substantiate this theory.

Definitions

As noted, the assumptions behind the theory should in turn be related to a set of empirical definitions. Hall and Lindzey (1957) further state that these definitions should be as precise as current conditions within the relevant field permit. Consequently, to examine the philosophical and theoretical precepts that underlie the theory, one must also carefully and selectively examine the terminology that serves as the building blocks for the theory. This effort is in line with Hall and Lindzey's proposition that a theory comprise terms that one can operationally define. This proposition is based on the belief that without such definitions one cannot test the validity and utility of a theory.

Culture seems to be the core concept around which the proposed theory revolves; however, in spite of its centrality, Sue, Ivey, and Pedersen fall short of defining the concept. More specifically, nowhere in the description of MCT do they present an explicit definition of culture. Such explicitness is necessary, because *culture* can have many different definitions; even within the field of psychology, culture has been defined in a multitude of ways (Pedersen, 1991; D. W. Sue, Arredondo, & McDavis, 1992). If MCT theory is to address how culture fundamentally affects the counseling process, then its authors must define what they mean by *culture*.

To make culture more explicit within MCT theory, its authors do not have to start from scratch. Their work can be easily expedited by using certain models that already attempt to define *culture*. For instance, Kluckhohn and Strodtbeck's (1961) model relies on universal values existing on a continuum. In this model each cultural group is seen as emphasizing different aspects of these values. Specifically, they include five cultural dimensions: (1) beliefs about human nature (good, bad, mixed), (2) relations of human nature (scientific, supernatural, harmonious), (3) activity orientation (doing, being, becoming), (4) time orientation (past, present, future), and (5) relationships (individualistic, collateral group, lineal group). Using such a model, therapists could try to understand how various cultural groups express their values along these continuums, then bring this understanding into play in conjunction with the current theory to identify which approaches are most appropriate with which groups.

Other researchers (James-Myers, 1991; Nichols, 1976; Nobles, 1972) see differences in worldview as a crucial aspect in defining what *culture* means. To these researchers, a *worldview* is a way in which individuals or cultural groups differentially perceive, define, and subsequently interact with their external environment as a result of past learning experiences. For example, Landrum-Brown (1994; Brown & Landrum-Brown, 1995) has proposed a theoretical model that encompasses eight different dimensions through which an individual or a cultural worldview affects the way one perceives the world: psycho-behavioral modality (doing, being, or behaving), axiology (values), ethos (guiding beliefs), epistemology (the process of knowing), logic (the process of reasoning), ontology (the nature of reality), concept of time, and concept of self (see Table 9-1, pp. 144–145). Using this particular model, research could explore how each of these dimensions affects the counseling process, then alter the process to optimize the quality of service to individuals with differing worldviews.

Another term that is important to MCT theory is *racism*. Again, this term is more implicit than explicit in the theory and as such needs to be defined. MCT theory discusses racism and oppression having adversely affected racial/ethnic minorities and also talks about how one must avoid unintentional racism. However, unless racism is tangibly defined, it remains an ephemeral concept that can be extremely difficult to address and overcome within the counseling process. While it may not be possible to identify all types of racist behaviors, selective identification of the variety of types that can impact the counseling process would be helpful.

While other terms besides culture and racism could benefit from more in-depth discussion, there is no room here to address them. However, to enable future research regarding the validity and utility of MCT theory, MCT theorists should continue to tease out those terms (e.g., culture-bound, ethnocentrism) that merit further definition as well as present examples that can help one apply the terms within the counseling process. Though this recommendation focuses on a more precise definition and operationalization of terms, one should in no way interpret it as a mandate for defining all terms with perfect precision. On the contrary, while seeking greater specificity for the majority of terms inherent in the theory, theorists should work from the perspective that definitions, while necessary, exist on a continuum ranging from complete and exact specification to very general and qualitative statements. In fact, early insistence upon complete specification of all terms encompassed by a theory can destroy many potentially fruitful paths of inquiry.

Philosophical Assumptions

It has already been mentioned that a theory should contain a cluster of assumptions systematically related to each other and to a set of empirical definitions. Additionally, the assumptions must be *relevant*, in that they bear on the empirical events with which the theory is concerned. MCT theory meets this criterion—its assumptions all deal with multicultural variables. However, the assumptions that underlie this theory seem somewhat superficial. Moreover, the basic philosophical assumptions appear to be missing from the presentation of the theory.

It seems apparent that a variety of assumptions and motivations underlying MCT theory are associated with its authors' conceptualization of multiculturalism. Though it is important not to underplay the complexity of this idea, developing an exact definition of this term and identifying the

TABLE 9.1
CULTURAL GROUP COMPARATIVE WORLDVIEW PROFILES

Worldview Components	Anglo American	African American
Psycho-Behavioral Modality	"Doing"	"Being"
Axiology (What Is Valued)	Competition Person-object Delay of gratification Emotional restraint Change Acquisition of property, goods Competition Individualism Youth Credentials (what one has) Directness/openness	Immediate gratification Cooperation Collective-responsibility Person-oriented Self-knowledge Authoritarian Childrearing Verbal expression Nonverbal expression Emotionally expressive
Ethos (Guiding Beliefs)	Independence Separateness Survival of fittest Mastery/control over nature	Interdependence Survival of group Harmony/oneness with nature
Epistemology (How One Knows)	Cognitive Counting and measuring Observation Formal education	Affective Symbolic imagery Feelings, rhythm "Vibes" Experience
Logic (Reasoning Process)	Dichotomous (either/or)	Diunital (both/and)
Ontology (What Is Reality)	Objective Material	Subjective Spiritual
Concept of Time	Precise Measurable Linear Future-focused	Event-focused Cyclical Present-focused
Concept of Self	Individual self (I think, therefore I am)	Extended self (I am because we are)

Note. From "Impacts of Culture on Teaching and Learning," by J. Landrum-Brown, September 28, 1994. Workshop given at University of California, Santa Barbara. Adapted by permission.

TABLE 9.1

(CONTINUED)

Latino/a Chicano/a	Native American	Asian American
"Being"	"Being"	"Becoming"

Immediate gratification
Interdependence
Person-person
Authority
Cooperation
Elders respected
Machismo
Personalismo
Saving face
Collective group
    identity
Hierarchy/authority
Familism
	Cooperation
	Interdependence
	Harmony with others and
	    nature
	Elders respected
	Cooperative relationships
	What a person is
	Nonverbal behaviors
	Harmony
	Accepts "what is"
	Tribalism
		Family-focused
		Humility
		Emotional restraint
		Tradition
		Transcendence
		Parental obedience and
		    obligation
		Conformity
		Interdependence
		Role rigidity
		Indirect expression
		Formality
		Harmony with universe
		Ancestor and elder
		    reverence

Authoritarianism Survival of group One with nature	Harmony with creation Survival of group	Harmony with nature
Affective Affect/symbolic Immersion in experience	Affective Conative Nature/symbolic Immersion in experience	Conative Object/symbol Transcendence Contemplative
Diunital	Diunital	Circular
Spiritual	Spiritual World-interconnected	Spiritual
Event-focused Cyclical	Event-focused Present-focused	Cyclical Eternal
Extended self	Extended self Part of nature	Extended self

assumptions behind it would be invaluable to researchers seeking avenues to support MCT theory. Carter and Qureshi (in press) present five main types of assumptions that underlie the various conceptualizations of multiculturalism: (1) *Universal*, which emphasizes the similarities between individuals above and beyond any consideration of an individual's culture; (2) *Ubiquitous*, which suggests that every facet of one's identity and circumstance contributes to one's culture, thus allowing individuals to belong to multiple cultures; (3) *Traditional Anthropological*, which states that one's upbringing and environment determine one's culture and that race as a social construct is unimportant; (4) *Race-Based*, which claims that race is the most important determinant of culture and that experiences associated with one's race are more salient than all other experiences; and (5) *Pan-National*, which is based on the idea that culture is global in nature and that one's race determines one's culture as well as one's power in society, regardless of the geosocial context.

Given its apparent assumptions, MCT theory seems largely based on the *Ubiquitous* conceptualization of multiculturalism. *Race-Based* multiculturalism also seems to have influenced the development of this theory, because of the prevalence of references to racism and the oppression of racial/ethnic minorities by traditional counseling approaches. An explicit statement of what role race plays in the formulation of an individual's culture and how this in turn has repercussions for the counseling process may clarify the theory.

Even so, just understanding the context for which MCT theory was developed is not enough. One must know the explicit assumptions and motivations behind this theory to provide direction for researchers who wish to verify and expand on it.

Utility

A theory is also evaluated by its utility. In line with Hall and Lindzey's criteria (1957), utility is based on two general components—verifiability and comprehensiveness. *Verifiability* refers to the capacity of the theory to generate predictions confirmed when the relevant empirical data are collected. *Comprehensiveness* refers to the scope or completeness of these derivations.

Relative to these two components, though MCT is presented as a fairly comprehensive theory, taking into consideration a myriad of variables, many of the major terms and variables that comprise MCT theory are not specifically defined. As such, the potential for developing research strategies to collect empirical data that could confirm any predictions generated by the theory is greatly weakened.

Heuristic Value

The last definitional criterion of Hall and Lindzey (1957) addressed in this chapter is the *heuristic value* of a theory. In essence, such value is substantiated by the capacity of a theory to generate studies by researchers who attempt to validate or invalidate all or parts of a proposed theory. MCT theory has great heuristic value. It provokes critical thought, and, with some fine-tuning regarding both the underlying philosophical precepts and the major terms that comprise the theory, it has the potential for engendering a substantive research agenda.

A CRITICAL REVIEW OF MULTICULTURAL RESEARCH

Research efforts related to MCT theory should seek to avoid the pitfalls that have plagued past multicultural research efforts. To this end, the material contained herein reflects a recent critical review of the literature conducted by Ponterotto and Casas (1991) covering a 6-year period and focusing on the following counseling journals: *The Journal of Counseling Psychology, The Journal of Counseling and Development, The Journal of Multicultural Counseling and Development, The Counseling Psychologist,* and *The Journal of Mental Health Counseling.*

Prior to initiating this review, however, Ponterotto and Casas (1991) reviewed selected writings of researchers who had expressed major concerns regarding the quality of the multicultural research (e.g., Atkinson, 1983, 1985; Casas, 1984, 1985a, 1985b; Pedersen, 1988; Ponterotto, 1989; D. W. Sue, 1981; Suinn, 1985). They identify 10 major criticisms directed at such research. The reason for identifying these criticisms was twofold: first, to use them as guidelines for critically assessing the research published over the aforementioned 6-year period; second, based on such assessment, to obtain the necessary data to either validate or refute these criticisms.

While not all of the criticisms were validated, they have received such extensive attention in the literature that they are important enough to use as guidelines to direct research endeavors to validate MCT theory. To this end, the following section not only identifies those that were validated, but it also directs attention to all 10 criticisms as the basis from which to offer suggestions regarding the type of research that needs to be conducted relative to the validation of MCT theory.

Criticism 1 (validated), regarding the *lack of conceptual/theoretical framework to guide research,* suggests that the initial research on MCT theory should focus on showing that the proposed theory meets a significant number of the requirements of a "good" theory (see Hall & Lindsey, 1957). As noted, without first establishing the fact that the theory meets such requirements, it is pointless to propose a research agenda regarding the applicability of the theory. To this end, initial research should systematically and carefully test particular hypotheses predicated in the proposed MCT conceptual/theoretical model. The findings of such research would serve to validate or disprove various theoretical tenets, which in turn would allow one to assess the strengths and weaknesses of MCT theory.

With respect to criticism 2 (only partially supported by the data), the *overemphasis on simplistic counselor/client process variables and a disregard for important psychosocial variables within and outside the culture that impact counseling,* to establish MCT's applicability, a number of essential topics other than process variables will merit research attention. Among them are the effective interaction between MCT theory and communication styles in minority groups, socializing practices, learning styles, psychocultural variables (such as loss of face among Asian Americans), and the effects of discrimination and poverty. It also appears that studies on the relationship between different levels of acculturation and/or racial identity development and the effectiveness of MCT theory are warranted. After all, as with any theory, it is such psychosocial variables that give shape and meaning to the client's (and counselor's) behavior in the counseling context (see Casas, 1984, 1985a; Lonner & Sundberg, 1985; Ponterotto, 1988).

Criticism 3 (not validated), is *overreliance on experimental analogue research.* As noted, though this criticism was not supported by Ponterotto and Casas's (1991) review of the literature, MCT theorists should take note that heavy reliance on analogue research, which is often more convenient to conduct in academic settings, will not suffice to staunchly establish the validity and applicability of MCT theory. To establish its validity and, in particular, its ability to be generalized across groups, settings, and presenting problems, MCT researchers will initially have to involve themselves extensively in "true experimental" studies conducted with actual clients and practicing counselors in natural counseling settings, such as a community mental-health clinic or a college counseling center.

Criticism 4 (validated), *disregard for within-group or intracultural differences,* is based on a concern expressed by a number of researchers, including Atkinson (1983, 1985), Casas, Ponterotto, and Gutierrez (1986), and S. Sue, Akutsu, and Higashi (1985), who claim that research designs comparing one ethnic group to another may result in each group being perceived as homogeneous. In fact, these researchers believe that interethnic group comparisons may do more to perpetuate ethnic categorizations and stereotypes than they do to prevent them (Campbell, 1967; S. Sue et al., 1985). However, given that MCT theory is new and in search of validation, it behooves MCT researchers to conduct studies both within and among racial/ethnic cultural groups. The studies among groups could serve to identify differential effects, if any, of using MCT with diverse racial/ethnic groups including Euro-Americans. In conducting such studies, however, the researchers should describe in great detail the demographics of each subject group. For the sake of generalizability, every effort should be made to match the subject groups on as many variables as possible, such as acculturation or racial-identity development level and socioeconomic status. Complementing these efforts, studies conducted within specific racial/ethnic groups are needed to identify the differential effects of MCT with people from the same racial/ethnic group.

Criticism 5 (validated), *the use of easily accessible college student populations*, is based on the concern expressed by Casas and others (Atkinson & Schein, 1986; Casas, 1984, 1985a; Casas et al., 1986) that a majority of the cross-cultural research published in the profession's most respected national journals relies too heavily on student samples. The concern here is that consumers of this research may generalize the results of student-based research to their nonstudent counterparts in the community. The counseling issues of minority college students, particularly on a predominantly White campus, may not reflect the larger minority community. Thus, maximizing the applicability of MCT research will require that researchers move beyond the "ivory towers" of the campus and conduct their studies within designated communities.

If MCT is to be validated for use within the diverse cultural contexts for which it is intended, criticism 6 (validated), *reliance on culturally-encapsulated psychometric instrumentation*, must receive serious consideration from MCT researchers. More specifically, this criticism is based on the fact that multicultural researchers have relied heavily on instruments developed to measure constructs conceptualized from a Western middle-class perspective (e.g., depression, self-concept, and assertiveness). Needless to say, the interpretive dangers of using such instruments developed with culturally different groups are many (see Lonner & Ibrahim, 1989; Pedersen, 1988; Ponterotto, 1988; D. W. Sue, 1989). For instance, Ponterotto (1988) asks, "What value is there in administering a depression rating scale to someone from a culture (e.g., some Asian cultures) that does not even conceptualize such a construct, that has no equivalent word for it in their vocabulary?" (p. 413). Unless more research attention is directed toward developing instruments relevant to racial/ethnic minority groups, it will be next to impossible to execute the empirically and systematically sound program to establish the validity and utility of MCT theory. If, however, MCT researchers believe that one can generalize a particular construct and the instrument used to measure it to a culturally different group, then they should develop culture-specific norms before initiating the designated study.

Attention has already been directed to criticism 7 (validated), *failure to adequately describe one's sample in terms of socioeconomic status (SES)*, within the context of the other criticisms noted above. Suffice it to say that to validate as well as maximize the generalizability of MCT theory will require conducting studies in which the subjects are described in detail, including (but not limited to) SES, acculturation and racial-identity development level, generational status, level of education, immigrant status, and age.

Criticism 8 (not validated), *failure to delineate the study's limitations*, is based on the belief that counseling studies in general (Scherman & Doan, 1985), and racial/ethnic minority counseling studies in particular (Ponterotto, 1988) have not adequately addressed and highlighted their generalizability limitations. While such criticisms in this area are not fully justified, it would be prudent for MCT researchers to take them into consideration as they initiate programmatic studies focusing on MCT theory. They should carefully articulate both the strengths of the studies and their limitations in order to facilitate the replication of such studies down the line.

Criticism 9 (partially supported by data) focuses on the *lack of adequate sample sizes*. It is well known that, from a statistical perspective, adequate sample size depends on research design. For instance, relative to survey research, which is the most common form of research used in cross-cultural studies (Ponterotto & Casas, 1991), the larger sample sizes in archival research are usually the most appropriate. With regard to true experiments and experimental analogue studies, in which subjects are randomly assigned to manipulated levels of an experimental treatment or stimulus, adequate sample size should be based on the research design and, in particular, on the number of variables inherent in the study. To ensure that all research emanating from MCT theory is empirically sound, researchers should make every effort to ensure that the sample size meets the methodological demands of the study (see Heppner, Kivlighan, & Wampold, 1992).

Criticism 10 (validated), *overreliance on paper-and-pencil measures as dependent variables*, was validated through the research efforts of Ponterotto and Casas (1991). As such, it merits serious consideration by MCT researchers. Because research (e.g., D. Sue, Ino, & Sue, 1983) has demonstrated that information obtained relative to certain characteristics or behaviors, such as assertiveness, can vary depending on the source of the information (e.g., surveys vs. behavioral observations), it behooves MCT researchers to use varied measures that focus on the same behavior. By doing so, they will provide more accurate and valid information with which to examine MCT theory.

METHODOLOGICAL CONSIDERATIONS

This section directs attention to the need to incorporate diverse methodological approaches in MCT research. More specifically, to adequately and comprehensively assess MCT theory, this section addresses the need to incorporate both quantitative and qualitative (i.e., descriptive designs) methodologies in such assessment.

From the review of the multicultural literature conducted by Ponterotto and Casas (1991), it is evident the majority of empirical studies in this area have been quantitative in nature. Essentially, such studies compare randomly selected groups with one another through collective mean differences. According to Heppner et al. (1992), such an approach is based on the "pure science myth," which holds up the experimental design paradigm as the "correct" or "best" mode of scientific investigation (p. 194). Furthermore,

> the received view of science tends to emphasize the testing and verification of theories, as well as comparisons among competing theories. Consequently, research in counseling has become largely a science of verification and less a science of description and discovery. Greenberg (1986) argued that counseling psychology should place more emphasis on discovery paradigms. He believes that the empiricist tradition with its emphasis on discovery on the controlled between-groups experiment has been overvalued by counseling researchers. We strongly agree. Consequently, a great deal of research in counseling is based on poorly described phenomenon [sic] and most likely is poorly understood. Too often researchers attempt to manipulate and control variables before enough is known about those variables. (p. 194)

This perspective shows that though quantitative experimental methodologies are valuable and provide reliable inferential (inferring to the sampled population as a whole) information, not all counseling research questions can be answered in this way, especially those that focus on the validation of new theories such as MCT theory. Thus, before one can test the adequacy of a theory in explaining a phenomenon, one must first obtain a detailed description of the phenomenon, which often can only be obtained through qualitative research methodologies. Consequently, MCT researchers should consider embracing those qualitative research methods that have been effectively used in the related disciplines of ethnology, cultural anthropology, and sociology (see Helms, 1989; Ponterotto, 1988). Furthermore, to maximize the cost effectiveness of MCT research efforts, both quantitative and qualitative methodologies should be used whenever possible.

Finally, in accordance with a recommendation by Ponterotto and Casas

(1991), as MCT researchers broaden their methodologies, they need also to consider an expansion of statistical techniques. For instance, such qualitative research methods as ethnographic reports, field techniques, oral histories, intensive interviews, and N = 1 studies could provide valuable observational information to the cross-cultural researcher that might not be attained through traditional quantitative research methods. The more research methodologies employed to examine MCT theory, the greater the probability of obtaining all the necessary data required to establish its validity.

SUMMARY

The purpose of this chapter has been to underscore and discuss the need for critical theoretical examination and validating research relative to MCT theory. To this end, the first section of the chapter critically examined, in a nonexhaustive manner, some of the philosophical and theoretical precepts that underlie the proposed multicultural theory as well as the terminology that serves as the basis for the theory. Such examination is necessary because unless the precepts and terminology that underlie a theory are precisely explained and defined, it is very difficult to design and conduct programmatic research to examine both the utility and validity of a theory.

The second section of the chapter offered a selective critical review of recent multicultural research. The intent of this review was to alert the MCT theorists of steps required to ensure the highest quality of research needed to validate MCT theory. This review included suggestions on topics that merit immediate research attention.

Finally, to ensure the maximum utility of such research, the third section of the chapter focused on the need to conduct studies based on a variety of methodological approaches. The information contained in this chapter is intended to provoke thought regarding the type of research necessary to examine and validate many of the ideas and suggestions contained in other chapters.

REFERENCES FOR CHAPTER 9

Atkinson, D. R. (1983). Ethnic similarity in counseling psychology: A review of research. *The Counseling Psychologist, 22,* 79–92.

Atkinson, D. R. (1985). A meta-review of research on cross-cultural counseling and psychotherapy. *Journal of Multicultural Counseling and Development, 13,* 138–153.

Atkinson, D. R., & Schein, S. (1986). Similarity in counseling. *The Counseling Psychologist, 14,* 319–354.

Brown, M., & Landrum-Brown, J. (1995). Counselor supervision: Cross-cultural perspectives. In J. Ponterotto, J. M. Casas, L. A. Suzuki, & C. Alexander (Eds.), *Handbook of multicultural counseling* (pp. 263–286). Newbury Park, CA: Sage.

Campbell, D. T. (1967). Stereotypes and the perception of group differences. *American Psychologist, 22*, 817–829.

Carter, R. T., & Qureshi, A. (in press). A typology of philosophical assumptions in multicultural counseling and training. In J. Ponterotto, J. M. Casas, L. A. Suzuki, & C. Alexander (Eds.), *Handbook of multicultural counseling.* Newbury Park, CA: Sage.

Casas, J. M. (1984). Policy, training and research in counseling psychology: The racial/ethnic minority perspective. In S. D. Brown & R. Lent (Eds.), *Handbook of counseling psychology* (pp. 785–831). New York: Wiley.

Casas, J. M. (1985a). A reflection on the status of racial/ethnic minority research. *The Counseling Psychologist, 13*, 581–598.

Casas, J. M. (1985b). The status of racial and ethnic minority counseling: A training perspective. In P. Pedersen (Ed.), *Handbook of cross-cultural counseling and therapy* (pp. 267–274). Westport, CT: Greenwood Press.

Casas, J. M., Ponterotto, J. G., & Gutierrez, J. M. (1986). An ethical indictment of counseling research and training: The cross-cultural perspective. *Journal of Counseling and Development, 64*, 347–349.

Chan, C. (1989). Issues of identity development among Asian American lesbians and gay men. *Journal of Counseling and Development, 68*, 16–20.

Espin, O. M. (1987). Issues of identity in the psychology of Latina lesbians. In Boston Lesbian Psychologies Collective (Ed.), *Lesbian Psychologies: Explorations and challenges* (pp. 35–51). Urbana: University of Illinois Press.

Greenberg, L. S. (1986). Change process research. *Journal of Consulting and Clinical Psychology, 54*, 4–9.

Hall, C. S., & Lindzey, G. (1957). *Theories of personality.* New York: Wiley.

Helms, J. E. (1989). At long last—paradigms for cultural psychology research. *The Counseling Psychologist, 17*, 98–101.

Heppner, P. P., Kivlighan, D. M., & Wampold, B. E. (1992). *Research design in counseling.* Pacific Grove, CA: Brooks/Cole.

James-Myers, L. (1991). Expanding the psychology of knowledge optimally: The importance of world view revisited. In R. Jones (Ed.), *Black psychology* (3rd ed., pp. 15–28). Berkeley, CA: Cobb & Henry Publishers.

Kendler, H. H. (1987). *Historical foundations of modern psychology.* Pacific Grove, CA: Brooks/Cole.

Kluckhohn, F. R., & Strodtbeck, F. L. (1961). *Variations in value orientations.* Evanston, IL: Row, Peterson.

Landrum-Brown, J. (1994, September 28). Workshop given on "Impacts of Culture on Teaching and Learning" at the University of California, Santa Barbara.

Lazarus, A. A., & Beutler, L. E. (1993). On technical eclecticism. *Journal of Counseling and Development, 71*, 381–385.

Lonner, W. J., & Ibrahim, F. A. (1989). Assessment in cross-cultural counseling. In P. B. Pedersen, J. G. Draguns, W. J. Lonner, & J. E. Trimble (Eds.), *Counseling across cultures* (3rd ed., pp. 299–334). Honolulu: University of Hawaii Press.

Lonner, W. J., & Sundberg, N. D. (1985). Assessment in cross-cultural counseling and therapy. In P. Pedersen (Ed.), *Handbook of cross-cultural counseling and therapy* (pp. 195–205). Westport, CT: Greenwood Press.

Nichols, E. (November, 1976). *The philosophical aspects of cultural differences.* Ibadan, Nigeria: World Psychiatric Association.

Nobles, W. (1972). African philosophy: Foundation for black psychology. In R. Jones (Ed.), *Black psychology* (1st ed., pp. 18–32). New York: Harper & Row.

Pedersen, P. B. (1988). *A handbook for developing multicultural awareness.* Alexandria, VA: American Association for Counseling and Development.

Pedersen, P. B. (1991). Multiculturalism as a fourth force in counseling. *Journal of Counseling and Development, 70.*

Ponterotto, J. G. (1988). Racial/ethnic minority research in the *Journal of Counseling Psychology:* A content analysis and methodological critique. *Journal of Counseling Psychology, 35,* 410–418.

Ponterotto, J. G. (1989). Expanding directions for racial identity research. *The Counseling Psychologist, 17,* 264–272.

Ponterotto, J. G., & Benesch, K. F. (1988). An organizational framework for understanding the role of culture in counseling. *Journal of Counseling and Development, 66,* 237–241.

Ponterotto, J. G., & Casas, J. M. (1991). *Handbook of racial/ethnic minority counseling research.* Springfield, IL: Thomas.

Ramirez, M. (1992). *Psychotherapy and counseling with minorities: A cognitive approach to individual and cultural differences.* New York: Pergamon Press.

Scherman, A., & Doan, R. E., Jr. (1985). Subjects, designs, and generalizations in Volumes 25–29 of the *Journal of Counseling Psychology. Journal of Counseling Psychology, 32,* 272–276.

Sue, D., Ino, S., & Sue, D. M. (1983). Nonassertiveness of Asian Americans: An inaccurate assumption? *Journal of Counseling Psychology, 30,* 581–588.

Sue, D. W. (1978). Eliminating cultural oppression in counseling: Toward a general theory. *Journal of Counseling Psychology, 25,* 419–428.

Sue, D. W. (1981). *Counseling the culturally different: Theory and practice.* New York: Wiley.

Sue, D. W. (1989, August). Effective multicultural counseling: Proposed research directions. In N. A. Fouad (Chair), *Cross-cultural research and training: Focus on critical issues.* Symposium presented at the annual meeting of the American Psychological Association, New Orleans, LA.

Sue, D. W., Arredondo, P., & McDavis, R. (1992). Multicultural counseling competencies and standards: A call to the profession. *Journal of Counseling and Development, 70,* 477–486.

Sue, S., Akutsu, P. O., & Higashi, C. (1985). Training issues in conducting therapy with ethnic-minority-group clients. In P. Pedersen (Ed.), *Handbook of cross-cultural counseling and therapy* (pp. 275–280). Westport, CT: Greenwood Press.

Suinn, R. M. (1985). Research and practice in cross-cultural counseling. *The Counseling Psychologist, 13,* 673–684.

CHAPTER 10

MCT THEORY AND ETHNOCENTRISM IN COUNSELING

Judy Daniels
Michael D'Andrea
University of Hawaii, Manoa

Assumption Audit

- MCT theory reflects the diversification of American society.
- MCT theory attacks the perpetuation of ethnocentrism.
- MCT theory recognizes the ethnocentrism of its own self-reference criteria.
- Ethnocentrism controls the research base of counseling.
- Ethnocentrism controls the training of counselors.
- MCT theory expands the epistemological foundation of counseling beyond ethnocentrism.
- MCT theory moves beyond ethnocentric perspectives in counseling practice.
- MCT theory acknowledges intentional and unintentional racism in the profession.
- MCT theory acknowledges the affective as well as the cognitive dimensions of ethnocentrism.
- MCT theory suggests constructive ways to overcome ethnocentrism.

In presenting their metatheory of MCT, Sue, Ivey, and Pedersen examine a number of issues of critical importance to the counseling profession. Their metatheory provides counselors with much more than interesting reading about a topic that is gaining popularity with both professionals and the general public. On reviewing the detailed synthesis of information provided in Chapters 1–3, one is led to consider a central and provocative question about the future of counseling and psychotherapy. That is, given the dramatic demographic transformation occurring in the United States, will the counseling profession make the types of changes necessary for it to continue to be a viable and relevant institution in the 21st century?

With the rapid diversification of American society and the limited relevance that the dominant counseling theories have for many people from diverse cultural, ethnic, and racial backgrounds, one might expect the multicultural movement to be enthusiastically embraced and integrated into the professional mainstream. In reality, despite being acknowledged as the "fourth force in counseling and psychology" (Pedersen, 1991), the MCT movement has consistently been met with much resistance in the past and is now only slowly gaining acceptance.

There are several important reasons to identify and overcome the barriers that continue to restrict the MCT movement. To name just one, counselors can extend greater respect and sensitivity to a broader range of clients when they overcome their own cultural biases (Atkinson, Morten, & Sue, 1993; see Chapters 1–3). Also, counselors and therapists who are not culturally competent are less likely to promote positive counseling outcomes among people from diverse backgrounds (Lee & Richardson, 1991; Sue, Arredondo, & McDavis, 1992).

In the first three chapters, Sue, Ivey, and Pedersen argue that the counseling profession continues to resist the idea that it must incorporate MCT paradigms into all aspects of the work practitioners, researchers, and trainers do. As a result of this ongoing resistance, much of the positive potential of MCT continues to go unrealized in the field. To move the profession beyond its current level of resistance, one must more fully understand why so many counseling professionals do not readily and willingly embrace the MCT movement.

Sue, Ivey, and Pedersen suggest that counselors' own professional and personal ethnocentrism fuels much of this resistance. Several other experts have also noted that the perpetuation of ethnocentrism represents a major barrier to the integration of MCT paradigms (Atkinson, Morten, & Sue, 1993; Locke, 1992). While general agreement exists about the negative impact of ethnocentrism in the counseling profession, few multicultural experts have clearly defined what they mean by *ethnocentrism* or have offered practical suggestions for overcoming it.

Given the importance of addressing these shortcomings, this chapter aims at helping professional counselors and psychotherapists better understand what ethnocentrism is and how it impacts their professional and personal development. First, *ethnocentrism* is defined. Each component of the definition is then examined in greater detail. Next, the chapter presents specific examples of ethnocentrism manifested in counseling practice, research, and training. These examples should help the reader better understand why many counselors resist the types of ideas Sue, Ivey, and Pedersen present in their metatheory.

Finally, this chapter offers a number of suggestions for identifying and overcoming those aspects of ethnocentrism that continue to trouble the counseling profession. It is hoped that the ideas and recommendations presented in this chapter will help counselors and psychologists become more aware of their own ethnocentrism and the need to use a multicultural perspective in their future work.

ETHNOCENTRISM DEFINED

Ethnocentrism is a psychological phenomenon characterized by the belief in the superiority of a set of values and a worldview that evolves from one's own cultural, ethnic, or racial group. The groups that one identifies with significantly influence the way one makes sense of life experiences and establish the norms for appropriate and inappropriate behaviors.

Everyone, including professional counselors and psychologists, is ethnocentric to some degree. No one really escapes the impact of being socialized within the context of a particular cultural setting. Consequently, the ways individuals interpret their life experiences are all consciously or unconsciously influenced by their cultural backgrounds and contacts.

Most individuals rarely take time, however, to consider the degree to which ethnocentrism determines their worldviews and behaviors. Usually a person who thinks or acts ethnocentrically does so automatically and unconsciously. This automatic unconscious process often leads individuals to assume that their way of thinking about and reacting to life events is "better" than the way people from other cultural groups interpret and respond to the same situations. Because ethnocentrism is rooted in the belief of the superiority of one's own culturally biased worldview, it represents a distorted interpretation of reality.

Most discussions about ethnocentrism in the counseling profession have focused on its cognitive dimensions. These discussions have generally centered on the types of conceptual biases that lead counselors and psychologists to act in certain predictable ways when they provide services to clients, conduct research, or train graduate students (Atkinson et al., 1993; D'Andrea & Daniels, 1991; see also Chapters 1–3).

Though ethnocentrism is largely cognitive, research suggests that it is also accompanied by an affective (emotional) component that reinforces a person's sense of cultural, ethnic, and/or racial superiority. A discussion of both the cognitive and the affective dimensions of ethnocentrism follows.

THE COGNITIVE DIMENSIONS
OF ETHNOCENTRISM

Ethnocentrism is, for the most part, a cognitive process that influences the way people think about and relate to others. Counselors and psychologists often manifest ethnocentrism in two fundamental ways. First, it occurs when counselors and therapists intentionally or unintentionally rely on theories rooted in a culturally specific worldview to assess their clients' concerns and needs. Second, ethnocentrism emerges when practitioners plan and implement counseling strategies that do not reflect sensitivity and respect for clients' cultural values, attitudes, and worldviews.

Sue and Sue (1990) define a *worldview* as the way "a person perceives his/her relationship to the world (nature, institutions, other people, etc.)," "one's conceptual framework," "one's philosophy of life," and the "way we make meaning in the world." They add that worldviews are the "reservoirs for our attitudes, values, opinions, and concepts; they influence how we think, make decisions, behave, and define life events" (p. 9). Every worldview emerges from a cultural context and is accompanied by a set of biases that influence the way individuals make meaning of their life experiences, operate in the world, and relate to others.

Ethnocentric Biases
in Psychological Theories

In their theory, Sue, Ivey, and Pedersen point out that traditional psychological theories have emerged from a Eurocentric worldview. The interplay between counselors' worldviews and their theoretical orientations to counseling and therapy determines the way they interpret their clients' needs and guides the types of approaches they use to achieve specific client outcomes.

Though traditional counseling theories usually provide an accurate description of the needs of people within the dominant (i.e., White, Western, middle-class) culture in the United States, they often fail to adequately explain the psychological development, concerns, and/or needs of people from non-Western, non-White backgrounds. Research suggests that interventions evolved from traditional Western theories are ineffective (and sometimes even harmful) when used with clients from diverse cultural backgrounds (Atkinson et al., 1993; Locke, 1992). Thus, the perpetuation and widespread use of traditional counseling theories with all clients, regardless of their cultural/racial background, continues to be one of the most common examples of ethnocentric bias in the profession today.

Cultural Biases in Counseling Research

Ethnocentric biases are also noted in many of the investigative methods counseling researchers use to test traditional counseling theories. The widely held notion that quantitative research methods are the "best" ways of conducting "legitimate" social scientific research provides a classic example of such bias (Goldman, 1989; Ivey, 1993). These investigative methods are rooted in a Western worldview that relies on a positivistic tradition of reductive experimentation, which embraces a quantitative, linear approach to social scientific inquiry (Goldman 1976; see also Chapters 1–3).

Cultural ethnocentrism impacts counseling research in many other subtle and not so subtle ways. For instance, the value that the dominant culture places on individualism shows up in the way many counseling researchers do their work. This predominately Western value results in a disproportionate number of research projects being conducted by individual investigators, often in isolation from other colleagues. Furthermore, the environment that generates most counseling and psychological research—the university—reinforces this isolation. The value of such individual research efforts typically emerges in discussions regarding faculty tenure and promotion decisions, in which single-authored research publications continue to be viewed more favorably than studies involving a collaborative effort. Though the individualistic approach to traditional counseling research continues to be highly valued within most academic circles, it limits the types of learning and competencies researchers themselves might gain as a result of collaborating with other racial/ethnic minority investigators (Sue, 1993).

Another example of cultural ethnocentrism played out in counseling research relates to the role of the researcher. In this regard, researchers have traditionally been urged to sustain objectivity, to refrain from developing personal relationships with individuals who participate in their studies. While the emphasis on remaining objective and impersonal reflects a specific cultural bias, it conflicts with the value many people from different cultural groups place on more informal and personal ways of relating to others. Thus, it is possible that by remaining impersonal and detached when conducting research with people from diverse cultural backgrounds, researchers may stimulate feelings of suspicion and even hostility among the participants (Sue, 1993). This in turn might lead investigators to make inaccurate interpretations about the data collected from these individuals (Parham, 1993).

One final characteristic of counseling research that reflects an important ethnocentric bias relates to the benefits derived from conducting psychological studies among subjects from racial/ethnic minority groups. As Sue (1993) explains, "Counseling research has often been used to benefit the persons conducting the research (obtaining research grants, promotions, and tenure) rather than contributing to the betterment of the group being researched" (p. 245). Counseling researchers continuing to benefit from conducting studies among people from diverse backgrounds, while the participants and their communities do not derive any advantages from participating, perpetuates a tradition of ethnocentrism and exploitation in the field.

Ethnocentrism in Counselor Training

Professional counseling and psychotherapy training programs play a major role in perpetuating many of the ethnocentric biases that exist in the field today. Professional training programs create a unique "cultural mindset" of their own by transmitting counseling and human-development theories, promoting the use of intervention strategies, and modeling counseling techniques that reflect a predominately White, middle-class, Eurocentric, male-dominated worldview (Atkinson et al., 1993; D'Andrea & Daniels, 1991; Gilligan, 1982; Locke, 1992).

One way this sort of ethnocentrism affects graduate programs stems from the continued adherence to an intrapsychic model of counseling by trainers in the field. The intrapsychic model is based on an individualistic, Western tradition that explains client problems in terms of their own personal disorganization and/or deficits (Aubrey & Lewis, 1988). Though generally holding individuals responsible for their own psychological health and problems, the intrapsychic model minimizes the effect that dysfunctional environments have on a person's well-being (Lewis & Lewis, 1989).

Because the problems of many clients, especially those from various racial/ethnic minority groups, are directly related to external injustices (such as racism, sexism, age bias), the intrapsychic framework tends to be relatively ineffective in many cases. Despite its limited effectiveness, however, this model continues to be dominant in counseling training programs throughout the United States (Atkinson et al., 1993; Bryson & Bardo, 1975; D'Andrea & Daniels, 1991; Katz, 1983).

Anthropologists and sociologists have long noted the varied ways that people from different cultures receive help with their personal problems. In the United States, however, counseling trainers generally promote a unique model of helping characterized by an office-bound, time-bound, individual-oriented framework. The strict reliance on the notion that professional helping is done in a specific setting, such as the counselor's office, for a certain length of time, usually 45–50 minutes, exemplifies the ways in which ethnocentric biases are perpetuated in many counseling training programs at the present time.

A third example of ethnocentrism in counseling training programs is the lack of contact graduate students have with people from diverse backgrounds. Because most of their learning opportunities continue to be structured within traditional classroom settings, most counseling students are effectively isolated from the life experiences of culturally different individuals. The inability and unwillingness of educators to provide graduate students with opportunities for meaningful contact with people from a variety of backgrounds shows again how ethnocentrism continues to be perpetuated in counseling training programs.

In light of the numerous cultural biases manifested in the way counseling practitioners, researchers, and trainers do their work, it is easy to understand why the profession continues to be handicapped by its own ethnocentrism. Unless immediate action is taken to move beyond the biases that limit the way professionals think about their own roles and relate to their clients, research participants, and students, this handicap will inevitably become more debilitating.

Overcoming the Cognitive Dimensions of Ethnocentrism

If counselors are to move beyond the ethnocentrism that characterizes the way they provide clinical services, conduct research, and train graduate students, the epistemological foundation that drives the counseling profession must expand. In other words, helping professionals must make a concerted effort to extend the way they think about their work so they can expand their methods of counseling/research/training to stay relevant in a pluralistic society.

Clearly, it will take time for the profession to develop new cognitive maps that

1. More accurately describe the psychological development of people from diverse backgrounds
2. Specify more effective and culturally responsive counseling intervention strategies (Pedersen & Ivey, 1993)

The formation and implementation of new conceptual paradigms is an evolutionary process. However, the speed with which MCT propositions and corollaries (such as those in Chapter 2) become accepted into the mainstream of the profession largely depends on the level of commitment practitioners, researchers, and educators make to overcome the cultural biases that continue to exist in the field. The following recommendations are offered as guidelines to ameliorate ethnocentrism in the counseling profession.

DEMONSTRATING A COMMITMENT FOR OPEN-MINDEDNESS. A fundamental prerequisite in striving to identify and move beyond one's own ethnocentric biases involves a willingness to demonstrate an open-minded disposition regarding culturally inclusive innovations in counseling and psychotherapy. This may seem an odd recommendation for members of a profession that pride themselves in being open-minded and nonjudgmental. However, research and field observations suggest a pervasive lack of open-mindedness concerning the incorporation of MCT theory into the mainstream of the profession (D'Andrea, Daniels, & Heck, 1991).

Making a commitment to overcome the ethnocentric limitations of one's personal and professional development requires a willingness to participate actively in lifelong learning designed to increase one's current level of multicultural counseling awareness, knowledge, and skills. Professional counselors and psychotherapists can realize this sort of commitment in a couple of practical ways.

First, all members of the profession are encouraged to join the Association for Multicultural Counseling and Development (a division of the American Counseling Association) and the Society for the Psychological Study of Ethnic Minority Issues (a division of the American Psychological Association). These professional groups regularly provide members with useful, up-to-date information related to MCT advancements.

Second, counselors and therapists are urged to make a commitment to participate in professional development programs offered at national and state-sponsored conferences that specifically focus on multicultural issues. In recent years, the number of workshops related to multicultural counseling issues, offered at the national conventions sponsored by the American Psychological Association and the American Counseling Association, has substantially increased. These professional development opportunities can help counselors and psychologists move beyond an ethnocentric way of thinking about their professional roles and responsibilities.

MOVING BEYOND ETHNOCENTRISM IN COUNSELING PRACTICE. To overcome their own ethnocentric perspectives, counseling practitioners must work very hard to develop an empathetic understanding of clients who are culturally different from themselves. This involves more than trying to imagine how the counselor would feel if she or he were in the client's shoes; it means accurately understanding how the client's culture impacts what she or he is actually thinking and feeling during the counseling session. In this regard, Pedersen and Ivey (1993) discuss the need to shift from a client-centered to a culture-centered counseling perspective.

To understand what culturally different clients are experiencing, one might simply ask them about their thoughts and feelings regarding the counseling process. Many counselors and psychotherapists, however, are not comfortable with soliciting this sort of information, because they have not been taught to inquire about these issues with their clients.

To address these issues, practitioners should realize that it is all right to acknowledge one's own lack of understanding by asking culturally diverse clients direct questions about their relevant thoughts and feelings. Taking time to check out these issues with their clients reduces the likelihood of making incorrect interpretations of their experiences during counseling and facilitates the development of a positive and culturally sensitive therapeutic alliance.

To overcome one's own ethnocentrism, one should pursue a variety of experiences with individuals from different backgrounds. One of the best ways of doing this is making a commitment to get involved in a community where most of the residents come from diverse cultural backgrounds. This might include volunteering time at a public school where most of the students are from racial/ethnic minority backgrounds, participating in a community service project, and/or attending meetings where local residents are involved in planning political action strategies designed to improve the quality of life in their neighborhoods.

OVERCOMING CULTURAL ETHNOCENTRISM IN COUNSELING RESEARCH. Counseling researchers can overcome cultural biases in research methodology by striving to move beyond the widely held notion that quantitative methods are the "best" and most "legitimate" ways of conducting psychological research. Hoshmand (1989) and Ponterotto and Casas (1991) stress the importance of becoming familiar and comfortable with using alternative investigative paradigms. Several research experts have noted that various qualitative research strategies offer much promise in studying complex psychological issues among culturally diverse people (Hoshmand, 1989; Ivey, 1993; Parham, 1993; Ponterotto, 1988).

Counselors and psychologists interested in conducting multicultural research are encouraged to direct their time and energies toward designing "within-group" studies that focus on various issues related to the normal psychological development of people from diverse backgrounds (Helms, 1993; Parham, 1993; Sue, 1993). In the past, counseling researchers have conducted an inordinate number of "between-group" studies in which White people were used as the normative group to which subjects from other populations were compared. By conducting within-group studies comprising people from the same cultural, ethnic, or racial background, researchers will expand their understanding of the unique similarities and differences that characterize individuals from various populations and avoid the ethnocentric tendency of using Whites as the standard.

Overcoming Ethnocentrism in Counselor Training

Trainers in professional counseling and psychology programs are also in pivotal positions to help reduce the level of ethnocentrism that exists in the profession. In the past, these individuals have largely been responsible for perpetuating an encapsulated view of counseling by adhering to a curriculum the content and process of which excluded any meaningful examination of cultural considerations (D'Andrea & Daniels, 1991; Wrenn, 1962).

The increasing number of training programs that require courses in MCT represent a concerted effort to overcome the biases that have historically characterized these programs (Hills & Strozier, 1993). However, a number of operational problems arise in using a one-course approach to ameliorate ethnocentrism in counseling. As Sue, Ivey, and Pedersen note in Chapter 1, such courses may

1. Continue to be ethnocentric and monocultural
2. Rely on unsophisticated attempts to adapt current Eurocentric theories to diverse populations
3. Fail to make clear the cultural biases and assumptions of the traditional counseling theories

Given the complex task of developing multicultural counseling competencies (Sue et al., 1992), it is further argued that a single-course approach is simply not an adequate way to prepare mental-health professionals for the challenges they will face in the future. In light of the rapid diversification of modern society, counselors and therapists need training opportunities that infuse issues related to clients' cultural, ethnic, and racial backgrounds into all aspects of the curriculum.

Despite the logic of this proposal, less than 1% of all counseling and psychology training programs in the United States currently use a cultural infusion framework in the preparation of professional counselors and therapists (D'Andrea & Daniels, 1991). Though few counseling programs have made the commitment to incorporate cultural considerations into all aspects of the curriculum, infusion models offer the greatest potential to reduce the level of ethnocentric bias plaguing the profession. Ina's (1994) multicultural counseling infusion model is an excellent resource for those interested in incorporating cultural issues into all aspects of their training program.

One of the most common barriers to developing infusion training models is the lack of support among faculty members. Practically speaking, it is not always feasible to generate faculty support for this training model. However, individual trainers can still make a difference and counteract the impact other colleagues have on graduate students by exposing their trainees to culturally sensitive theories and approaches.

To help students overcome the types of ethnocentric thinking reinforced by traditional training programs, individual trainers must provide students with information, support, and encouragement to develop a broad range of alternative helping roles. Specifically, graduate students should be given opportunities in which they can confidently and skillfully learn to take on the role of adviser, advocate, consultant, change agent, and facilitator of indigenous support systems when working with a diverse client population (Atkinson, Thompson, & Grant, 1993). By promoting these alternative helping models, students will be encouraged to consider the benefits of implementing services that emphasize a systems, preventive, and developmental approach to counseling.

Most important, providing numerous opportunities for graduate students and faculty members to interact with people from diverse backgrounds should be an integral part of every professional training program. Having real-life experiences with individuals from diverse backgrounds is simply the best way to learn about how culture, ethnicity, and race impact a person's psychological development. Though these types of experiences need to be included at all levels of the curriculum, they are especially important in practicum and internship courses.

Some professional counseling and psychology training programs may offer many excuses for not implementing this recommendation. This institutional resistance should not, however, deter graduate students from taking the initiative to seek out experiences with people from culturally different groups. Students enrolled in training programs that do not offer these experiences can still take time to overcome their own ethnocentrism by attending cultural celebrations/festivals in their communities or becoming actively involved in neighborhood projects within racial/ethnic minority communities.

ACKNOWLEDGING THE IMPACT OF RACISM IN THE PROFESSION. Another major stumbling block to moving beyond ethnocentrism involves the reluctance of many counselors and psychologists to acknowledge the different ways racism shows itself in the field. There is no reason to believe that counselors and therapists are any less vulnerable to manifesting various types of intentional and unintentional racism than other members of society (Locke, 1992).

Many have outlined ways that racism continues to appear in counseling practice, research, and training (Atkinson et al., 1993; D'Andrea, 1992; D'Andrea & Daniels, 1994; Ponterotto & Pedersen, 1993). In terms of the present discussion, the types of resistance and apathy many counselors and therapists exhibit toward the multicultural movement reflect an exclusionary sentiment often rooted in ethnocentric and racist attitudes. It will be difficult to truly ameliorate ethnocentrism in the field without confronting how racism is manifested in the profession.

Although difficult to do, White counselors and psychologists must initiate and encourage open discussions about the manifestations of racism and ethnocentrism in the profession. These ongoing discussions should be done within training programs and at state, regional, and national conferences and conventions. In doing so, counseling practitioners, researchers, and trainers would have opportunities to learn more from their colleagues about these issues and identify practical ways of addressing them.

Clearly, the amelioration of ethnocentrism will require a dramatic change in the way helping professionals think about their roles and responsibilities. It will mean that counselors and psychologists will have to learn about the different ways individuals from diverse backgrounds develop psychologically. The way one thinks about such basic concepts as "mental health" and "psychological well-being" will also need to be expanded as one comes to understand that the meaning of these constructs is culturally determined and not necessarily universally accepted.

THE AFFECTIVE DIMENSIONS
OF ETHNOCENTRISM

Ethnocentrism is not simply an intellectual phenomenon composed of a set of cognitions that reflect a certain way of thinking about the world and the different types of people who live in that world. In addition to these cognitive components, ethnocentrism is also supported by various feelings individuals have about themselves, people from diverse cultural/ethnic/racial backgrounds, and the multicultural counseling movement itself. This section provides a description of the affective dimensions of ethnocentrism and describes their manifestations in the counseling profession.

Although multicultural counseling theorists have done a good job of discussing the cognitive dimensions of ethnocentrism (Atkinson et al., 1993; D'Andrea & Daniels, 1991; Ivey, Ivey, & Simek-Morgan, 1993; Pedersen, Draguns, Lonner, & Trimble, 1989; see also Chapter 3), they have generally failed to address the affective components of this problem. The *affective* dimensions of ethnocentricism refer to those positive feelings counselors and psychotherapists experience as a result of perpetuating a culturally biased worldview in their work.

Field-based observations have led researchers to identify several common sources of personal satisfaction and comfort that counselors experience in conducting their work. This includes positive feelings that result from providing counseling and psychological services in a competent manner, having meaningful connections with colleagues, experiencing substantial economic success and security, and being involved in a personally challenging and gratifying career. Further, it is very difficult for most individuals to criticize the field from which they ultimately gain a great deal of personal satisfaction.

In attempting to address the problem of ethnocentrism in the profession, one must consider the degree to which affective benefits contribute to the perpetuation of culturally biased theories, research paradigms, and training procedures. By taking into account the affective dimensions of ethnocentrism, MCT advocates will be better able to develop strategies to address this problem.

The Sense of Personal Loss in the Shift to Multicultural Counseling

As the United States becomes increasingly diverse, counselors and therapists will be pressed to develop a host of new competencies that will enable them to work effectively with people from various cultural backgrounds. MCT advocates argue that the profession must undergo major changes if it is to remain a relevant and viable institution in a pluralistic society. These changes will require counselors and therapists to abandon their ethnocentric biases and provide culturally responsive services to their clients (Pedersen & Ivey, 1993).

When attempting to make these changes, many mental-health professionals are likely to experience a genuine sense of loss as they strive to move beyond many well-established ethnocentric traditions and practices that have provided them with much personal meaning, comfort, and satisfaction. Kegan (1982) notes that this sense of personal loss is a normal psychological response that typically accompanies significant changes in one's life.

Several other theorists have written about the psychology of personal loss and the types of grief reactions adults have to significant changes (Daniels, 1990; Kübler-Ross, 1969). In this regard, the work of Kübler-Ross is particularly useful in understanding the types of personal losses many counselors and therapists experience when challenged to move beyond their own level of ethnocentricity.

Using Kübler-Ross' (1969) framework as a guide, one can describe five common affective responses counselors and therapists have been noted to exhibit when confronted with the types of issues Sue, Ivey, and Pedersen outline in their metatheory:

1. *Denying That a Problem Exists.* Many counselors and therapists deny that traditional counseling theories/approaches are culturally biased

and refuse to acknowledge that they do not adequately address the mental-health needs of people from non-Western backgrounds (Lloyd, 1987). By denying that cultural biases exist in the profession, counselors and therapists effectively avoid dealing with many of the concerns raised by Sue, Ivey, and Pedersen (1995) earlier in this book.

The following statements exemplify such denial. "This multicultural counseling stuff is much to do about nothing. Good counseling is good counseling. Multicultural counseling is a minority problem and really has nothing to do with me."

2. *Expressing Anger.* Some counselors and therapists express anger when confronted with the types of ethnocentric biases that exist in the counseling profession. This sort of reaction often occurs when they become frustrated by specific concerns raised by multicultural counseling advocates. Some counselors show anger when they feel that their own effectiveness in working with racial/ethnic minority clients is being questioned.

The following statements reflect various examples of this affective response. "I am sick and tired of hearing all this talk about multicultural counseling. Why should I be expected to make all these changes? I have been in this business for more than 25 years and I am an effective therapist. All this noise about multiculturalism is just a fad and I am tired of it."

3. *Bargaining.* When attempting to cope with the numerous changes that the multicultural movement brings with it, some counselors and psychologists will manifest what Kübler-Ross has described as "bargaining strategies." These strategies are characterized by attempts to soften the impact of incorporating a multicultural perspective in counseling practice, research, and training.

The following statements provide examples of possible bargaining by professional trainers. "I am in favor of instituting a course in multicultural counseling in our program. This demonstrates our commitment to multiculturalism. However, I do not think it is necessary to have these issues raised in all of our courses. If the multicultural counseling instructor does an effective job teaching the one course, that should be enough."

4. *Expressing Guilt Without Action.* Some counselors say that they should probably know more about multicultural counseling issues than they do. Despite this expression of guilt, though, they make little effort to move beyond their ethnocentric biases.

The following statements reflect specific examples of how this sort of "guilt without action" might sound. "I realize the importance of becoming more aware and knowledgeable about multicultural counseling issues. I only wish I had the time to participate in workshops that would help me improve in this area."

5. *Accepting and Supporting Multicultural Counseling.* Acceptance of multicultural counseling includes two components. First, individuals acknowledge the need for change both in the profession at large and in their own way of thinking and operating as professionals. Second, they take specific actions to help them overcome their own ethnocentrism, such as attending multicultural counseling workshops and training seminars or joining the Association for Multicultural Counseling and Development or the Society for the Psychological Study of Ethnic Minority Issues.

The following statements exemplify the ways professionals might demonstrate genuine support and acceptance for the multicultural counseling movement. "I really learned a great deal from that multicultural counseling workshop. In fact, I learned how much more I need to know to become an effective counselor in today's world. I am planning to attend another workshop in this area next month and want to talk to my supervisor about the possibility of getting other staff members to attend as well."

Overcoming the Affective Dimension of Ethnocentrism

Because they are harder to identify than the cognitive components of ethnocentrism, the affective dimensions are more difficult to address and modify. Counselors and therapists must nonetheless deal with these affective reactions, because they help perpetuate many of the cultural biases discussed earlier in this chapter. The following points are offered as guidelines that counselors and therapists are encouraged to consider when dealing with their own affective reactions to the MCT movement.

1. It is important for professionals to acknowledge that affective reactions contribute to much of the resistance to the MCT movement.

2. Counselors and therapists need to recognize that these emotional responses represent normal grief reactions that often emerge when individuals feel that they are losing something that is familiar and valuable to them. This sense of loss may occur when counselors and therapists are pressed to give up many of their traditional ways of thinking and operating as professionals.

3. Professionals should understand that unintentional and latent racist attitudes may lie at the root of much of the resistance and apathy that counselors and psychologists manifest toward the MCT movement.

4. Counselors and therapists are encouraged to consider which affective reaction(s) they typically use in responding to the MCT movement.

5. In overcoming the affective dimensions of ethnocentricism, counselors must demonstrate an unusual level of openness and sensitivity toward personal and professional change.

6. Counselors and therapists are encouraged to initiate discussions regarding the positive benefits to the profession of incorporating MCT paradigms in all aspects of their work.

7. Counseling practitioners, researchers, trainers, and graduate students need to obtain real-life experiences in racial/ethnic minority communities. These experiences should extend beyond their participation in professional workshops and required courses (i.e., practicum and internship placements) so that individuals from diverse cultural backgrounds will be viewed as "real people" and not just as "clients" with whom they may someday work.

8. Organizational and institutional incentives are needed to support those counselors and therapists who initiate efforts that address ethnocentrism in the profession. These might include (a) allocating resources for them to participate in professional development activities that further increase their level of multicultural counseling competencies, (b) introducing new staff development projects that address diversity issues within the workplace, (c) establishing institutional policies that support the right of all clients to receive services sensitive to and respectful of their unique cultural identities, and (d) creating organizational rewards (i.e., promotions, merit pay increases, etc.) for those who demonstrate a commitment to multiculturalism in their work.

CONCLUSION

This chapter served a threefold purpose. First, it examined the various ways ethnocentrism arises in the counseling profession. Second, it discussed two dimensions of ethnocentrism—the cognitive and affective components. Third, a number of recommendations for overcoming the cognitive and affective components of ethnocentrism were presented.

A couple of issues should also be addressed in future discussions about ethnocentrism in the profession. The first relates to the commonly held belief that cultural and ethnocentric biases are primarily a problem for White counselors and therapists. Although this perspective has dominated scholarly discussions in the past, all professionals (regardless of their cultural backgrounds) impose ethnocentric thoughts and feelings at different times in their personal and professional lives.

Since these thoughts and feelings are closely tied to one's cultural heritage, it is difficult for all people to divorce themselves from the biases, prejudices, and preferences that underlie the interpretations they make of their daily experiences. With this in mind, all counselors and therapists should try to understand the ways in which their own ethnocentric biases impact the manner in which they interact with clients and other colleagues in the profession.

Second, in attempting to reduce the level of resistance against the multicultural counseling movement, national professional associations must complement the efforts of individual counselors who demonstrate a willingness to overcome their own ethnocentrism. Specifically, the American Psychological Association (APA) and the American Counseling Association (ACA) must become much more visible in facilitating the "diversification" of the profession by demonstrating greater support for the inclusion of multicultural paradigms in counseling practice, research, and training.

In closing, it is clear that the sociopolitical reality of the United States will continue to undergo dramatic changes well into the 21st century. The challenge to the profession can be summed up in the following question. Will counselors and therapists demonstrate the type of commitment and take the necessary action to continue to be a relevant and viable force in this nation's mental-health-care system, or will they become victims of their own professional arrogance and ethnocentrism?

REFERENCES FOR CHAPTER 10

Atkinson, D. R., Morten, G., & Sue, D. W. (1993). *Counseling American minorities.* Dubuque, IA: Brown & Benchmark.

Atkinson, D. R., Thompson, C. E., & Grant, S. K. (1993). A three-dimensional model for counseling racial/ethnic minorities. *The Counseling Psychologist, 21,* 257–277.

Aubrey, R. F., & Lewis, J. A. (1988). Social issues and the counseling profession in the 1980s and 90s. In R. A. Hayes & R. F. Aubrey (Eds.), *New directions for counseling and human development* (pp. 286–303). Denver, CO: Love Publishing.

Bryson, S., & Bardo, H. (1975). Race and the counseling process: An overview. *Journal of Non-White Concerns, 4,* 5–15.

D'Andrea, M. (1992). The violence of our silence: Some thoughts about racism, counseling and development. *Guidepost, 35*(4), 31.

D'Andrea, M., & Daniels, J. (1991). Exploring the different levels of multicultural counseling training in counselor education. *Journal of Counseling and Development, 70,* 78–85.

D'Andrea, M., & Daniels, J. (1994). The different faces of racism in higher education. *Thought and Action, 10*(1), 73–89.

D'Andrea, M., & Daniels, J. (1995). Promoting multiculturalism and organizational change in the counseling profession: A case study. In J. Ponterotto (Ed.), *Handbook of multicultural counseling.* Newbury Park, CA: Sage.

D'Andrea, M., Daniels, J., & Heck, R. (1991). Evaluating the impact of multicultural counseling training. *Journal of Counseling and Development, 70,* 143–150.

Daniels, J. (1990). *Loss: A developmental approach to transition and its impact on the work environment.* Unpublished doctoral dissertation, Vanderbilt University, Nashville, TN.

Gilligan, C. (1982). *In a different voice: Psychological theory and women's development.* Cambridge, MA: Harvard University Press.

Goldman, L. (1976). A revolution in counseling research. *Journal of Counseling Psychology, 23,* 543–552.

Goldman, L. (1989). Moving counseling research into the 21st century. *The Counseling Psychologist, 17,* 81–85.

Helms, J. E. (1989). At long last—Paradigms for cultural psychology research. *The Counseling Psychologist, 17,* 98–101.

Helms, J. E. (1993). I also said, "White racial identity influences White researchers." *The Counseling Psychologist, 21,* 240–243.

Hills, H. I., & Strozier, A. L. (1993). Multicultural training in APA approved counseling psychology programs: A survey. *Professional Psychology, 18,* 45–53.

Hoshmand, L. L. (1989). Alternative research paradigms: A review and teaching proposal. *The Counseling Psychologist, 17,* 3–79.

Ina, S. (1994). *Multicultural curriculum infusion in counselor training: An innovative consultation model.* Paper presented at the annual meeting of the American Counseling Association, Minneapolis, MN.

Ivey, A. E. (1993). On the road to reconstruction of our present practice of counseling and psychotherapy. *The Counseling Psychologist, 21,* 225–228.

Ivey, A. E., Ivey, M. B., & Simek-Morgan, L. (1993). *Counseling and psychotherapy: A multicultural perspective.* Boston: Allyn and Bacon.

Katz, D. (1983). Factors affecting social change. *Journal of Social Issues, 39*(4), 27.

Kegan, R. (1982). *The evolving self.* Cambridge, MA: Harvard University Press.

Kübler-Ross, E. (1969). *On death and dying.* New York: MacMillan.

Lee, C. C., & Richardson, B. L. (1991). *Multicultural issues in counseling: New approaches to diversity.* Alexandria, VA: American Association for Counseling and Development.

Lewis, J., & Lewis, M. (1989). *Community counseling: A human service approach.* Pacific Grove, CA: Brooks/Cole.

Lloyd, A. P. (1987). Multicultural counseling: Does it belong in counselor education? *Counselor Education and Supervision, 26,* 164–167.

Locke, D. C. (1992). *Increasing multicultural understanding: A comprehensive model.* Newbury Park, CA: Sage.

Parham, T. A. (1993). White researchers conducting multicultural counseling research: Can their efforts be "mo betta"? *The Counseling Psychologist, 21,* 250–256.

Pedersen, P. B. (1991). Multiculturalism as a fourth force in counseling. *Journal of Counseling and Development, 70.*

Pedersen, P. B., Draguns, J., Lonner, J., & Trimble, J. (1989). *Counseling across cultures* (3rd ed.). Honolulu: University of Hawaii Press.

Pedersen, P. B., & Ivey, A. (1993). *Culture-centered counseling and interviewing skills: A practical guide.* Westport, CT: Praeger.

Ponterotto, J. G. (1988). Racial/ethnic minority research in the *Journal of Counseling Psychology:* A content analysis and methodological critique. *Journal of Counseling Psychology, 53,* 410–418.

Ponterotto, J. G., & Casas, J. M. (1991). *Handbook of racial/ethnic minority counseling research.* Springfield, IL: Thomas.

Ponterotto, J. G., & Pedersen, P. B. (1993). *Preventing prejudice: A guide for counselors and educators.* Newbury Park, CA: Sage.

Sue, D. W. (1993). Confronting ourselves: The White and racial/ethnic minority researcher. *Counseling Psychologist, 21*(2), 244–249.

Sue, D. W., Arredondo, P., & McDavis, R. J. (1992). Multicultural counseling competencies and standards: A call to the profession. *Journal of Multicultural Counseling and Development, 20,* 64–88.

Sue, D. W., & Sue, D. (1990). *Counseling the culturally different: Theory and practice.* New York: Wiley.

Wrenn, G. C. (1962). The culturally encapsulated counselor. *The Harvard Educational Review, 32*(4), 444–449.

PART III

MCT THEORY AND SPECIFIC POPULATIONS

A primary test of MCT theory concerns its appropriateness or inappropriateness when applied to specific populations. MCT theory is additive rather than subtractive and must balance the culture-universal and culture-specific. The difficulty of this task raises the question of whether a metatheory truly allows one to formulate principles applicable across populations. How adequate is MCT theory when seen from the perspective of African-American, Native-American, Asian-American, Latina(o)-American, and women's worldviews? Where is it applicable and inapplicable, and in what direction must MCT theory evolve to become a viable alternative to traditional formulations?

Space limitations and other factors prevented the expansion of the section to include any number of culturally different groups: gay/lesbian, Middle-Eastern and Arab, physically challenged, and others. In no way does this omission deny the importance of these group distinctions, for MCT must ultimately be tested against them as well. This book is intended as a springboard for you to deal with your own critical analysis of MCT theory with respect to the many diverse groups in society. How do you think MCT applies to groups not discussed here?

Each of the following chapters, written from the perspective of a particular worldview, raises some very important theoretical and practical implications. You may find the reactions, ideas, and challenges raised by the authors not only enlightening and challenging, but occasionally controversial. Again, please continue your "assumption audit" of each chapter.

CHAPTER 11

MCT Theory and African-American Populations

Thomas A. Parham
University of California, Irvine

Assumption Audit

- MCT theory moves one in the direction of addressing not only "what to do" but "how to do it" as well.
- MCT theory does a good job of commenting on the limitations of traditional theories.
- It is important to note, however, that traditional psychology is not oppressive because it adheres to different assumptions, mores, values, and customs, but rather in how that theory is operationalized.
- Euro-American psychology has deliberately attempted to ignore and/or erase the historical influences of ancient African ideas on Western civilizations.
- The profession may not be poised for a paradigm shift.
- Some may have reservations about whether the generic MCT approach is the most fruitful direction to take.
- MCT theory shares several points of common ground with an African-centered worldview: holistic integration of person and environment, "self as collective," liberation of consciousness, and need for systemic interventions.
- MCT theory needs to define culture as a design for living and a pattern for interpreting reality.
- MCT theory needs to address the issue and possibility that the inclusion of a culturally specific "skill" may be at odds with a theoretical orientation that does not share similar assumptions or worldviews.
- For MCT theory to be relevant to African-Americans, it must help clinicians understand the moral mandate to create social change ("social engineering").

- MCT theory must avoid dancing around the issues of environmental oppressions and call them what they are: racism! sexism! classism!
- MCT theory cannot be totally effective in its application to black people without addressing the fundamental components of the African personality and the African character.
- MCT theory cannot just rely on consensus validation of multicultural "experts" to measure the relevance of the theory. It must be proven through empirical study and measured against a set of principles or standards that are culturally specific regardless of the evaluators.

The growing interest in MCT has stimulated an unprecedented increase in the number of presentations and publications that concern themselves with providing mental-health services to culturally different people. While some of those research efforts have traveled the road of merely highlighting or synthesizing what has already been done in the literature, others have sought a road that allows them to make a substantial and significant contribution to the field. Without question, Sue, Ivey and Pedersen have traveled the latter and taken center stage with their latest theory on MCT. This timely effort represents the intent to fill a void that has plagued the cross-cultural literature for some time. Though information on multicultural counseling exists (Ivey, Ivey, & Simek-Morgan, 1993; Lee, 1989; Locke, 1993; Pedersen & Marsela, 1980; Sue & Sue, 1992), the void exists as a body of literature that has reached its limitations because it has accomplished what it initially intended to do.

During the past 25 years, the psychological literature (especially that related to Blacks) has focused considerable attention on critiquing traditional psychology's view of people of African descent (R. L. Jones, 1972, 1980; Myers, 1988; Thomas & Sillen, 1972; White, 1972). The authors of these writings are extremely pointed in their questioning of both the racist paradigms promoted by Whites in psychology (Guthrie, 1976; Nobles, 1972) and the utility of using traditional theories of psychotherapy (Jackson, 1980) and assessment instruments (Samuda, 1975; Williams, 1972) with Black populations. Though these critiques are important contributions in and of themselves, they suffer from a major limitation. As a body of scholarship, they skillfully point out what is fundamentally wrong with the study and application of traditional psychology to Black people. However, the research does not effectively present viable alternatives. For example, the utility of Freudian (E. Jones, 1982), behavioral (Hayes, 1972), and humanistic (Jenkins, 1980) theories have all been heavily scrutinized. But if they are inappropriate, what is the culturally specific alternative? Few have been offered.

The current popularity of multiculturalism has given rise to an echoing of sentiments from the past that highlight the limitations of traditional Euro-American approaches. Not only have these efforts implored psychologists and counselors to increase their cultural awareness and sensitivity (Locke, 1993; Sue & Sue, 1992), but they have also invited counselors to develop a greater level of clinical/counseling competence with different populations (Sue, Arredondo, & McDavis, 1992). And so, while many in counseling now know *what* to do (i.e., be culturally sensitive), Parham and Parham (in press) argue that there is a less crystallized body of knowledge that assists them in knowing *how* to do it. Consequently, MCT theory takes on a greater salience in light of the growing interest in being more culturally sensitive in specific ways.

GENERAL REACTIONS

The authors of MCT theory have done a good job of commenting on the limitations of traditional theories. Sue, Ivey, and Pedersen are absolutely correct when they assert that theories grounded in a Euro-American worldview (1) inadequately explain the complexities associated with the personalities and life experiences of people of color, (2) are culture bound and inflexible in their inclusion of alternative explanations for psychological phenomena, and (3) usually focus on only a single dimension of the personality.

Sue et al. have also pointed out how psychology and its related theories have been used as a tool of oppression against culturally different people. However, the authors should make clearer that traditional psychology is not oppressive just because it adheres to the assumptions, mores, values, and customs of Western cultures. After all, there is a fundamental difference between the core constructs of a theory and how that theory is operationalized and applied. In fact, many of these approaches to counseling might have some redemptive value if they could avoid the "difference equals deficiency" logic, in which everything different is assumed to be inferior.

Traditional psychology has been oppressive in its application and the way it has been operationalized. Further, as Nobles (1986) has argued, a major shortcoming of Western psychology is that its major theorists have practiced a form of scientific colonialism. That is, Euro-American psychology has deliberately attempted to influence the dissemination of ideas directly by engaging in a systematic process of falsification. Nobles further suggests that scientific colonialism has three components:

1. Unsophisticated falsification—where certain facts or ideas are simply destroyed or falsified;
2. Integrated modificationism—where original facts, information,

and ideas are distorted, suppressed, or modified in order to fabricate "new" facts and ideas; and

3. Conceptual incarceration—where the person's knowledge base becomes a prisoner of "alien ideas" by utilizing a set of predetermined concepts which influence one's willingness to use an expanded perspective in evaluating those ideas. (p. 19)

Euro-American writers ignoring and otherwise erasing the historical influences of ancient African ideas on Western civilizations is a good example of scientific colonialism. It doesn't take much effort to find the African concepts of complementarity of feminine and masculine attributes of the Creator reflected in the theories of several prominent scholars, with no mention of their ancient African roots. Guthrie (1976) offers numerous other examples of scientific colonialism as he describes the blatant expressions of racism advanced by many prominent Euro-American psychologists. One of the earliest examples of this racist posture comes from Hall (1904), who not only describes Blacks as members of the adolescent races, but uses these conclusions as evidence to support the mandate for Blacks to be placed in socially subservient roles to Whites. Terman (1916) provides yet another example of racism in his use of IQ testing. His efforts resulted in labeling Blacks as retarded, incapable of mastering abstractions, and prone to criminal activity. Ferguson (1916) exacerbates these peculiar conclusions by stating that because of their IQ scores, Blacks should be relegated to training as manual laborers. A final example is illustrated in the work of Thorndike (1940), who tries to justify slavery and racial segregation by asserting that Blacks are born inferior to Whites and are doomed, because of their limited intellectual and genetic capacity, to be exploited by Whites.

The proliferation of racist theories and their advocacy by influential leaders of the time led others to institute academic, research, and clinical practices equally detrimental to African people. Thomas and Sillen (1972) chronicle how studies in psychiatry and psychology have been used as tools of oppression in concluding higher rates of mental illness, misdiagnosis of psychological conditions, and mistreatment of Black people in the mental-health system. Furthermore, they go on to document psychology's characterization of Black family life as pathological and deviant and the exclusion of Blacks from certain forms of treatment (i.e., psychoanalysis) because they were presumed to lack the personality characteristics necessary for successful outcomes. Because the space and focus of this article do not permit a more thorough discussion of this argument, readers should also consult texts by Nobles (1986), James (1976), and Diop (1976).

Though heartened by Sue et al.'s enthusiasm for transforming the counseling profession from less to more culturally sensitive, I disagree with their point that the discipline is poised for a major paradigm shift. The

African tradition states that "ideas are the substance of behavior." Essentially, this means that truth lies in the congruence between what is spoken and what is practiced. While one can point to several corners of the psychology profession where speaking loudly about multiculturalism is fashionable, those same corners have failed to respond with meaningful change in areas such as diverse faculty and staff in training programs, curriculum modification, recruitment and retention of underrepresented students, equitable distribution of power in professional associations, changes in licensing laws to cover cultural competence as a professional and ethical mandate, more culturally sensitive research efforts, and changes in the valuation of culturally specific scholarship in matters of tenure and promotion. Indeed, the profession is talking loudly, but saying very little when it comes to operationalizing diversity and multiculturalism—all the more reason why MCT is a significant addition to the struggle for greater cultural advances in psychology.

MCT theory attempts to provide a generic framework for understanding the myriad helping approaches advanced by different cultural groups. Despite the fact that some literature is critical of generic approaches, Sue, Ivey, and Pedersen boldly step forward and offer a metatheory that offers exciting possibilities. In light of their assertions, however, one can question whether a generic theory is the most fruitful direction to take. Having to be all things to all people is a burden difficult to meet under the best of circumstances. Yet, like most things in life that require one to take the good with the bad, the MCT theory offers several advantages and disadvantages, which its authors describe. Clearly, they seem to be in accord with an African principle that states, "Life at its best is a creative synthesis of opposites in fruitful harmony." Essentially, this means that sometimes your greatest strength can also be your greatest weakness, depending on the context. Accordingly, the MCT theory provides an adequate synthesis of its strengths and its limitations.

AFRICAN-CENTERED WORLDVIEW

To understand the applicability of MCT theory to African-American people and an African psychological perspective, specific areas of congruence and incongruence between the MCT theory and the African-centered worldview should be briefly discussed.

The African-centered worldview begins with a recognition that things within the universe are innerconnected (*consubstantiation*). The sense of interrelationship between all things is essential for understanding the relationship between African-American people and the context of their lives. As such, any analysis of behavior must include this context rather than merely focus on the individual. The notion of interrelatedness is also important for understanding the connections among the spiritual, cognitive, affective, and behavioral dimensions of the personality. Though some psychological perspectives seek to focus only on one isolated dimension of the personality, the African worldview recognizes that there is a spiritual essence or life force that permeates everything that is. Thus, the personality one develops is believed to be a manifestation of spiritual, mental, emotional, behavioral, and biogenetic factors that interact with the environment in a holistic way (Kambon, 1992; Myers, 1988; Parham & Parham, in press).

The African-centered worldview also focuses on the group or tribe, not the individual, as the most salient element of existence. Thus, individual achievement and competition is valued less than efforts that contribute to cooperation among people and efforts that facilitate group survival (Nobles, 1972; Parham, 1993; White, 1984; White & Parham, 1990). White (1984) and White and Parham (1990) also comment on the African worldview's fluid time perspective and the notion of "being" in the moment, emphasis on the emotional vitality and legitimacy of feelings, use of the oral tradition and the relationship between speaker and listener, orientation toward living in harmony with the universe, and tendency to define one's worth in relation to how one contributes to the community.

Further, one can make natural extensions from an African-centered perspective to the understanding of an African-American psychology. In this regard, Parham and Parham (in press) have offered a definition that may facilitate this analysis of areas of convergence and divergence with MCT theory. This definition emerged out of a 1992 retreat held by the Western Region of the Association of Black Psychologists. Though this definition is currently being revised, it provides the essence of an African-centered framework:

> African psychology examines processes which allow for the illumination and liberation of the spirit (one's spiritual essence). Relying on the principle of harmony within the universe as the natural order of human existence, Africentric psychological perspectives recognize the spiritness that permeates everything that is, the notion that everything in the universe is innerconnected; the value that the collective is the most important dimension of existence; and the idea that self-knowledge is the key to mental health. African psychology then is the dynamic manifestation of the unifying African principles, values, and traditions whereby the application of knowledge is used to resolve personal and social problems and promote optimal human functioning.

Given this definition of an African-centered psychological perspective, let us now focus on areas of convergence and divergence with MCT theory.

MCT THEORY AND
AFRICAN-CENTERED WORLDVIEWS

Areas of Congruence

In reviewing the MCT theory, one finds several points in common with an African-centered worldview. I applaud Sue et al. for recognizing that everyone possesses an identity formed in multiple levels of experience and context. Their focus here implies a holistic integration between person and environment, an assumption they most clearly articulate in Corollary 2B.

Equally impressive, they advocate an expanded definition of self, moving from "self as individual" to "self as collective." In keeping with the focus on a more holistic approach, MCT theory also invites users to consider more than one dimension in discussions and assessment of personality. It is also encouraging to see Sue et al. acknowledge that therapy, healing, etc., must focus on the liberation of consciousness, although they never really define *consciousness* in the text. Lastly, they recognize the need for systemic interventions when counselors work with clients in therapy. Numerous articles and book chapters have been written about the need to intervene systemically when environmental factors have largely caused a client's psychological distress (Gunnings & Simpkins, 1972; White & Parham, 1990).

Areas of Divergence

In contrast to the specific areas of congruence, there appear to be several areas of divergence that should not escape closer scrutiny. Unless these areas are adequately addressed in the theory, the mass of African-American clinicians and others who treat African-American clients in culturally sensitive ways may find it hard to recognize the MCT theory's utility. The first area of divergence lies in the authors' definition of *culture*. In Corollary 2E, Sue et al. seem to reduce the definition of culture to mere demographics. While I suspect their intention was different than the outcome, culture cannot be simply defined as "any group that shares a theme or issue(s)" (p. 16). Admittedly, culture is a complex constellation of behaviors, ideas, attitudes, communication styles, value systems, rituals, etc., practiced in the life of each person. However, what is most important to know about culture is not that everyone has one; that seems rather obvious. Rather, as Nobles (1986) suggests, culture provides a general design for living and a pattern for interpreting reality. Consequently, the most salient information a helping professional can know about a client's culture is how the various rules for living and patterns for interpreting reality affect a client's view of the world. In this regard, I would think it wise for the clinician to speak with clients about their cultural orientations, including questions about how they make sense out of situations in their life. Relevant data might include value systems, assumptions about life events and other people, goals in life, perceived advantages and obstacles, expected outcomes, and clients' motivations for responding to life events in the particular ways they do. Based on the feedback derived from the client, the clinician should be able to develop a deeper understanding of the client's culture and how it might influence treatment planning.

Another divergence stems from Proposition 1 and its discussion of the usefulness of various theories. Sue et al. argue for a recognition that (all) theories are neither inherently "right or wrong," "good or bad," regardless of their cultural origins. However nice it is to validate each theory as valuable, one must also recognize that a theory may be good or bad in its application to a particular group. It seems confusing to argue on the one hand, for example, that Western theories have major shortcomings when used with people of color and may actually do harm, and then later argue that those same theories are neither right nor wrong, inherently. For a particular cultural group, a specific theory may be right or wrong or congruent or incongruent with specific cultural precepts. In arguing this point, one must understand the distinction between the core constructs of a theory and the way a theory is operationalized by that practitioner. An example of this distinction can be provided by using a client-centered approach. Among other things, Rogers's theory, as articulated by Corey (1982), suggests that validation, support, approval, and genuine regard from significant others in a person's life are necessary for that person to feel good about him/herself. As such, personal distress in a client's life is often related to an absence of those qualities he or she was able to obtain developmentally. Therapy then becomes a forum where the client can discuss his or her concerns in an atmosphere of empathy, genuineness, and unconditional positive regard provided by the therapist.

A limitation of this approach lies in the attribution of clients' distress to individual causes and the subsequent focus of the counseling interaction, which is dictated by the therapist. For instance, if the counselor assumes that distress can be alleviated by creating a more nurturing atmosphere for a client to explore feelings, etc., this approach may prove detrimental to Black clients, whose issues of distress may be instigated by a larger society's degradation of their humanity as African-Americans. This scenario requires more recognition of systemic factors in the client's life and more activity by the therapist to impact the client's social condition.

Another scenario can be provided using a cognitive-behavioral approach. Ellis's theory of rational-emotive therapy (RET) argues that clients' distress is caused by their perception of an event, rather than the situational phenomenon itself. In focusing on a client's irrational belief system, the therapist seeks to challenge and dispute faulty thinking and replace it with what is believed to be more realistic appraisals of a client's life experiences. In the context of counseling and therapy, client perceptions are matched with 1 of 10 or 11 (depending on the sourcebook) irrational beliefs as the therapist describes the faulty aspects of a client's thought process. What practitioners often fail to understand is the culturally latent value structure that supports the labeling of certain beliefs as rational or irrational and how this can conflict with a client's cultural value system. African Americans, for example, are not just group oriented; their orientation toward collective survival mandates that they be extremely concerned about the general welfare and emotional states of others. Also, in recognizing the divine nature of all humans and the innerconnectedness of people, African Americans value treating others and being treated with utmost respect, kindness, and decency. Imagine the dissonance created when worrying excessively about another's problems or expecting others to act kindly toward you are characterized as irrational and indications of "masturbatory thinking" (Ellis & Grieger, 1977). Of course, one can also criticize the RET theory itself for assuming a client's distress is intrapsychic as opposed to sociocultural. In each of these examples, the theories themselves, as well as the way they are operationalized, can potentially prove detrimental to clients of African descent.

Still another point of divergence lies in the discussion of appropriate treatment modalities (Proposition 4). Sue et al. seem to advocate the use of culturally congruent modalities. Yet, they maintain that MCT theory strives to expand the existing repertoire of helping skills regardless of theoretical orientation. This seems potentially inconsistent. While I agree with and support their goal of clinicians expanding their existing skill base, I can conceive of a time when the inclusion of a culturally specific "skill" would work against a theoretical orientation that does not share similar assumptions. Imagine for a moment a clinician learning a skill of "joining" as advocated by Phillips (1990) in his model of NTU psychotherapy or Boyd-Franklin (1989) in her family therapy approach. "Joining" in these cases represents an innerconnectedness between the client and therapist in which each seeing him/herself in the other facilitates the process of healing. How might clinicians who endorse a more psychodynamic approach to therapy resolve the dilemma that arises from choosing to "join" in this way even though it violates their bias for objective distance from the client, potentially stimulating a reaction (i.e., transference) that might be considered resistance? In a similar vein, how does a skill of advocating for and actively working toward systemic change correspond to a theoretical orientation that presents the target of therapeutic intervention as intrapsychic? Unless one could modify a fundamental principle of a particular theory to incorporate the expanded view, the potential for dissonance between a therapist's objective and the theory's proposed goals of intervening would be enhanced. Thus, though extending one's skill repertoire is prudent, I question whether such efforts can be successful "regardless of theoretical orientation."

The Need for Further Expansion

Regardless of the specific areas of convergence and divergence previously discussed, MCT theory has enormous potential. However, for MCT theory to be considered relevant to African-American people (if that is even possible) and adopted by African-American clinicians as a useful metatheory, Sue et al. may want to consider adding several propositions. The first proposition suggests that MCT theory's effectiveness (and maybe credibility) lies in its ability to help clinicians understand the moral mandate to create social change. In the context of an African-American psychology, White and Parham (1990) assert that the keys to a third phase of a Black psychology movement would be "applied psychology and social engineering." Any theory that merely recognizes environmental constraints such as oppression and fails to address them or help the client address them in meaningful ways helps to perpetuate the status quo. If therapists only help their clients "feel" better or "think" more clearly about oppressive conditions in their lives, all therapists do potentially is create mentally healthy people who are still vulnerable to the same social pathology that instigated their distress in the first place. Clinicians must do more than validate client reactions to oppression. They must become, and teach their clients to become, social engineers. This social engineering can occur as close to home as helping to change some of the practices within the professions of psychology and counseling or as far away as working within the larger society. For instance, a clinician in a university counseling center might consider lobbying the school's administration to adopt diversity training in response to student concerns of racial harassment and intolerance on campus. Academicians may want to consider lobbying professional associations and licensing boards to require training in MCT of those who seek licensure and certification or who serve ethnic clientele. Perhaps a psychologist/counselor who practices in the community with clients who share frustrations about racist and discriminatory social policies will get involved in community initiatives designed to change those policies. Such efforts not only help to change social circumstances many find oppressive, but also provide an important source of validation for the client.

A second proposition, like the first, recognizes the need to label clients' experiences accurately for them. MCT theory's discussion of "person-environment interactions" and "recognizing environmental oppression" that impacts on clients' lives tidies up a more sordid reality that must be addressed. That is, MCT theory must avoid dancing around the issues of environmental oppressions and call them what they are: Racism! Sexism! Classism! MCT theory cannot be relevant to African-American people if it does not teach them (clients, families, children, etc.) to confront and understand racism. I believe this is a critical mental-health issue. It is no accident that some of the best African-American clinicians, including psychologists (Akbar, 1984; Kambon, 1992; Myers, 1988), psychiatrists (Cress-Welsing, 1991), counselors (Locke, 1993), and clinical social workers (Gibbs, 1988) devote a considerable amount of time in their writing to this purpose. The focus on racism here in particular is not accidental, because it is one of the most insidious mental disorders, too often making its victims believe there is something wrong with them. An MCT theory must do something to address this fundamental issue and help African-American clients understand what Fuller (1969) means when he writes, "If you do not understand (racism) and White supremacy, what it is, and how it works, everything else that you think you understand will only confuse you" (p. 169).

The importance of this recognition lies in the principles of self-love and empowerment. First, recognizing racist systems and how they work potentially renders African Americans less vulnerable to being manipulated by Whites, whose actions and intentions are sometimes oppressive. Second, learning to reject racist notions may impact an individual's ego and self-image positively. Third, recognizing the what and how of racism may help identify ways a client/student/person can confront those inequities in his or her life.

A third proposition necessary to enhance the utility of an MCT theory is the need to understand what it means to be an African American (or for that matter, a member of any other group). Nobles (personal communication) has suggested that a psychological perspective relevant to Black people must address both the meaning of human beingness and the essential elements of human functioning. Consequently, MCT theory cannot be totally effective in its application to Black people without addressing the fundamental components of the African personality and the African character. Sue et al. argue in Proposition 6 that a basic goal of MCT theory is the liberation of consciousness. In this regard, a clinician would find it difficult if not impossible to facilitate the therapeutic process of healing (liberate consciousness) in Blacks if he or she has no idea of what constitutes the mental health of African people. It is commendable to talk about liberating consciousness, but what exactly does that mean for African Americans? This point can be illustrated with a brief explanation.

Consciousness represents our capacity to know and experience reality. Fundamentally, African-American people experience reality as a union of the spiritual with the material. Myers (1988) believes these two dimensions become real through the use of our five senses. As the personality interacts with the environment, people make choices to respond to their reality in certain ways. Some of those responses are in harmony with one's cultural essence while other responses are in direct conflict with one's nature. Consequently, for African people, mental health is analogous to living in accord with one's nature or natural essence (Parham, 1993; Parham & Parham, in press). The awareness of who one is (self-knowledge) as a spiritual being is central to this notion. As such, a healthy personality requires the illumination (and liberation) of the spirit such that energy or life force channeled through the cognitive, affective, and behavioral dimension of the personality organizes them to meet the needs of the organism as a whole. The manifestation of those dimensions is accompanied by a consciousness that recognizes the divine nature of the self, the ability to grow, the ability to acquire wisdom, the ability to exercise free will, the necessity to be morally and socially responsible in interactions with other people, and the mandate to live by the standard of "Maat." (Maat was represented by the seven cardinal virtues of truth, justice, righteousness, harmony, order, balance, and reciprocity [Karenga, 1990]). Clinicians who might attempt to employ MCT with African-American clients would be required to know these fundamental precepts of the African character and personality before and if any "liberation of consciousness" could take place. They may then serve to help African-American clients more fully understand, appreciate, and express their Africanness.

CONCLUSION

In commenting (however briefly) on the usefulness and relevance of MCT theory for African-American people, this chapter has attempted to present a balanced view. I do, however, want to reiterate my enthusiasm for this effort at trying to help the profession become more culturally sensitive in meaningful ways. This MCT theory is "no small step"; rather, it represents "one giant leap" in that direction, and I applaud my colleagues for this work. In closing, I also want to invite Sue, Ivey, and Pedersen to consider a challenge. Recognizing that there is a lack of homogeneity among cultural groups raises issues of relevance to all of them. Consequently, a larger question seems to be whether a generic metatheory has enough of the specificity needed to be relevant to particular cultural groups simultaneously? Only time and use of the theory will answer that question.

While personal opinions of various multicultural "experts" are important considerations, Sue et al. must be careful not to rely on consensus validation alone as a yardstick to measure the relevance of their MCT theory. A theoretical discussion that seeks to support or correct various components of the MCT theory is an insufficient test of the theory's integrity. I, for one, have never been a fan of "democratic sanity, where ideas seem credible just because a group of people endorse them" (even when I am among that group of people).

Rather, MCT theory's utility for African-American people must be proven through empirical study and must be measured against a set of principles or standards that are culturally specific regardless of the evaluators. For African Americans, those standards can be extrapolated from a body of literature that communicates several common themes (Akbar, 1984; Asante, 1986; Azibo, 1989; Cress-Welsing, 1991; Kambon, 1992; Myers, 1988; Nobles, 1986; Parham, 1993). These themes are consistent with the Ancient Kemetic and historically African worldview, and should be considered essential to the application of any theory to African-American clients. These prerequisites include the following:

1. The need to define the African personality, including its spiritual essence, clearly. Clinicians cannot treat what they do not understand.

2. The knowledge of how to support and nurture the spirit of African people. Because spirit is so fundamental to everything that is, clinicians must learn to embrace and nurture the spirit in ways that give it guidance, reassurance, and unconditional love.

3. The need to define appropriate human functioning, including definitions for ordered and disordered behavior. Indeed, what is normal must have a culturally centered frame of reference.

4. The need to promote the liberation of the African mind in helping African Americans move toward a greater sense of self-determination. Woodson (1933) was clear when he wrote that if you control the way a person thinks, you do not have to assign them to an inferior status; if necessary, they will seek it for themselves. MCT theory must help Black people recognize and use a culturally congruent source of validation.

5. The need to express culturally specific treatment strategies and techniques that might help clinicians serve African-American people and help African Americans themselves achieve a greater sense of harmony and congruence with their own cultural essence.

Ultimately, a theory that seeks to help clinicians work with the human personality cannot help but mirror some of its attributes. One dimension of the African personality is the process of human transformation toward perfection (Karenga, 1990). This dimension recognizes that while who we are represents our beingness at a moment in time, all of us have the capacity to grow into a fuller expression (manifestation) of ourselves. Similarly, MCT theory is a *significant contribution* in its current version. However, its potential is even more exciting. For the sake of the helping professions, I hope it continues to become "mo' betta."

REFERENCES FOR CHAPTER 11

Akbar, N. (1984). *Chains and images of psychological slavery*. Jersey City, NJ: New Mind Productions.

Asante, M. (1986). *The Afrocentric idea*. Philadelphia: Temple University Press.

Azibo, D. A. (1989). African centered thesis on mental health and a nosology of Black personality disorders. *Journal of Black Psychology, 15*(2), 173–214.

Boyd-Franklin, N. (1989). *Black families in therapy*. New York: Guilford Press.

Corey, G. (1982). *Theory and practice of counseling and psychotherapy* (2nd ed.). Monterey, CA: Brooks/Cole.

Cress-Welsing, F. (1991). *The Isis papers*. Chicago: Third World Press.

Diop, C. A. (1976). *The African origin of civilization*. Westport, CT: Lawrence, Hill & Co.

Ellis, A., & Grieger, R. (1977). *Handbook of rational emotive therapy* (Vol. 1). New York: Springer.

Ferguson, G. O. (1916). *The psychology of the Negro*. New York: The Science Press.

Fuller, N. (1969). *United independent compensatory code/system/concept: Textbook for victims of White supremacy*. Washington, DC: Library of Congress.

Gibbs, J. T. (Ed.). (1988). *Young, Black, and male in America*. Dover, MA: Auburn House.

Gunnings, T., & Simpkins, G. (1972). A systemic approach to counseling disadvantaged youth. *Journal of Non-White Concerns, 1*, 4–8.

Guthrie, R. (1976). *Even the rat was White*. New York: Harper & Row.

Hall, G. S. (1904). *Adolescence*. New York: Appleton.

Hayes, W. (1972). Radical Black behaviorism. In R. L. Jones (Ed.), *Black psychology*. New York: Harper & Row.

Ivey, A. E., Ivey, M. B., & Simek-Morgan, L. (1993). *Counseling and psychotherapy: A multicultural perspective* (3rd ed.). Needham Heights, MA: Allyn and Bacon.

Jackson, G. (1980). The African genesis of a Black perspective in helping. In R. L. Jones (Ed.), *Black psychology* (2nd ed.). New York: Harper & Row.

James, G. (1976). *Stolen legacy*. San Francisco: Julian Richardson.

Jenkins, A. (1980). *The psychology of the Afro-American*. Oxford, England: Pergamon Press.

Jones, E. (1982). Psychotherapist impressions of treatment outcomes as a function of race. *Journal of Clinical Psychology, 38*(4), 722–731.

Jones, R. L. (Ed.). (1972). *Black psychology.* New York: Harper & Row.

Jones, R. L. (1980). *Black psychology* (2nd ed.). New York: Harper & Row.

Kambon, K. (1992). *African personality in America.* Tallahassee, FL: Nubian Productions.

Karenga, M. (1990). *The book of coming forth by day.* Los Angeles: University of Sankore Press.

Lee, C. (1989). Editorial: Who speaks for multicultural counseling? *Journal of Multicultural Counseling and Development, 17,* 2–3.

Locke, D. C. (1993). *Increasing multicultural understanding.* Newbury Park, CA: Sage.

Marsela, A., & Pedersen, P. (1980). *Cross-cultural counseling and psychotherapy.* New York: Pergamon Press.

Myers, L. J. (1988). *Understanding the Africentric worldview.* Dubuque, IA: Kendall Hunt.

Nobles, W. (1972). African philosophy: Foundations for Black psychology. In R. L. Jones (Ed.), *Black psychology.* New York: Harper & Row.

Nobles, W. (1986). *African psychology: Toward its reclamation, reascension, & revitalization.* Oakland, CA: Black Family Institute.

Parham, T. A. (1993). *Psychological storms.* Chicago: African American Images.

Parham, T. A., & Parham, W. D. (in press). *Therapeutic approaches with African American populations.* Newbury Park, CA: Sage.

Phillips, F. (1990). NTU psychotherapy: An Afrocentric approach. *Journal of Black Psychology, 17*(1), 55–74.

Samuda, R. (1975). *Psychological testing and American minorities.* New York: Harper & Row.

Sue, D. W., Arredondo, P., & McDavis, R. (1992). Multicultural competencies/standards: A pressing need. *Journal of Counseling and Development, 70*(4), 477–486.

Sue, D. W. & Sue, D. (1992). *Counseling the culturally different* (2nd ed.). New York: Wiley.

Terman, L. (1916). *The measurement of intelligence.* Boston: Houghton-Mifflin.

Thomas, A., & Sillen, S. (1972). *Racism in psychiatry.* Secaucus, NJ: Citadel Press.

Thorndike, E. L. (1940). *Human nature and the social order.* New York: Macmillan.

White, J. L. (1972). Toward a Black psychology. In R. L. Jones (Ed.), *Black psychology.* New York: Harper & Row.

White, J. L. (1984). *The psychology of Blacks.* Englewood Cliffs, NJ: Prentice-Hall.

White, J. L., & Parham, T. A. (1990). *The psychology of Blacks: An African American perspective.* Englewood Cliffs, NJ: Prentice-Hall.

Williams, R. L. (1972). Abuses & misuses of testing Black children. In R. L. Jones (Ed.), *Black psychology.* New York: Harper & Row.

Woodson, C. G. (1933). *Miseducation of the Negro.* Washington, DC: Associated Publishers.

CHAPTER 12

MCT Theory and Native-American Populations

Teresa LaFromboise
Margo Jackson
Stanford University

Assumption Audit

- MCT theory emphasizes the essential function of culture and social contexts in the process of helping and in the roles that helpers play both inside and outside the helping encounter.
- Knowledge of and respect for a Native-American worldview and value system are fundamental for creating a trusting counselor-client relationship and for defining the counseling interventions most appropriate for each client.
- MCT theory notes that different cultures may hold very different worldviews or beliefs about what defines well-being, health, and illness.
- Native-American worldviews traditionally hold more spiritual, holistic, harmonious, and collective beliefs than Eurocentric worldviews about what constitutes health and well-being.
- Basic to most Native-American beliefs and traditional healing methods is the concept that wellness is harmony and that unwellness is disharmony in spirit, mind, and body.
- The most important element, the essence of the being, is the spirit.
- MCT theory's recognition of the importance of seeing the client in his or her cultural and social contexts may lead to finding more culturally appropriate solutions that may vastly change the way therapy is conducted.
- MCT theory also recognizes the equal or greater salience of collective identity for many culturally different groups; in many Native-American tribes, identity is not defined apart from the group but rather in relation to community, family, or clan.

- It makes sense to include as helpers not just counselors acting one-on-one, but also respected community leaders, traditional leaders, elders, and larger social units such as the extended family and other relevant groups.
- MCT theory's emphasis on coconstruction between the client and the counselor may be at odds with the mores surrounding appropriate help-seeking behavior with traditional healers and advice givers within the Native-American community.
- Traditional Native-American healing processes usually involve the client, therapist or healer, significant others, and community members.
- MCT theory's emphasis on expanding therapeutic interventions to involve the network of support systems surrounding the individual client validates the role of community involvement and outreach in multicultural counseling.
- Some Native Americans have mixed feelings regarding MCT theory's implication that counselors should learn about specific indigenous methods of helping and healing from Native-American cultures to supplement conventional Western approaches.
- Some Native Americans suspect that an overture by non-Native Americans to use indigenous therapeutic approaches (whether well intentioned or not) is just another attempt to devalue and appropriate Native cultural traditions.
- Particularly relevant is the issue of Native-American empowerment through interventionist strategies including raising the client's self-esteem, mobilizing interpersonal and material resources, creating or strengthening familial and extrafamilial support systems, and informing people about their tribal as well as societal rights and entitlements.
- Psychodynamic counseling approaches, in particular, have not only been ineffective with Native-American clients but also have caused counselors to misinterpret and dismiss Native cultural values.
- Client-centered approaches may create barriers for effective intervention with Native Americans because of the centrality of the client-therapist relationship that occurs as a one-on-one interaction outside the context of the community, family, or clan.
- Because cognitive-behavioral theory emphasizes person-environment interactions, it can lend itself readily to cultural adaptation consistent with Native-American worldviews.
- MCT theory's suggestion that the tenets of cognitive-behavioral theory—namely, its cause-effect, linear approach with emphasis on the future—conflicts with Native-American worldviews is challenged.
- MCT theory focuses on liberating clients from self-blame and helping them see themselves, their problems, and their own development in relation to their cultural context.
- Community-based cognitive-behavioral interventions provide one framework for counselor involvement in advocacy for empowerment.
- *Conscientizacao* suggests that the source of the problems presented in MCT

may not lie "in the client" but rather in the client's understandable responses to multiple societal oppression—that is, racism, classism, and economic deprivation.

• Outreach approaches grounded primarily in conventional Western counseling approaches cannot insure that counselors will understand the cultural and social context enough to develop trusting and credible relationships with Native-American communities.

Some aspects of MCT theory are relevant to developing culturally sensitive counseling interventions with Native Americans. These aspects include MCT theory's emphasis on the essential function of culture and social contexts in the helping process and in the roles that helpers play both inside and outside the helping encounter.

THE CULTURAL CONTEXT
OF COUNSELING

Proposition 1 (MCT is a metatheory of counseling and psychotherapy) and Corollary 1C (Different worldviews lead to different constructions of client concerns) of MCT theory suggest that understanding the worldviews of different cultures helps counselors more effectively conceptualize and treat culturally different clients. Knowledge of and respect for a Native-American worldview and value system—which varies according to the client's tribe, level of acculturation, area of residence, and other personal characteristics—is fundamental not only for creating the trusting counselor-client relationship vital to the helping process but also for defining the counseling interventions most appropriate for each client.

Definitions of Health and Well-Being

MCT theory notes that different cultures may hold very different worldviews or beliefs about what defines well-being, health, and illness. In contrast to Eurocentric (White, male, European) worldview assumptions underlying current dominant theories of counseling and psychotherapy, Native-American worldviews traditionally hold more spiritual, holistic, harmonious, and collective beliefs about what constitutes health and well-being (Trimble, Manson, Dinges, & Medicine, 1984).

Locust (1988) describes one aspect of traditional Native-American beliefs about well-being that contrasts with Western beliefs. Basic to most

Native-American beliefs and traditional healing methods is the concept that wellness is harmony and that unwellness is disharmony in spirit, mind, and body. The most important element, the essence of the being, is the spirit. Unlike traditional Native-American caregiving, Western medicine tends to treat the body for illness, and may refer a patient with emotional or mental problems to a mental-health specialist. That is, Western medicine treats the body and perhaps the mind, but not the spirit.

For this reason, a Native American with a broken leg, for example, may seek treatment not only from a physician to care for the physical injury but also from a medicine man or woman to care properly for the spirit:

> Treating the spirit is the process of finding out why the broken leg occurred, understanding the events in a spiritual rather than a physical sense, and then beginning the process of changing whatever it was in the body, mind, or spirit that was out of harmony enough to warrant a broken leg. (Locust, 1988, p. 321)

MCT theory's recognition of the importance of seeing the client in his or her cultural and social contexts may lead to finding more culturally appropriate solutions that may vastly change the way therapy is conducted.

Psychosocial Unit of Identity

MCT theory also recognizes the equal or greater salience of collective identity for many culturally different groups. Unlike the Eurocentric value placed on individualism, in many Native-American tribes, identity is not defined apart from the group but rather in relation to community, family, or clan. Given these contexts, it makes sense to include as helpers not just counselors acting one-on-one, but also respected community leaders, traditional leaders, and elders and larger social units such as the extended family and other relevant groups. However, MCT theory's emphasis on coconstruction between the client and the counselor may be at odds with the mores surrounding appropriate help-seeking behavior with traditional healers and advice givers within the Native-American community.

Expanding the Helping Roles/Relationships

Propositions 2, 5, and 6 advocate broadening the perspective of the helping relationship. Similarly, according to certain traditional Native-American views, an individual's psychological welfare must be considered in the context of the community. When problems arise in Native communities, they become not only problems of the individual but also problems of the community. The family, kin, and friends reconvene into an activated network to observe the individual, find comprehensible reasons for the individual's behavior, draw the individual out of isolation, and integrate the individual back into the social life of the group (LaFromboise, 1988). Strong social bonds among the extended family network surface to maintain a disturbed member within the community with minimal coercion (Attneave, 1969, 1982; Speck & Attneave, 1973).

Thus, unlike conventional psychological interventions, traditional Native-American healing processes usually involve more than the client and therapist or healer. Often, the client's significant others and community members are asked to participate (LaBarre, 1964; Wallace, 1958). The "cure" may require more than recognized healers; for instance, intercession with the spirit world. Thus the collective treatment of psychologically troubled individuals in tribal groups serves not only to heal the individual but also to reaffirm the norms of the entire group. MCT theory's emphasis on expanding therapeutic interventions to involve the network of support systems surrounding the individual client validates the role of community involvement and outreach in multicultural counseling. Yet, there are mixed feelings regarding MCT theory's implication that counselors should learn about specific indigenous methods of helping and healing from Native-American cultures to supplement conventional Western approaches. Opinion is divided among Native Americans on this issue; many suspect that an overture by non-Native Americans to use indigenous therapeutic approaches (whether well intentioned or not) is just another attempt to devalue and appropriate Native cultural traditions.

Helping As Empowerment

MCT theory underscores the importance of empowerment throughout the helping process. *Empowerment* refers to helping clients develop skills enabling them to exert interpersonal influence, improve role performance, and maintain effective support systems. It means doing whatever possible to help clients control their own lives. The underlying assumption of empowerment is that people are capable of taking control but often choose not to do so because social forces and institutions hinder their efforts. Particularly relevant is the issue of Native-American empowerment through interventionist strategies, including raising the client's self-esteem, mobilizing interpersonal and material resources, creating and strengthening familial and extrafamilial support systems, and informing people about their tribal as well as societal rights and entitlements (LaFromboise & Rowe, 1983).

For over two decades, many Native-American people have been "consumed with the tasks of revitalizing their culture, languages, and religions which are the heart of tribalism" (Fixico, 1985, p. 33) to revive their community empowerment. Native-American scholars have labeled this movement *retraditionalization*, which relies on the use of cultural beliefs, customs, and rituals as a means of overcoming problems and achieving Native self-determination. Tribal customs and traditions are used as sources of strength that provide culturally consistent coping mechanisms (Swinomish Tribal Community, 1991). For example, to cope with professional challenges, a client might recall an honoring ceremony performed for him or her on graduating from college.

STRENGTHS AND LIMITATIONS OF EURO-AMERICAN THEORIES APPLIED TO NATIVE AMERICANS

MCT theory implies that all theories have merit for culturally diverse clients. Below is a review of psychodynamic, client-centered, and cognitive behavioral theories for their respective consistency with Native-American life experiences and consequent merit in working with Native clients. MCT theory argues that elements of each of these theories could be combined to the extent that they are relevant to the client's concerns.

Psychodynamic Approaches

One might think that psychodynamic theory would be a forum of choice for Native-American clients who struggle with the yet unsolved problem of how personhood is achieved against the ever-present threat of being museumized or cast as a thing. In an article exploring individual therapy with clients from a Plains tribe, Gustafson (1976) reports how his secretary once presented him "with a cartoon showing an Indian, lying out of sight of the analyst on the analytic couch, saying 'I have a fear of vanishing'" (p. 238). Some 20 years later, a documentary on Native Americans, produced by Turner Broadcasting and entitled "The Invisible People," aired on national networks, confirming this fear of marginalization.

Psychodynamic counseling approaches, however, have not only been ineffective with Native-American clients but also have caused counselors to misinterpret and dismiss Native cultural values (Devereux, 1951; Trimble & Medicine, 1976). One aspect of psychodynamic counseling theory and process that conflicts with indigenous approaches concerns the role of the ego in therapy. On the one hand, psychodynamic therapy aims at strengthening the ego. On the other hand, therapy in Native-American communities aims at encouraging the client to transcend the ego by experiencing the self as embedded in and expressive of the community:

> Spiritual disciplines seek to limit the significance and range of the ego.
> Though they encourage effective ego functioning, it is only up to that
> point where the ego can run smoothly and cease to demand attention

and special treatment. The ego must remain a tool to be used by higher spiritual forces. The goal is not to strengthen the ego, but to transcend it. (Katz & Rolde, 1981, p. 370)

From the point of view of Native-American approaches, inner motivations and unique experiences involving repression, self-esteem, ambivalence, or insight are typically ignored. Alternatively, symptoms are interpreted as elements of social categories rather than personal states. New solutions to problems or new ways to see old problems become possible through interconnectedness with the community (LaFromboise, Trimble, & Mohatt, 1990).

From his psychoanalytic practice with Plains Indians in Montana and Wyoming, Gustafson (1976) has concluded that his clients needed to be a part of something larger than themselves. He argues that the narcissistic transference relationship of mirrored empathy that develops over time between the client and therapist in successful psychoanalysis was rarely an effective approach with Native-American clients. They did not typically seek such costly, long-term individual therapy focused on self and ego. Instead, such clients needed to transcend the ego and be more wholly involved in the community so as not to be lost in the bleakness of their surroundings. They sought a more problem-focused approach and a stronger connection to the continual ritual, traditions, and spirituality of the group.

Another central defining element in psychodynamic approaches to therapy—and a source of misconception in counseling Native Americans—is the therapeutic technique of transference interpretation. Because of the dictates of their theory, psychodynamic therapists tend to view clients "as gratifying infantile impulses, being defensive, having developmental defects, and resisting the therapy" (Bergin & Garfield, 1994, p. 477). In contrast, the high levels of therapeutic interpretation (generally considered to be necessary for a successful outcome in psychodynamic therapy) may be perceived by Native-American clients as intrusive control and experienced as hostile dominance. Such interactions are an altogether too familiar aspect of Native Americans' historical experience with oppressive majority-group members and institutions. Furthermore, psychodynamic transference interpretations focus on intrapsychic processes for analyzing unconscious motives and defenses rather than on cultural-context issues such as sociopolitical constraints or community empowerment through retraditionalization.

Katz and Rolde (1981) report that mental-health consumers have been increasingly combining psychodynamic therapy with alternatives such as spiritual approaches based on various meditations. Clients pragmatically viewed psychodynamic and alternative approaches not as conflicting but as complementary sources of help. Similarly, Native Americans often consulted different community resources for different purposes (Locust,

1988). However, Katz and Rolde found that, in contradiction to the clients' interests, most of the psychodynamically oriented therapists condemned clients' double involvement as "acting out" and resisting "working through" the transference.

Client-Centered Approaches

Although client-centered therapy's emphasis on internal values and autonomy is broadly consistent with traditional Native-American values, several aspects of this approach may create barriers for effective intervention with this population. The first problem lies with the centrality of the client-therapist relationship that occurs as a one-on-one interaction outside the context of the community, family, or clan. The effectiveness of client-centered therapy also depends on the length and quality of the client-counselor relationship. Cultural mistrust and cultural involvement may obstruct the ability to develop the ongoing alliance necessary for clinical influence.

This type of helping not only focuses on the client individually but also fails to take into account the role that the client may perform within the larger community system and the impact of the client's attitudes and behavior on that system. The client-centered approach generally emphasizes self-process and self-insight without considering the social or political issues involved.

In addition, a typical client-centered communication style between counselor and client emphasizes summarization, restatement, reflection of feeling, and minimal encouragers. This style may not work well with clients who cannot comfortably express or reflect on feelings (Dauphinais, Dauphinais, & Rowe, 1981). Traditionally raised Native-American clients place a high value on restraint of emotions and the ability to suffer in silence (Basso, 1970). The selective use of counseling responses consistent with these values has yet to be evaluated for their effectiveness when used with Native-American clients.

Cognitive-Behavioral Approaches

A third form of counseling intervention implemented in Native-American communities involves cognitive-behavior therapy. This form of therapy assumes a reciprocal influence between behavior and thoughts, feelings, physiological processes, and the consequences of behavior. A strength of cognitive-behavioral therapy is its action-oriented focus on the present rather than the past. Because cognitive-behavioral theory emphasizes person-environment interactions, it can lend itself readily to cultural adaptation consistent with Native-American worldviews. With this approach, counselors can readily attend how a client develops within his or her culture.

They can and should also consider the influence of external factors in a client's problem formation to empower the client to maintain his or her unique cultural perspective, rather than help the client adapt to dominant social standards.

Consider for example the development and validation of the Zuni Life Skills Development Curriculum, a cognitive-behavioral suicide-prevention program for high-school youth in the pueblo of Zuni (LaFromboise, 1995). A functional analysis of the problem revealed cultural differences in determining adaptive coping mechanisms: *cognitive* problems included negative views of self, the world, and the future; *behavioral* problems included the normalization of self-destructive behaviors and social isolation; and *emotional* problems included the restraint of emotions, especially depression and hopelessness, and conflicts surrounding acculturation demands (Belgarde & LaFromboise, 1988).

Although the responsibility for change rested on the individual students, the knowledge and experience of Zuni life proved essential to every aspect of the intervention. The intervention would never have occurred were it not for the collaboration of the community with counselors and teachers in initiating, designing, and delivering the intervention. Cognitive work on social and political injustices formed a major part of the intervention. Depression-management activities addressed profound loss, rejection, and abandonment. Counselors considered the historical roots of distrust and anger caused by oppression and the disregard for tribal rights when they coached clients on the expression of legitimate anger as well as forms of introspection and self-talk for anger regulation. Decision-making and goal-setting skills included determining how individual goals complemented short-term and long-term community goals. The effectiveness of this intervention was evaluated using a form of social validation (peer and trained Native-American assessments of skill development) as well as student self-reports of feelings, beliefs, and behaviors associated with preventing suicide (LaFromboise & Howard-Pitney, 1995). An assessment of community empowerment as a result of this community-based and extensive effort would have also been appropriate.

One caution that Trimble (1992) puts forth regarding cognitive-behavioral interventions with Native Americans involves the absolute necessity of home and community support for the intervention. "Teaching youths prevention skills within the context of a community rife with drug and alcohol use is likely to create emotional tension for them, cause them to question what is normative, and erode respect and allegiance to kin" (p. 269).

One can take issue with MCT theory's suggestion that the tenets of cognitive-behavioral theory—namely, its cause-effect, linear approach with emphasis on the future—would conflict with Native-American worldviews.

This theoretical approach has been modified effectively in numerous clinical applications with Native-American youth (assertion training, LaFromboise, 1983; professional skills development, LaFromboise, 1989; substance-abuse prevention, Schinke et al., 1988; and the reduction of tobacco use, Schinke, Moncher, Holden, Botvin, & Orlandi, 1989).

LIBERATION AND CRITICAL CONSCIOUSNESS

Corollaries 6A and 6B of MCT theory (p. 22) suggest that the theory strives to liberate consciousness at all levels, which brings together contextual and traditional approaches. These corollaries are drawn from Freire's (1972) seminal work. Sue, Ivey, and Pedersen believe that the role of the MCT counselor includes facilitating the process of *conscientizacao*, or critical consciousness. In other words, MCT theory may focus on liberating clients from self-blame and helping them see themselves, their problems, and their own development in relation to their cultural context. Community-based cognitive-behavioral intervention efforts provide one framework for counselor involvement in advocacy for empowerment. *Conscientizacao* suggests that the sources of the problems presented in MCT may not lie "in the client" but rather in the client's understandable responses to multiple societal oppressions—that is, racism, classism, and economic deprivation (Ivey, Ivey, & Simek-Morgan, 1993). This perspective supports the proposal, mentioned earlier, that counselors who hope to work effectively with Native-American clients must start from a conceptually grounded framework that includes an understanding of the sociopolitical history of oppression and current constraints that form the cultural context for their clients' presenting concerns.

Perhaps an even more important goal for counselors facilitating *conscientizacao*—in helping clients see themselves better in relation to their families and to the cultural influences on their development—is to focus on the wisdom, strength, coping resources, and unique competence involved in existing indigenous methods of helping and healing. Trimble et al. (1984) recommend that counselors search for alternative frameworks to conceptualize the relationship between Native Americans and their mental-health status, from which point counselors could focus on cultural competence as defined and operationalized by Native-American people. Such a reorientation would shift attention away from improving inherently biased nosologies and measures and, alternatively, "toward identifying the situations, developmental tasks, and skills required for an Indian person to meet particular needs and to achieve life goals in his or her own terms" (p. 212).

Nevertheless, outreach experience alone—particularly if grounded primarily in conventional Western counseling approaches—cannot insure that counselors will understand the cultural and social context enough to develop trusting and credible relationships with Native-American communities.

REFERENCES FOR CHAPTER 12

Attneave, C. L. (1969). Therapy in tribal settings and urban network interventions. *Family Process, 8,* 192–210.

Attneave, C. L. (1982). American Indian and Alaskan native families: Emigrants in their own homeland. In M. McGoldrick, J. Pearce, & J. Giordano (Eds.), *Ethnicity and family therapy* (pp. 55–83). New York: Guilford.

Basso, K. H. (1970). "To give up on words": Silence in the Western Apache culture. *Southwestern Journal of Anthropology, 26*(3), 213–230.

Belgarde, M. J., & LaFromboise, T. D. (1988, April). *Zuni adolescent suicide.* Paper presented at the annual meeting of the American Educational Research Association, New Orleans, LA.

Bergin, A. E., & Garfield, S. L. (Eds.). (1994). *Handbook of psychotherapy and behavior change.* New York: Wiley.

Dauphinais, P., Dauphinais, L., & Rowe, W. (1981). Effects of race and communication style on Indian perceptions of counselor effectiveness. *Counselor Education and Supervision, 21,* 72–80.

Devereux, G. (1951). Three technical problems in the psychotherapy of Plains Indian people. *American Journal of Psychotherapy, 5,* 411–423.

Fixico, M. (1985). The road to middle class Indian America. In C. E. Trafzer (Ed.), *American Indian identity: Today's changing perspectives* (pp. 29–37). Sacramento, CA: Sierra Oaks Publishing Company.

Freire, P. (1972). *Pedagogy of the oppressed.* New York: Herder and Herder.

Gustafson, J. P. (1976). The group matrix of individual therapy with Plains Indian people. *Contemporary Psychoanalysis, 12*(2), 227–239.

Ivey, A. E., Ivey, M. B., & Simek-Morgan, L. (1993). *Counseling and psychotherapy: A multicultural perspective.* Boston, MA: Allyn and Bacon.

Katz, R., & Rolde, E. (1981). Community alternatives to psychotherapy. *Psychotherapy: Theory, Research and Practice, 18*(3), 365–374.

LaBarre, W. (1964). Confessions as cathartic therapy in American Indian tribes. In A. Kiev (Ed.), *Magic, faith, and healing* (pp. 36–49). New York: Free Press.

LaFromboise, T. D. (1983). *Assertion training with American Indians: Cultural/behavioral issues for training.* Las Cruces, NM: Educational Resources Information Center Clearinghouse on Rural Education and Small Schools.

LaFromboise, T. D. (1988). American Indian mental health policy. *American Psychologist, 43*(5), 388–397.

LaFromboise, T. D. (1989). *Circles of women: Professional skills training with American Indian women.* Newton, MA: Women's Educational Equity Act Publishing Center.

LaFromboise, T. D. (1995). *American Indian life skills development curriculum.* Madison: University of Wisconsin Press.

LaFromboise, T. D., & Howard-Pitney, B. (1995). The Zuni Life Skills Development Curriculum: Description and evaluation of a suicide prevention program. *Journal of Counseling Psychology, 42*(4), 479–486.

LaFromboise, T. D., & Rowe, W. (1983). Skills training for bicultural competence: Rationale and application. *Journal of Counseling Psychology, 30,* 589–595.

LaFromboise, T. D., Trimble, J. E., & Mohatt, G. V. (1990). Counseling intervention and American Indian tradition: An integrative approach. *The Counseling Psychologist, 18*(4), 628–654.

Locust, C. (1988). Wounding the spirit: Discrimination and traditional American Indian belief systems. *Harvard Educational Review, 58*(3), 315–330.

Schinke, S., Moncher, M., Holden, G., Botvin, G., & Orlandi, M. (1989). American Indian youth and substance abuse: Tobacco use problems, risk factors and preventive interventions. *Health Education Research, Theory and Practice, 4,* 137–144.

Schinke, S., Orlandi, M., Botvin, G., Gilchrist, L., Trimble, J., & Locklear, V. (1988). Preventing substance abuse among American Indian adolescents: A bicultural competence skills approach. *Journal of Counseling Psychology, 35,* 87–90.

Speck, R., & Attneave, C. (1973). *Family process.* New York: Pantheon.

Swinomish Tribal Community. (1991). *A gathering of wisdoms. Tribal mental health: A cultural perspective.* LaConner, WA: Swinomish Tribal Mental Health Project.

Trimble, J. E. (1992). A cognitive-behavioral approach to drug abuse prevention and intervention with American Indian youth. In L. Vargas & J. Kos-Chioino (Eds.), *Working with cultures* (pp. 246–275). San Francisco: Jossey-Bass.

Trimble, J. E., Manson, S. M., Dinges, N. G., & Medicine, B. (1984). American Indian conceptions of mental health: Reflections and directions. In P. Pedersen, N. Sartorius, & A. Marsella (Eds.), *Mental health services: The cross-cultural context* (pp. 199–220). Beverly Hills, CA: Sage.

Trimble, J. E., & Medicine, B. (1976). Development of theoretical models and levels of interpretation in mental health. In J. Westermeyer (Ed.), *Anthropology and mental health* (pp. 161–200). The Hague, Netherlands: Mouton.

Wallace, A. (1958). Dreams and wishes of the soul: A type of psychoanalytic theory among seventeenth century Iroquois. *American Anthropologist, 60,* 234–248.

CHAPTER 13

MCT THEORY AND ASIAN-AMERICAN POPULATIONS

Frederick T. L. Leong
The Ohio State University

Assumption Audit

- MCT theory summarizes crucial issues in counseling.
- MCT theory delineates the shortcomings of existing theories according to their lack of attention to culture.
- MCT theory has integrated the experiences of many multicultural counselors and therapists.
- By recognizing human interactions, MCT theory has adopted the new science of complexity.
- MCT theory provides the foundation for empirical exploration.
- MCT theory advocates openness to new information.
- It is essential to recognize multiculturalism as a fourth force in psychology.
- MCT theory has established why such a theory is needed, what the theory looks like, and how one would use the theory.
- MCT theory helps avoid stereotypes of Asian Americans by focusing on within-group differences.
- MCT theory discusses such variables as worldviews.
- MCT theory addresses the power imbalance between therapists and clients.
- MCT theory should be expanded to provide a multilevel ecological perspective.
- MCT theory needs to be more closely tied to clinical utility, specifying how the counselor selects culturally appropriate strategies, tactics, and tools.
- The field is not on the verge of a major paradigm shift; MCT theory is more like a wish list.
- Counselors and therapists are not likely to embrace MCT theory for some time.

- MCT theory is understood better in the complexity of the client's perspective than in that of the counselor's perspective.
- MCT theory needs to demonstrate incremental validity.
- MCT theory needs more of an interdisciplinary base.

This chapter has three sections. In the first, I shall summarize my perceptions of the strengths of the MCT theory proposed by Sue, Ivey, and Pedersen. In the second, I shall comment on how the theory relates to specific issues for Asian-American populations. In the third, I shall present some constructive criticisms and suggestions regarding the theory.

Before you proceed, I offer the following information about my background, theoretical leanings, and potential biases. I am a first-generation Chinese American who immigrated to the United States from Malaysia for undergraduate studies. During my training as a counseling psychologist at the University of Maryland, I developed several additional interests. First, my personal and professional interest in cross-cultural issues in counseling and psychology began there. For instance, I met my wife in college. Further, because she is European by descent both my daughters are Amerasians. Second, I did a two-year internship at Dartmouth Medical School that focused on long-term psychodynamic psychotherapy. Third, I also have a strong interest in industrial/organizational psychology. Therefore, in addition to teaching and supervising graduate students in cross-cultural counseling and psychodynamic psychotherapy, I actively consult with organizations regarding career development and cross-cultural issues.

STRENGTHS OF THE
MCT THEORY

The MCT theory proposed by Sue, Ivey, and Pedersen has much to recommend it. This theory masterfully summarizes some of the most crucial issues in applying the cross-cultural dimension to the current field of counseling and psychotherapy. As the proponents of this theory, Sue, Ivey, and Pedersen each bring a rich and unique perspective on cross-cultural counseling to their theory. Each is a leading figure in the field with significant and long-standing contributions to the profession's understanding of cross-cultural counseling. MCT theory represents an excellent distillation and integration of their thinking into a unified theory.

As with many new theories, the primary impetus for its development is the inadequacy of existing theories (Kuhn, 1981). MCT theory clearly and comprehensively delineates the shortcomings of current counseling theories with regard to culturally different clients. First, many of these contemporary theories do not take into account the importance of culture and operate according to the myth of client uniformity (see Leong, 1986). Second, MCT theory points out the political framework of the counseling and therapy enterprise as embedded in the larger social context. In doing so, MCT theory provides specific philosophical perspectives regarding the need for a theory of multicultural counseling and therapy and how one would implement such a theory. Sue et al. also argue convincingly that using MCT theory would be superior to operating without it.

The current MCT theory is also quite valuable in that it has integrated many experiences of various cross-cultural counselors and therapists. Thus, counselors and therapists who have been working with culturally different clients will find MCT theory quite consistent with their clinical experiences. In other words, MCT theory has a high level of external validity for those involved in cross-cultural training and practice.

MCT theory has also adopted the new science of complexity by recognizing that individuals and various groups are indeed complex, adaptive systems that are nonlinear, multi-variate, non-equilibrium (constantly changing with no stability), open, multiple equilibria (with many different states of equilibrium), pattern forming, information processing, adapting, evolving, co-evolving, self-organizing, and consisting of emergent properties (Leong, in press). The reaffirmation of the complexity of human interactions, particularly cross-cultural interactions, provides a long overdue antidote to the linear, unidimensional, and reductionistic thinking that has so dominated psychology and the social sciences in the past few decades. I also find the use of the constructionist perspective helpful toward understanding culture's influence on counseling and therapy. Gergen (1985), among many others, has provided cogent arguments for the need to adopt this constructionist perspective.

As everyone knows, a good theory consists of testable hypotheses. MCT theory has gone a long way toward making the implicit assumptions of the field explicit. By presenting these assumptions in a series of propositions and corollaries, MCT theory has provided the foundation for empirical exploration of the key variables in cross-cultural counseling and therapy. Though I have some concerns about the propositions' specificity, discussed in the last section of this chapter, MCT theory has taken some important first steps in the right direction. A useful aphorism comes to mind: "You cannot solve a problem until you have measured it."

MCT theory also advocates an openness to new information. This respect for multiple and alternative perspectives is essential. As you know, psychology as the study of human behavior recognizes the dynamic nature of human interactions; only an evolving and dynamic theory of counseling can keep pace with the phenomena under consideration. Sue et al. show great courage in "practicing what they preach" by their openness to opinions regarding their evolving theory, inviting others to respond openly to their formulations.

Both experienced counselors and therapists as well as those in training would gain a great deal by reading MCT theory. All counselors and psychotherapists would benefit from applying the theory's recommendations for becoming a better therapist. Unless they choose not to serve a large segment of the population, counselors and therapists will have to recognize multicultural counseling as the fourth force in psychology (Pedersen, 1991). More and more counselors and psychologists, including those on accrediting committees, are coming to recognize cross-cultural counseling competencies as fundamental—that is, they can no longer be relegated to the interests of those in specific work environments such as inner cities. MCT theory will serve as the guide for counselors and therapists who embark on this journey of multicultural counseling. In summary, MCT theory has clearly set forth why a theory of multicultural counseling is needed, what that theory should look like, and how one would use that theory.

IMPLICATIONS FOR ASIAN-AMERICAN POPULATIONS

Any discussion of Asian-American therapy must begin with the caveat that the phrase *Asian Americans* represents a diverse set of ethnic groups with as much between-group variation as within-group variation. As such, because this section presents generalizations, you should keep a constant eye out for within-group variance. Interestingly, much of the knowledge base on the psychology of Asian Americans has been developed in the last two decades (see the historical review by Cheung, 1994, and the historical monograph by Leong, 1993). Much of this knowledge base was dominated early on by the writings of two brothers, Derald and Stanley Sue (e.g., D. W. Sue & Kirk, 1972, 1973, 1975; D. W. Sue & S. Sue, 1972; S. Sue, 1977; S. Sue & Kitano, 1973; S. Sue & McKinney, 1975; S. Sue & Wagner, 1973). Hence, certain books became the clinical and theoretical foundation for counseling and psychotherapy with Asian Americans (D. W. Sue, 1981; S. Sue & Morishima, 1982). A comprehensive bibliography on Asian Americans (Morishima, Sue, Teng, Zane, & Cram, 1979) was also a valuable resource. Also, a series of critical reviews integrated the existing literature (e.g., Leong, 1986; Root, 1985; Toupin, 1980; Yamamoto, 1978).

Considerable progress in this knowledge base has been made in the past decade (see in particular D. W. Sue & D. Sue, 1990; Uba, 1994). A more recent bibliography on Asian Americans has been produced by the American Psychological Association (Leong & Whitfield, 1992). Critical reviews on counseling and therapy with Asian Americans continue to appear regularly (e.g., Kinzie, 1989; Marsella, 1993; True, 1990). Indeed, several journals have recently published special issues on the mental health of Asian Americans (e.g., Leong, 1994; S. Sue, Nakamura, Chung, & Yee-Bradbury, 1994).

This information provides a context for the implications of MCT theory for Asian-American populations. The brief review also identifies important resources for those interested in reading more about counseling and therapy with Asian Americans. While such literature continues to grow, several major themes have emerged that can serve as focal points in the following discussion, which claims to be neither comprehensive nor exhaustive.

Cultural Identity

One of these themes is the nature and extent of ethnic identity and acculturation conflicts among Asian-American clients. MCT theory has appropriately made the client's and the counselor's cultural identity a central component in the theory (see Propositions 2 and 3). This is consistent with many recent theoretical formulations within the field of cross-cultural counseling in general (e.g., Atkinson, Thompson, & Grant, 1993) and those concerning Asian Americans in particular (see Leong, 1986; D. W. Sue & D. Sue, 1990; S. Sue & Morishima, 1982; Uba, 1994). Just as racial identity has been a key variable in understanding African-American worldviews, ethnic identity and acculturation are quickly becoming the focal point of much research on Asian Americans (see Leong & Chou, 1994; Tata & Leong, 1994).

Given the importance of cultural identity and the acculturation process for understanding the mental health of Asian Americans, I was very encouraged to see the central position given to this theme in MCT theory. For example, Proposition 2 states that "both counselor and client identities are formed and embedded in multiple levels of experiences . . . and contexts," while its various corollaries spell out its specific implications. A full understanding of this issue will serve as a safeguard against using general information about Asian Americans in a stereotypical fashion. For example, though many Asian Americans somaticize their emotional problems (Leong, 1986; S. Sue & Morishima, 1982; Uba, 1994), not all Asian Americans do so; thus, an assessment of the Asian-American client's acculturation level and cultural identity would provide the most guidance (see Atkinson et al., 1993).

Using Culture-Specific Variables

Another major theme in the relevant literature is the need for counselors to learn and use culture-specific variables about Asian Americans. These variables have ranged from the importance of harmony in interpersonal relations and the associated need to avoid loss of face to the preference for more subtle and indirect forms of communication. Value differences provide another central culture-specific variable. For example, the value orientation of individualism versus collectivism is becoming a key variable for understanding how Asian Americans might differ from Euro-Americans (Markus & Kitayama, 1991; Tata & Leong, 1994). MCT theory has created a central place for these culture-specific variables by discussing them as worldviews (Proposition 1) and as cultural values (Proposition 4).

One can illustrate the importance of culture-specific variables in yet another component of MCT theory. Corollary 3D, concerning the inherent power imbalance in which the therapist is one-up and the client one-down, implies the need for counselors to monitor and correct such power differentials, moving toward an egalitarian relationship with clients. Such a hierarchy of power between counselors and clients is real; however, its effect varies depending on cultural differences. For example, it is well known that among Asian Americans, those who are "traditional" or less acculturated will tend to expect a hierarchical relationship with mental-health professionals as well as physicians. Any change in that hierarchy will result in these clients' frustration and a perception that the mental-health professional lacks the expertise or knowledge to be of assistance. Herein lies a major dilemma of any theory of multicultural counseling. Though MCT theory must recognize and delineate culture-specific variables, the more specific the theory becomes in its recommendations, the greater the danger of running counter to the values of a given cultural group, as in the case of egalitarianism and Asian Americans. Thus, it should not surprise one that MCT theory consists primarily of philosophical propositions in contrast to specific prescriptions (more about this problem later).

Underuse of Western Services

Another major theme that arises in literature about Asian Americans is their tendency to underutilize formal and Western-oriented mental-health services (S. Sue & Morishima, 1982). The formulations in MCT theory regarding this theme remind me of a cartoon I read in which two goldfish in a bowl argue as to whether there's life outside of their bowl. In the first frame, one fish argues that there cannot be life outside water. The second frame shows two people sitting in front of the television looking out the window arguing if there is life on other planets. Within that second frame, of course, sits the same goldfish bowl. I share this cartoon to emphasize that in psychology one needs to regularly remind oneself of the importance of a multilevel ecological perspective (Bronfenbrenner, 1977).

Like the first goldfish, however, the current MCT theory is engaged primarily in only one level of analysis. For many Asian-American clients, the other levels of analysis within their culture-specific ecology are just as important, if not more important. Rogler, Malgady, and Rodriguez (1989) offer an ecological model of mental-health services that is particularly helpful here. They point out in their framework for research that to increase one's understanding of the mental health of Hispanics, one needs to recognize that there are five phases within the ecology of mental-health services. Culture serves as a major determinant in each phase, with one phase serving as a "filter" leading onto the next phase. The model begins with the emergence of mental-health problems in the community, or *psychiatric epidemiology*, or the kinds of mental-health problems in the community, how they are manifested, and they are dealt with. In this regard, MCT theory does pay some attention to the notions of indigenous healers and to the fact that conceptions of mental health and mental illness vary across cultures.

Rogler et al.'s (1989) second phase is the help-seeking process, or what others have referred to as *mental-health-service utilization*. Here again, culture serves as a filter according to which certain individuals within those communities, when they experience a particular threshold of problems, will seek professional psychological help. Many individuals within these communities, for a variety of reasons, tend not to seek help from the formal mental-health system despite high levels of stress and significant psychological disorders. That is, Asian Americans tend to "drop out" at this second stage.

Once someone does make contact with the mental-health system, the third phase occurs: *diagnosis and assessment.* In this phase, mental-health professionals begin to formulate the nature, extent, and severity of the problems being presented. Once again, culture is assumed to be a central determinant.

In the fourth phase, actual *interventions* are recommended and implemented for the person seeking help. Finally, at the end of the prescribed treatment, whether terminated mutually or prematurely by the client, comes the fifth and final stage. In the *therapeutic outcome*, the individual returns to the community.

MCT theory is primarily located in the third and fourth phase of this model—namely, assessment and psychotherapeutic interventions—and while it acknowledges the other components and phases, it pays relatively little attention to them. This is particularly important for the Asian-American population because many Asian Americans will experience mental-health problems in the community and will not seek help for a variety of reasons, which is why the studies of help-seeking behavior among Asian

Americans are so crucial. Because many Asian Americans tend not to enter counseling and therapy (S. Sue & Morishima, 1982), MCT theory is really tackling only a small part of the problem in addressing mental-health services for Asian Americans. Hence, while MCT theory is valuable for improving the kind of therapy provided to those Asian Americans who do come in for services, it does not address the issues of the many Asian Americans who need the mental-health services but choose not to come in. Hence, MCT theory needs to provide much more information on phases one and two. To summarize, I believe that it would be useful for MCT to expand the theory to provide a multilevel ecological perspective as illustrated by either Bronfenbrenner (1977) or Rogler et al.'s (1989) model.

CONSTRUCTIVE CRITICISMS AND SUGGESTIONS

I offer the following constructive criticisms and suggestions for MCT with the recognition that as the theory improves, it will better serve all the participants in the cross-cultural counseling enterprise, including Asian-American populations. Theories vary along various dimensions, from parsimoniousness to testability. In general, MCT theory fares quite well in terms of its hypotheses and also its inclusion of multiple perspectives. However, in terms of clinical utility, MCT theory currently scores only fairly well. In other words, the theory at present only provides somewhat useful ideas for clinical use; it must offer much more specific information for it to be practical for practicing counselors and therapists. For example, in Corollary 1B, MCT theory does not specify *how* the counselor would go about selecting the most culturally appropriate and consistent approach to use with clients, just that they should. Though MCT theory has done an excellent job in providing general strategies and recommendations for approaching the culturally different client, it has not provided any specific *tactics* and *tools* for working with the culturally different client.

As mentioned earlier, an inherent dilemma exists in any theory of multicultural counseling because of cultural relativism. Given the numerous cultures involved and the associated complexity, such a theory is limited to generalizations that would apply across all or most cultural groups. Furthermore, such generalizations and philosophical perspectives have limited clinical utility. MCT's principles tell the counselor how to approach clients in general (e.g., use a counseling modality consistent with the client's cultural values) but not how to counsel a particular client (e.g., a White therapist discussing the issue of an authoritarian father of a second-generation Chinese-American college student). The dilemma lies in the fact that cultural relativism as manifested in group differences makes proposing specific guidelines appropriate to all groups extremely difficult (see my earlier example of power issues for Asian Americans). In psychodynamic language, MCT formulations are akin to the principle that psychodynamic therapy's primary goal is "making the unconscious conscious." While psychodynamic theory goes on to offer dream analysis, projective tests, interpretation of transference, etc., as tools for achieving this goal, MCT lacks this specificity. MCT theory thus needs specific tools and guidelines on when to use them.

Some of these new tools may be developed by adapting those from other theoretical models. For example, according to psychodynamic theory, the therapeutic alliance is the coming together of the mature observing ego of the therapist and that of the client. This therapeutic or working alliance forms the foundation for the analysis of the neurotic and transferential elements in the client's personality. In integrating this notion of the therapeutic alliance into MCT theory, one sees that the therapist needs to monitor the cultural issues that are occurring within the counseling dyad. Without a doubt, the client is engaged in the same process in forming the alliance. In essence, what this take on MCT theory is proposing is that counselors need to define, assess, and measure this cultural axis within the therapeutic alliance. To the extent that they serve as barriers, cultural issues are essential to the dynamics of the situation, for they are the actual psychopathology or neurosis that is being treated. In other words, the therapeutic alliance consists of at least two axes—namely, the personality axis and the cultural axis—both of which are crucial to the counseling relationship. The perfect example to illustrate this distinction is Ridley's (1984) formulation of functional and cultural paranoia among African Americans and the importance of not confusing the two phenomena. The former is of course a personality problem, while the latter is a cultural adapational style that should not be pathologized.

On a broader note, the authors of MCT theory imply that the field is on the verge of a major paradigm shift. Personally, I am somewhat more pessimistic. According to Kuhn's (1981) ideas of scientific revolutions and when particular paradigms will shift, the current MCT formulation is more like a wish list; I believe that the paradigm shift is quite far from realization. While minorities are becoming significantly important in this country, a disproportionate number of majority clients still benefit from the dominant traditional Western-based theories of counseling and therapy. I do not believe that multicultural counseling and therapy as proposed in this book will become a dominant paradigm in the next two decades. To put it more concretely, if the American Psychological Association conducted a psychotherapy survey at the beginning of every decade, MCT theory would not be listed among the top five theoretical orientations by therapists for many decades to come. I assume that this particular theory of MCT has been proposed in an attempt to expand traditional Western theories so that the experiences of racial/ethnic minorities will be recognized, respected, and addressed. One must remember, though, that the majority of Americans, of European descent, will cling to what is most comfortable to them culturally and most therapists will continue to practice Western-oriented counseling and psychotherapy given the demand. Such is the politics of numbers.

I am happy to see that MCT theory has incorporated many elements of the science of complexity into its formulations. The characteristics of the complex adaptive systems are indeed important to understanding cross-cultural interactions. Many unidimensional theories of counseling are inadequate because they are limited to linear and nondynamic formulations (Leong, in press). However, just as cultural relativism makes it extremely difficult for MCT theory to offer specific prescriptions, the theory's use of the science of complexity may result in many counselors moving even further away from the Western scientific aspects of psychotherapy. Part of this danger comes from MCT theory's recognition that clients, counselors, the relationships they form, and the cultures they come from are complex phenomena that one cannot reduce to linear equations. It should not surprise you that many counselors would embrace MCT formulations, since these counselors deal daily with the complexity of their clients' lives. However, as they find support for their daily experience of complexity in counseling their clients, they become even more convinced of the limited value of science in guiding what they do. Such a polarization of the scientific and practical sides of the field would be detrimental in the long run. The challenge is how to introduce the elements of complexity into science so that it becomes more relevant while at the same time not abandoning the values of the scientific method. Without science, much of what one does becomes journalism, carrying as much weight as personal opinion.

I also recommend that MCT theory consider incremental validity in its future revisions (Sechrest, 1963). The concept of incremental validity may be illustrated with an example. In a situation where several predictors are used to predict a particular outcome, each predictor accounts for a certain amount of variance in the outcome. For example, one may evaluate the role of client-centered therapy (predictor) as applied to a particular problem (depression) and measure the outcome (improvement). If one adds any elements, concepts, or models to client-centered therapy, the value of that additional element is determined by whether it increases the validity with regard to the prediction of the outcome. Hence the use of antidepressants (the new element) would be said to have *incremental validity* if it increased the variance predicted (amount of improvement) for client-centered therapy alone. In other words, for new variables or models to have incremental validity, it must increase the success of the outcome.

In the same way, MCT theory should be conceptualized within the framework of incremental validity. Specifically, studies should compare two groups of therapists: one group is taught only traditional Western-oriented therapy, while the second group is taught traditional Western-oriented therapy *and* MCT. MCT would be considered to have incremental validity if the latter group accounted for higher variance (i.e., produced a better outcome for their clients) than the former group. Only then could one say that MCT theory had added anything substantive to the current enterprise of providing effective counseling and psychotherapy. While the authors of MCT theory do discuss this, I would recommend that they more specifically address the issue of how to measure the incremental validity of MCT.

Finally, I would recommend that the authors of MCT theory look to disciplines beyond counseling and therapy for their knowledge bases. While MCT theory has referred to these issues, it has tended not to integrate these models directly. Specifically, MCT theory would benefit tremendously from the use of various social-psychological theories that account for the current state of affairs. In other words, why have cultural differences been ignored in therapy that springs from Eurocentric approaches? Just as theories and models of counseling and therapy are cultural constructions, cultural constructions are the outcomes of social-psychological phenomena—namely, intergroup and group dynamics. The future for advancing the fourth force in counseling and therapy lies in understanding these social-psychological dynamics.

REFERENCES FOR CHAPTER 13

Atkinson, D. R., Thompson, C. E., & Grant, S. K. (1993). A three-dimensional model for counseling racial/ethnic minorities. *The Counseling Psychologist, 21,* 257–277.

Bronfenbrenner, U. (1977). Toward an experimental ecology of human development. *American Psychologist, 32,* 513–531.

Cheung, F. K. (1994). Asian American and Pacific Islanders' mental health issues: A historical perspective. *Asian American and Pacific Islander Journal of Health, 2,* 94–107.

Gergen, K. J. (1985). The social constructionist movement in modern psychology. *American Psychologist, 40,* 266–275.

Kinzie, J. D. (1989). Therapeutic approaches to traumatized Cambodian refugees. *Journal of Traumatic Stress, 2,* 75–91.

Kuhn, T. (1981). *The structure of scientific revolution* (2nd ed.). Chicago: University of Chicago Press.

Leong, F. T. L. (1986). Counseling and psychotherapy with Asian Americans: Review of the literature. *Journal of Counseling Psychology, 33,* 196–206.

Leong, F. T. L. (1993). History of Asian American Psychology. *Monograph Series, Asian American Psychological Association, 1.*

Leong, F. T. L. (1994). Special issue on the mental health of Asian Americans and Pacific Islanders: Guest Editor's Introduction. *Asian American and Pacific Islander Journal of Health, 2,* 89–91.

Leong, F. T. L. (in press). Towards an integrative model for cross-cultural counseling and psychotherapy. *Applied and Preventive Psychology: Current Scientific Perspectives.*

Leong, F. T. L., & Chou, E. L. (1994). The role of ethnic identity and acculturation in the vocational behavior of Asian Americans: An integrative review. *Journal of Vocational Behavior, 44,* 155–172.

Leong, F. T. L., & Whitfield, J. R. (Eds.). (1992). *Asians in the United States: Abstracts of the psychological and behavioral literature, 1967–1991.* (Bibliographies in psychology, no. 11). Washington, DC: American Psychological Association.

Markus, H. & Kitayama, S. (1991). Culture and the self: Implications for cognition, emotion, and motivation. *Psychological Review, 98,* 224–253.

Marsella, A. J. (1993). Counseling and psychotherapy with Japanese Americans: Cross-cultural considerations. *American Journal of Orthopsychiatry, 63,* 200–208.

Morishima, J. K., Sue, S., Teng, L. N., Zane, N. W. S., and Cram, J. R. (1979). *Handbook of Asian-American/Pacific Islander Mental Health* (Vol. 1). Rockville, MD: National Institute of Mental Health.

Pedersen, P. B. (1991). Multiculturalism as a generic approach to counseling. *Journal of Counseling and Development, 70,* 6–12.

Ridley, C. R. (1984). Clinical treatment of the nondisclosing black client: A therapeutic paradox. *American Psychologist, 39,* 1234–1244.

Rogler, L. H., Malgady, R. G., & Rodriguez, O. (1989). *Hispanics and mental health: A framework for research.* Malabar, FL: Krieger Publishing Company.

Root, M. (1985). Guidelines for facilitating therapy with Asian American clients. *Psychotherapy, 22,* 349–356.

Sechrest, L. (1963). Incremental validity: A recommendation. *Educational and Psychological Measurement, 23,* 153–158.

Sue, D. W. (1981). *Counseling the culturally different: Theory and practice.* New York: Wiley.

Sue, D. W., & Kirk, B. A. (1972). Psychological characteristics of Chinese-American students. *Journal of Counseling Psychology, 19,* 471–478.

Sue, D. W., & Kirk, B. A. (1973). Differential characteristics of Japanese-American college students. *Journal of Counseling Psychology, 20,* 142–148.

Sue, D. W., & Kirk, B. A. (1975). Asian Americans: Use of counseling and psychiatric services on a college campus. *Journal of Counseling Psychology, 22,* 84–86.

Sue, D. W., & Sue, D. (1990). *Counseling the culturally different: Theory and practice.* (2nd ed.). New York: Wiley.

Sue, D. W., & Sue, S. (1972). Counseling Chinese-Americans. *Personnel and Guidance Journal, 50,* 637–644.

Sue, D. W., & Sue, S. (1987). Cultural factors in the clinical assessment of Asian Americans. *Journal of Consulting and Clinical Psychology, 55,* 479–487.

Sue, S. (1977). Community mental health services to minority groups: Some optimism, some pessimism. *American Psychologist, 32,* 616–624.

Sue, S., & Kitano, H. H. L. (1973). Stereotypes as a measure of success. *Journal of Social Issues, 29*, 83–98.

Sue, S., & McKinney, H. (1975). Asian-Americans in the community mental health care system. *American Journal of Orthopsychiatry, 45*, 111–118.

Sue, S., & Morishima, J. K. (1982). *The mental health of Asian-Americans.* San Francisco: Jossey-Bass.

Sue, S., Nakamura, C. Y., Chung, R. C. Y., & Yee-Bradbury, C. (1994). Mental health research on Asian Americans. *Journal of Community Psychology, 22*, 61–67.

Sue, S., & Sue, D. W. (1971). Chinese-American personality and mental health. *Amerasia Journal, 1*, 36–49.

Sue, S., & Sue, D. W. (1974). MMPI comparisons between Asian-American and non-Asian students utilizing a student health psychiatric clinic. *Journal of Counseling Psychology, 21*, 423–427.

Sue, S., & Wagner, N. (1973). *Asian Americans: Psychological perspectives.* Palo Alto, CA: Science and Behavior Books.

Tata, S. P., & Leong, F. T. L. (1994). Individualism-collectivism, network orientation, and acculturation as predictors of attitudes towards seeking professional psychological help among Chinese Americans. *Journal of Counseling Psychology. 41*, 280–287.

Toupin, E. S. W. A. (1980). Counseling Asians: Psychotherapy in the context of racism and Asian-American history. *American Journal of Orthopsychiatry, 50*, 76–86.

True, R. H. (1990). Psychotherapeutic issues with Asian American women. *Sex Roles, 22*, 477–486.

Uba, L. (1994). *Asian Americans: Personality patterns, identity, and mental health.* New York: Guilford.

Yamamoto, J. (1978). Therapy for Asian-Americans. *Journal of National Medical Association, 70*, 267–270.

CHAPTER 14

MCT THEORY AND LATINA(O)-AMERICAN POPULATIONS

Patricia Arredondo
Empowerment Workshops, Inc., Boston

Assumption Audit

- MCT theory is a transitional object and reference point to guide and support visions for competence and ethics in inclusive research, training, and practice.
- MCT theory is based on multiple methodologies and realities from a broad base of populations.
- MCT theory emphasizes the importance of the client's viewpoint.
- MCT theory goes beyond existing theories to create meaning about human behavior in many contexts.
- MCT theory reflects the priorities of "Workforce 2000" in its complexity.
- The MCT propositions are interrelated.
- MCT theory promotes the centrality of cultural identity for Latina(o)s and others.
- MCT theory is relevant for Hispanics because of its heterogeneous definition of *culture*.
- MCT theory rightly emphasizes spirituality and belief systems.
- MCT theory links interventions with the client's belief system.
- MCT theory validates historical reality and determinants.
- MCT theory interprets behavior in its cultural context, such as the importance of family in Latina(o) culture.
- MCT theory emphasizes the importance of self-awareness and self-assessment.
- MCT theory points out that meaning is formed and embedded in symbolic words such as *aliens* and *illegals.*
- MCT theory emphasizes strengths, not deficits; empowerment, not criticism.

When I'm out with workers, they teach me every single day. It's an amazing thing. Obviously, I don't know everything, I just know a little bit. Perhaps because I've made more mistakes than anybody else, I've had a chance to learn more than anybody else. But still, the workers teach me every single day as I teach them.

Cesar Chavez (Levy, 1974, p. 520)

The words of Cesar Chavez, a leader and hero to thousands of Mexican migrant workers, also inspire those of us engaged in defining and creating new ways to recognize the value and worth of all people. By example, not words alone, Chavez demonstrated the importance of "expanding personal, family, group, and organizational consciousness," as Sue, Ivey, and Pedersen advocate (p. 22). His mission, like that of counselors and therapists, is about paradigm change, with cultural constructs as keys to multicultural knowledge-building and practice, a legacy for future counseling generations. The proposed MCT theory is both the transitional object as well as reference point that will guide and support visions for more competent, ethical, and inclusive counseling research, practice, and training.

The six propositions in Chapter 2, describing shortcomings in contemporary theories, reflect the thinking of many counselors and educators who have carried the multicultural banner for over 20 years. What makes these propositions compelling is that they are based on multiple methodologies and realities and research and interventions with broad-based populations, unlike almost all theories taught today. Counselors who have worked deliberately with culturally, economically, linguistically, and racially diverse groups can readily identify with the proposed theory because it articulates the need to understand and work with clients from their own contexts, viewing people as multicultural entities with a range of dimensions that relate to their sense of personal identity (Arredondo, 1994). MCT theory promotes the valuation of culture-specific helping roles and approaches, and acknowledges that the cultural identity of client and counselor must be evaluated in the context of a society built on dominant-subordinate relationships. Furthermore, with relationships and helping as their focus, counselors must be prepared to learn anew, admit what they do not know, and be willing to adapt their thinking and practice to become culturally competent and ethical (Sue, Arredondo, & McDavis, 1992). In short, the proposed MCT model goes far beyond existing theories because it is derived from data emerging from research designs that try to create meaning about human behavior in context—sociocultural, historical, and sociopolitical. These approaches apply to the population-at-large, not just persons of color.

From a historical perspective, the need for preparing culturally effective counselors based on MCT theory is even greater today than 15–20 years ago. It requires, though, a planned educational program of theory and intensive practice with regard to multicultural populations (Arredondo-Dowd & Gonsalves, 1980). Domestic and international changes introduce new challenges to the counseling profession daily. Be they international migrations, health-care reform, high dropout rates among minority youth, downsizing of U.S. businesses, the AIDS epidemic, or violence in the workplace, these changes require counselors' purview of awareness, knowledge, and skills to expand. Developing and increasing multicultural competency is the approach that will give counselors the foothold existing theories alone cannot provide. Through this framework of cultural, historical, and contextual meanings, one can better understand and address pressing issues.

The world of business offers a parallel. With the publication of *Workforce 2000* (Johnson & Packer, 1987), the concept of workforce diversity became more "believable." The numbers spoke. Projections about demographic trends and their implications for the workplace caught the attention of major businesses. For contemporary counselors, the same message about shifts in demographic diversity applies. I have been reminded by a colleague on more than one occasion that 80% of the world population is comprised of persons of color. Based on this fact alone, an MCT theory becomes a necessity, a fact of life.

In this chapter, I shall attempt to create links between the proposed MCT theory and the Latina(o)/Hispanic-American experience in the United States. Given the heterogeneity and complexity of the population based on far-ranging sociocultural and demographic considerations, the comments cannot be taken as absolutes but rather be viewed on a continuum: This will apply "more or less" in "certain situations" and "for some individuals" and not others. In the course of the discussion, variables that impact individuals as well as subgroups within the culture will be examined. I will also try to avoid categorizing based on labels of traditional versus nontraditional. This personal preference comes from how I have often heard *traditional* used—as a judgment by which people dismiss or minimize rather than try to seek further cultural/contextual explanation. For example, certain behavioral practices in choice of health care or childrearing may be more culture-specific than ones that appear to some as culture-bound, or Western. To categorize these as traditional or nontraditional does not allow for understanding of other factors, including belief system, level of acculturation, socioeconomic status, and urban versus rural life experience.

As an invited commentator, I believe it is important to articulate my long-standing self-interest in cultural issues and my personal study of Latina(o) culture in order to be a more informed consultant in this area. Therefore, I am both influenced and biased by my own perspectives as a Mexican-American woman of a working-class background who has earned higher-education degrees. Other factors include my age, my own sense of biculturalism and bilingual capacity, and my different modalities for help-ing. Understandably, these factors as well as the limitations of space will affect what I choose to say, and what I shall omit.

While the MCT propositions are presented independently, they are interrelated. Therefore, my discussion will be fluid, somewhat like an orga-nized stream of consciousness corresponding to one or more propositions simultaneously. My comments will be both broad and specific, though not exhaustive. Minimally, however, this analysis will open the door to further discussions about counseling from a Latina(o) frame of reference.

LATINA(O) CULTURE WITHIN THE PURVIEW OF MCT THEORY

What does the MCT theory offer to Latina(o)/Hispanic populations, to other culture-specific populations, and to other domains of counseling? For Latina(o)s, first of all, it offers potential for recognition of their cultural and racial diversity, their power of self-definition, the core values that con-tribute to their worldview and lifestyles, and the history of colonization that impacted their ancestors and that has had consequences in the current lives of many from North and South America. While self-determination is not a core Latina(o) cultural value, MCT theory promotes the centrality of cul-tural identity and difference as mediating forces for all groups and individu-als. For Latina(o) professionals, the challenge lies in self-empowerment by becoming creators, consumers, and critics of theory and practice.

Indigenous and Western Models of Health Care

The MCT metatheory is said to accommodate both indigenous helping models as well as those developed in the Western world (Western Europe and the United States). For Latina(o)s, use of such models is relevant because of the heterogeneity of the culture. Latina(o)s in the United States are of African, Asian, European, and Indian heritage, of many shades of skin color and phenotype (Hall, 1994), various levels of acculturation, urban and rural lifestyles, many educational and economic backgrounds, and varied English/Spanish language proficiency. Government institutions use the label *Hispanic* to try to easily categorize multiple nationalities that have roots in Latin-American countries and Spain. The most notable but not exclusive common denominators for the general population are the

Spanish language and the Roman Catholic religion. According to the Bureau of the Census Report (1990), people of Hispanic origin numbered an estimated 22,554,000 (p. xxii).

Because they are deeply rooted in the culture and the history of Latina(o)s in the New World, religion and spirituality have influenced belief systems and practices with regard to physical and mental health. The dominant holistic view, moral in nature, suggests one's behavior causes one's health or illness. Individuals must conform to the norms of their family and community and precepts of the Church (Giachello, 1985). For example, a person who abuses alcohol is deemed to be lacking in moral character and thereby responsible for the embarrassment or harm he or she inflicts on family members. Illness is also attributed to environmental conditions and supernatural causes. Environmental conditions include "bad air, germs, dust, excess of hot and cold, bad food or poverty" (Giachello, 1985, p. 163). Because they occur beyond a person's control, however, these conditions do not lead to moral judgments. One can say the same about supernatural causes. Whether it be bad luck, harmful spirits, or witchcraft, individuals cannot possibly control what is inflicted on them. Further, such beliefs about inner and external control influence prevention and utilization practices. For example, in a study of breast exam screenings, those who believed they could have personal control over health outcomes were less likely to seek out screenings with medical professionals (Bundek, Marks, & Richardson, 1993).

Counselors working from an MCT framework will be able to understand the correlations between symptoms and possible causes as described. For example, in general, Latina(o)s have lower cancer rates but a higher incidence of diabetes, gastrointestinal disorders, and strokes. Emotional distress manifests itself in *nervios*, *ataques de nervios*, and *ataques*. These conditions have been most prevalent among people of Puerto Rican, Cuban, and Central-American heritage, and primarily women. Though often used interchangeably, the three conditions involve distinct experiences. *Ataques de nervios* are acute episodes that involve bodily shaking, heat or pressure on the chest, weakness of limbs, a mind blank or loss of consciousness, and/or a loss of memory about what transpired during the experience. *Nervios* refers to nerves, a reaction to anxiety-provoking life situations, and these are usually precursors to an *ataque de nervios*. A mother whose son has joined active military duty might attribute *nervios* to her fears, uncertainty, and lack of control. Refugees who have fled violence may develop a case of *nervios* in the United States.

Ataques are distinguished as a specific type of *ataque de nervios* whereby the individual may lapse into a state of unconsciousness followed by seizure-like behavior. *Ataques* have been chronicled in the psychiatric literature as far back as the late 1950s and early 1960s. Often referring to it as the "Puerto Rican Syndrome," army psychiatrists initially characterized it as a psychopathological reaction pattern and hysterical personality (Guarnaccia, De la Cancela, & Carrillo, 1989). They also attributed this condition to flaws in Latina(o) culture, including child-rearing practices. A multicultural approach, however, allows counselors to understand ataque-like behavior contextually and culturally. In fact, *ataques de nervios* refer to different behavioral experiences, including "the emotional expression of grief and anger and the social experiences of family disruption, migration, and leaving family behind" (Guarnaccia et al., 1989). They are culturally sanctioned as an acceptable way to express powerful emotions. Zavala (1981) has emphasized that colonial experiences of oppression for Puerto Ricans have influenced this form of expression. She describes them as a culture-specific and culture-appropriate outlet for repressed anger.

This belief system also influences the type of intervention Latina(o)s seek. Historically, naturalistic/homeopathic and spiritual/religious traditions have influenced Latina(o) culture. Aztecs, Incas, Mayans, and Tainos, among others, have influenced so-called non-Western practices. The use of herbs, teas, and other home remedies is still well regarded by many now living in the States. It is not unusual to hear that someone who has visited the home country has returned with remedies to treat different illnesses and discomforts. Giachello (1985) describes the *curandero*, akin to a general practitioner, as one who ministers to physical ailments, including fractures and fevers. She describes the *espiritistas* as the "highest-ranking curanderos" (p. 164). They are often sought out for dealing with emotional problems and other illnesses of a supernatural dimension, including *susto* (fright), *mal ojo* (evil eye), and *empacho* (upset stomach). I remember working with a man from El Salvador who was convinced that his 7-year-old daughter, who was experiencing convulsions, had been given a *mal ojo* by an enemy of the family. Even though she improved once she received appropriate Western medication, he was still convinced that only an espiritista could rectify the situation by getting even with the person who willed the *mal ojo*.

Of course, one cannot assume that all people from El Salvador or Latina(o)s in general subscribe exclusively to the supernatural, environmental, or psychological models of illness and cures. Padilla (1981) found that people living in urban settings tended to seek out Western health practices. Those in rural areas, with presumably less access to private and government-sponsored services, relied more on indigenous models. With respect to mental-health practices, in Latin America the dominant model has been psychoanalytic psychotherapy. This is the result of the migration of Eastern and Western Europeans, primarily of Jewish heritage, to these continents during World War II. These individuals established this form of practice, which has been subscribed to primarily by people of relatively high socioeconomic means. Often, Latina(o)-American immigrants seeking a private practitioner ask for a psychiatrist or assume psychoanalysis as the mode of treatment.

The challenges for counselors are evident. With an MCT approach, however, they can understand and respect both holistic and Western orientations. Health-care providers, therefore, need to inquire about an individual's belief system while asking about symptoms, assess the impact of acculturation and experiences upon health-care practices, and be informed about the role of economics and institutional racism and language differences as possible gatekeeping (discriminatory) factors.

Latina(o) Self-Identification and Experience

According to Proposition 2, "Counselor and client identities are formed and embedded in multiple levels of experience . . . and contexts" (p. 15). This premise is essential if counselors are to understand the idea of a "different psychology of human existence" (p. 5) as it relates to the worldview of Latina(o)s and the contributing factors that have shaped the culture.

Historical determinants contribute to the psychology of individuals categorized as Hispanics/Latina(o)s. These determinants include colonialism; the imposition of Roman Catholicism as the "right" religion; the denial of the basic rights of primarily indigenous persons; slavery as a means to control one group for the benefit and power of another; the denial of cultural, linguistic, religious, and economic identity; and dichotomous thinking (right and wrong) based on Catholic tenets. The last to a great degree have also influenced the definition of gender roles as recognized in Latina(o) culture.

In the United States, the largest Latino subgroup is Mexican, followed by Puerto Rican, then Cuban. All are very nationalistic. Differences among the groups' socioeconomic status are based on historical relations with the United States. Most Latin-American countries share a history of difficult political struggle with the United States, principally because of colonization. While each group has its stories, racism and other forms of oppression have rendered groups and individuals powerless. This, I believe, lies in the recesses of the Latina(o) collective psyche. It is an imprint not easily erased.

Generations later, these historical experiences, still emotionally ripe for many, play out in sociopolitical ways. For example, there continues to be a movement among Puerto Ricans to become independent of their U.S. Commonwealth status. Mexicans in the southwest and California, who also identify themselves as *Chicanos*, have many mixed feelings about their ethnic identity. The Treaty of Guadalupe Hidalgo of 1848 made Mexicans foreigners on their own land. The consequences of this physical and psychological "displacement" show up in the limits of power, economics, and education of the group. Of the three largest Latina(o) groups, only the Cubans can report an invited entry to the United States. In the 1950s and 1960s, those of sufficient economic means to flee the regimes of the Batista and Castro governments did so with U.S. aid. Among all groups, Cubans today hold the most political and economic clout.

The heterogeneity across and within groups must also be put in perspective. As a whole, Latina(o)s are the most economically disadvantaged subgroup in the country. "In 1991, Latino men earned 60 cents for each dollar of white men's median earnings, while Latinas earned 78 cents for each dollar of white women's median earnings" (*Latino Poverty and Public Policy*, 1994, p. 4). Varying health-care studies indicate that underutilization rates of Latina(o)s indicate a greater "at risk" tendency. Lack of access to preventive services, language differences, poverty, and beliefs are cited as contributing factors.

Relationships, Family Structure, and Other Core Values

Proposition 4 suggests that counselors must operate from a client-related-to-cultural-context perspective. This clearly places responsibility on counselors to have the knowledge and skills that will engage clients through culturally appropriate modalities. Relationships are central to Latina(o) self-definition and day-to-day practices. Through this discussion, counselors may gain some insight about some of the similarities between the meanings of *relationship* in the counseling and the Latina(o) cultures, particularly the depth of meaning it holds for the latter.

Key words in Spanish, such as *personalismo, amistad, simpatía, respeto, dignidad,* and *familismo* highlight the value of relationships, their interdependent and authority-based nature, and the centrality of family. In fact, the family is the primary source of self-definition and self-esteem, the structure and support of the individual. In the literature, this is described as an allocentric orientation, one that fosters a sense of group identity versus individualism, mutuality, and reciprocity rather than competition and achievement for personal glory. In counseling situations, it is quite common to have both men and women describe their personal conflict about choices that would primarily benefit them as individuals, such as accepting a promotion that would involve family relocation or moving away from home to create new opportunities. Counselors need to be aware, however, that Latina(o)s make these decisions with a great sense of responsibility and *respeto* to the family.

Another example of the Latina(o) sociocentric orientation is the extended family structure of *compadrazgo* (Padilla, 1981), signifying the relationship with *comadres* and *compadres*, demonstrating *familismo*. *Comadres* and *compadres* are often godparents, confirmation sponsors, or maids-of-honor or best men. Through *compadrazgo*, trust, confidence, and loyalty are mutual and assumed.

What do these values suggest about Latina(o)s' relationship style in the family and out of it? Within the family, *respeto* is learned early on, with unquestionable authority expected for parents, grandparents, and other adults. Research has shown (Hostede, 1980) that because Latina(o) culture is hierarchical and authority-oriented, it can also be characterized as a high-power distance culture. "Power distance is the degree of inequality in power between a less powerful and a more powerful individual" (p. 71), between an individual and an organization, and within and between groups in a national culture. This national tendency manifests in other social systems, inducing greater conformity and behavior that is role- and status-based. In the family, men hold the overt role of authority and women the silent power. Loyalty to family is taught and children are told that family comes first, not their personal wants. Some people do behave individualistically or on their own, but others see this behavior as selfish and undesirable.

To reinforce family values, precepts are used to exert control over one's behavior. These precepts show up in terms such as *orgullo* (pride) contrasted with *verguenza* and *sinverguenza* (shame, shamelessness). Pride and *dignidad* (dignity) are strongly promoted as values, pride in one's family and oneself as a Mexican, Puerto Rican, etc. On the other hand, one's bad behavior can be a source of *verguenza* for the entire family. *Chismes* or gossip about *fulana* and *mengana* (so-and-so) are used as deterrents, warnings that one's reputation as well as the family's will suffer if one steps out of line. For instance, children are continuously reminded of the need to manage their behavior in school or in any outside activities so as not to cast any discredit on the family.

In a related circumstance, school personnel often criticize Latina(o) parents for not becoming more involved in school functions. One can understand this, though, by examining culture, acculturation, and economic factors. In Latin-American countries, teachers are seen as learned authority figures who know what is best for the child. Parents therefore tend to defer to their knowledge. The culturally different expectations in the United States are unfamiliar and countercultural for most Latina(o) parents. Furthermore, having to face school officials who do not understand Spanish can be experienced as intimidating as well as shameful. When someone other than the parents—a grandparent, aunt or uncle, or comadre—comes to school with the child, school staff may see it as not satisfying the norm. Greater acculturation and higher economic status may also affect the parents' relationship with the school, engendering greater familiarity and ease of involvement. Without an understanding of the centrality of family structure, *respeto,* and other cultural values, a counselor's ethnocentric perspective might impose unintentional judgment on a family or an individual who is seeking help.

Cultural Values and Gender Role Socialization

Socialization based on gender and role expectations is very demarcated in Latina(o) culture. For men, gender identity is strongly associated with the emphasis on *machismo,* the "cult of virility . . . arrogance and sexual aggressiveness in male-to-female relationships" (Stevens, 1973, p. 315). It is also about demonstrating the capacity to provide for and having firm control of one's family. In some communities, it would be an affront to a man if his wife had to seek employment, because her behavior would intimate that he cannot provide sufficiently. More recent attention to this concept suggests the following: (1) Machismo has been seriously underresearched and therefore subject to stereotyped portrayals of men. (2) It is not unique to the Latina(o) culture and machismo-defined criteria are found in most cultures worldwide (Casas, Wagenheim, Banchero, & Mendoza-Romero, 1994). Double standards that tolerate infidelity and value education for boys over girls are two examples. (3) The culture is actually matriarchal because of the status accorded to motherhood (Benavides, 1992).

In support of Benavides' assertion, women are referenced in terms of *marianismo,* "the cult of female spiritual superiority which teaches that women are semi-divine, morally superior to and spiritually stronger than men" (Stevens, 1973, p. 315). Marianismo is directly connected with the veneration of the Virgin Mary in Latina(o) Catholicism. Women are expected to remain virgins until they marry. Should an unmarried woman lose her virginity, she is automatically labeled promiscuous (Espin, 1985). On the other hand, if a young woman has a child out of wedlock, the family will care for both the child and the young mother in the home. For parents who want to raise their daughters according to learned cultural and religious values, a more open society that promotes sexual relationships without a marriage commitment creates familial stress and conflict.

The reverence for motherhood presents many paradoxes for women who are portrayed as submissive caretakers and who learn how to *aguantarse* (endure and repress personal wants). For women of post–World War II generations, employed and professionals, the norms for saintly and silent behavior do not necessarily work well. Awareness of one's sense of self, one's rights and access to different forms of expression (education, writing), and societal changes with regard to women have upset the dynamic in many personal relationships. Some professional men with whom I have worked have discussed their desire for their partners' development, but have also expressed their fears that the women will "outdo" them. Some women, conversely, worry about outshining their partners. It is as though the women have to protect the men's sense of masculinity and take a back seat, much like the cultural script they learned.

Variations exist among individuals based on demographic factors as well. Studies across different Latina(o) ethnic groups have found that a husband's authority varies by region and socioeconomic class, with men of the middle and upper classes exercising less authority than men of a lower economic status (Vazquez-Nuttall & Romero-Garcia, 1989). Other studies found that male dominance in marital decision making is not necessarily the norm (Cromwell & Ruiz, 1979).

With respect to homosexuality, researchers have found disparate attitudes that range from intolerance to flexibility. A gay or lesbian identity may be judged immoral based on religious beliefs, including marianismo. For men, machismo does not include homosexuality as an acceptable identity.

Acculturation and Ethnic Identity

Acculturation has been described as a process "whereby attitudes and/or behaviors of persons from one culture are modified as a result of contact with a different culture" (Moyerman & Forman, 1992, p. 163). For Latina(o)s, this process can be considered in two primary ways: (1) as it impacts the immigrant who must adjust to a new culture, language, and sociocultural and sociopolitical trappings and (2) as it is experienced by the Latina(o) born in the United States, who has been categorized as a minority or person of color by the dominant culture.

Factors that impact acculturation include the similarity or difference between the immigrant's culture and the new one, the new country's receptiveness to newcomers based on the country's economic conditions, and the political relationship between the home country and the new one. (Arredondo-Dowd, 1981). Furthermore, people whose skin color and phenotype is less European-looking might have a more stressful adaptation process because of the lack of receptivity of the host culture. For most Latina(o) immigrants, the concept of categorization as a minority or Hispanic is new. Some of these factors may also hold true for those Hispanic-Americans who can usually "pass" based on skin color, English-language usage, and other behaviors deemed acceptable by the dominant culture.

Latina(o)s and other "visible racial/ethnicity groups" (Helms, 1990) who grow up in dual and often oppositional cultures must evaluate their individual and group identity against differing worldviews, norms, and scripts about ethnic/racial identity. Studies (e.g., Denton & Massey, 1989) indicate that for Caribbean Hispanics, there is double minority status, based on racial and ethnic differences in the United States. Once in the country, they experience the pressures of bipolar racial categorization, which particularly contribute to biases in their employment and residential opportunities. For many Latina(o) immigrants, national identity supercedes racial identity until they arrive in the States.

Researchers have operationalized ethnic identity as a multidimensional construct, embodying attitudes and values, feelings, social affiliations, use of language, and knowledge of the Latina(o)/American cultures and behaviors defined in terms of the two (Felix-Ortiz, Newcomb, & Myers, 1994). Based on studies with Mexican-American populations, ethnic identity is defined as a person's self-established ideas about ethnic group membership including self-concept (Bernal, Saenz, & Knight, 1991). Counselors working with youth in school settings need to be aware that feedback from staff, teachers, and peers will impact the development of these students' ethnic identity.

Phinney (1991) describes the key elements of ethnic identity as follows: (1) self-identification as a group member, (2) attitudes and evaluations relative to one's group, (3) attitudes about oneself as a group member, (4) extent of ethnic knowledge and commitment, and (5) ethnic behavior and practices. These elements make up a dynamic process that again points to the relevance of context to understanding Latina(o)s in general as well as in various life and work situations.

Ethnic Identity in the Counseling Encounter

Other considerations emanate from Proposition 3, which speaks of ethnic identity development as a "major determinant of counselor and client attitudes toward the self [and] toward others" (p. 17). A counselor of Latina(o) heritage therefore is often considered the most appropriate person to treat, interview, or test another Latina(o). A bilingual counselor may facilitate the process for a client who prefers to speak in Spanish. Using his or her primary language to express emotions enables the client to experience engagement and a sense of empowerment (Guarnaccia et al., 1989).

Latina(o) counselors are also deemed more desirable because of their presumed familiarity with the cultural values. However, this knowledge varies, depending in part on ethnic identity. A Latina counselor may have an integrated sense of cultural identity, enabling her to be both subjective and objective regarding a Latino client's concerns. That is, she would be able to understand issues in a cultural context, recognize her feelings about them, and still provide empathy and support. Counselors with mixed feelings about their Latina(o) cultural identity may not be able to separate their unresolved issues from those of their clients. For example, a counselor who knows only English may be intolerant of people who speak grammatically incorrectly and with accents. This counselor might operate from the belief that everyone should learn English and that if one does not, she or he is just lazy. Then there is the counselor, of any background, who identifies primarily with the Eurocentric culture. This person may criticize the Latina(o) client's cultural ways, imposing his or her biases on the client. This type of counselor has a need to label the client's attitudes and behavior as "traditional" and as the cause of the client's problems. For example, school and family counselors often see Latina(o) parents as too old-fashioned and unwilling to allow their children to Americanize. Counselors operating from this mindset will likely increase family disharmony. Martinez (1994) cautions that counselors must neither describe culture in dysfunctional terms nor dismiss the cultural context as irrelevant in the American setting. For example, to describe a Latina(o) family as "enmeshed" may be a reflection of a counselor's lack of knowledge about the interdependence of families.

According to Sue et al. (1992), counselors must have an awareness of their own assumptions, values, and biases; knowledge of their own self-definition; how this definition influences their personal and professional behavior; and how they impact others. Latina(o)s, like other persons of color, must go through this type of self-assessment in order to practice competently with all clients. Thus, one cannot always say that same-culture dyads are the best ones. Because of the cultural similarity between counselor and client, and the sense of familiarity and comfort it provides, they are often recommended; however, they offer no guarantees.

What does a non-Latina(o) counselor do if there is no choice of a Latina(o) counselor for referral? First, the counselor should not assume that he or she cannot treat the client, language differences notwithstanding. The counselor can proceed with caution, trying to inquire about the client's concerns and expectations. With the client's permission, a consultation should be made with a counselor knowledgeable of the Latina(o) culture. Other resources in the community might help as well. Even so, the counselor needs to (1) be willing to learn from the client and (2) be ready to embark on a multicultural course of study.

Relevance of Latina(o)-Specific Knowledge to Counseling Practice

These culture-specific data provide understanding about the different psychology of Latina(o)s in terms of gender socialization and group identity and about the range of variability within the culture and among the different nationalities. For example, previous discussions have strongly supported the need to honor the Latina(o) culture's value of relationships in counseling practice, whether it be in therapy, assessment, or research. In counselor training, rapport building is considered the foundation of the client-counselor relationship. Similarly, with Latina(o) clients, research studies report that *simpatia* is likely to influence an individual's behavior. According to Marin and Marin (1991) *simpatia* "emphasizes the need for behaviors that promote smooth and pleasant social relationships" (p. 9), involving a certain level of conformity and demonstration of empathy that show respect, allow harmonious interpersonal relationships, and help avoid interpersonal conflicts. Individuals will tend to be more agreeable, even acquiescent. Researchers (Hostede, 1980; Marin & Marin, 1991) have found that Latina(o) subjects have a tendency to give socially desirable responses and to avoid conflict in certain social situations (Kagan, Knight, & Martinez-Romero, 1982). *Simpatia* also increases a client's agreeableness in therapy encounters and research studies.

Self-disclosure is a norm of counseling interventions, whether it be in testing, research, or therapy. Though, as previously noted, *simpatia* may affect these transactions, values of *dignidad* (dignity) and *orgullo* (pride), counteracted by *verguenza* (shame), will also impact client behavior. Clients do not want to intimate that there are problems, because it may disparage the family system. In studies of counseling with college-age Latinas, these women's double bind of allocentrism versus individualism emerged: *How can I be a good daughter if I left my mother to do all the work?* or *What's the point of being in medical school when my father just lost his job?* These expressions speak to the young women's concerns about role expectation and family loyalty (Arredondo, Psalti, & Cella, 1993).

Latina(o) clients with whom I have worked have also expressed guilt or labeled themselves selfish for achieving more educationally and economically than their parents. While parents may work to enable this evolvement for their children, it can also serve as a double-edged sword. Because education is a tool of acculturation, for many families it may result in the children's loss of traditions, values, and language, and perhaps result in an intercultural marriage.

Knowledge of the cultural implications of Spanish and its use is particularly important for counselors. For instance, non-Latina(o) counselors who want to speak in Spanish during an interview must be cautious about how they address the client. In Spanish, there are two ways to address another: formal and informal. Adults usually address children informally, but other adults formally until familiarity is established. Thus, one might ask a child "¿Cómo estás?" but an adult "¿Cómo está?"—both meaning "How are you?" A good rule of thumb is to ask the client how she or he would like to be addressed: Señor, Señora, Señorita, Miss, Mister or Mrs.? To call an adult by a first name without asking permission would be a sign of disrespect.

Another useful tool to put the client at ease, particularly during an initial interview, is *la plática*, or small talk. This allows for exchanges that neutralize a potentially power-bound relationship and at the same time encourages the client to participate in a culturally familiar role. Story telling and the use of *dichos* (sayings) and other culture-specific metaphors become points of connection in the counseling exchange. I have worked with a range of Latina(o) clients, women and men alike, who emphasized their need to know me without violation of their personal space.

Similar to counseling in general, Latinas will more often tend to be clients. As in the U.S. male culture of self-reliance, Latinos find it difficult to seek help. When they do, scripts about *machismo* will be particularly relevant. Predictably, the dynamics with male counselors will differ from those with female counselors. It is counter-cultural for men to be dependent on women, unless as a child. Thus, as would be the case working with most men and understanding this norm, the female counselor must assert clear boundaries about her role in the relationship.

Over the years, studies have examined the underutilization of therapy by low-income, Latina(o) clients. Many clinicians, in fact, subscribe to the myth that Latina(o)s do not care for therapy. More often than not, findings about the lack of use or dropout from services indicate the following: (1) Community-based services not easily accessible to public transportation are not used; (2) The welcoming or unwelcoming signals that are sent at an agency, school, or hospital will influence a client's decision about returning; (3) The respect or disrespect demonstrated by the counselor will be a signal; or (4) The client's expectations about the counselor's role were not satisfied. If counselors are to provide culturally relevant services to a Latina(o) population, they must be aware of how these four factors may either facilitate or discourage the use of mental-health services.

Psychologists (Arredondo, Orjuela, & Moore, 1989; De La Cancela, 1991; Arredondo-Dowd, 1981) have raised other issues regarding safety and trust as they apply to political refugees or other undocumented individuals. Because of proximity to the United States, as well as this nation's historical interventions in Latin-American countries, multiple realities and contexts would need to be considered in the treatment process (see Chapters 1–3). Political strife in Central America during the past 20 years has forced the displacement of thousands of individuals and families, many of whom were already traumatized from viewing or being victims of violence themselves (De La Cancela, 1991). Their undocumented status has prevented them from establishing connections with necessary support systems, leaving many instead in new states of fear and isolation, fearful of authority figures, including counselors. Refugees have shared their concerns that counselors might be government agents or simply people who might harm, not help.

For counselors, knowledge of political events that impact Latina(o) newcomers and assessment about the counselor's own biases or assumptions about these events will affect counseling situations, such as schools, hospitals, and social service agencies. De La Cancela (1991) advocates what he calls "progressive counseling," an empowerment-based form of intervention that is action oriented, "integrating social reality with psychotherapy" (p. 26). Through this approach, the counselor enables the refugee family or client to address adaptation issues practically and psychologically.

Proposition 2 reminds us that counselors' identities consist of multiple experiences and contexts. For example, the terms *aliens* or *illegals* are often used in the media to refer to undocumented individuals. Both connote a negative and demeaning association, not one that signifies the refugees' economic deprivation or political distress. Because there is power in language and images that depersonalize others, when serving people so characterized, counselors need to recognize how these portrayals will affect their ability to relate to these clients respectfully.

The data regarding politically displaced refugees can be particularly helpful toward understanding a client's behavior. By avoiding eye contact, is the client deferring to the counselor out of respect or because she or he fears that the counselor is an agent of the police? My work with immigrants and refugees also suggests that individuals go through an involuntary loss and grief process that often manifests itself in depression or over-compensation, such as working two or three jobs and denying their feelings of loss. Counselors in schools working with children and young adults need to be particularly attuned to symptoms of loss and grief, posttraumatic stress disorder, and what I call "healthy paranoia"—reality-based fears and mistrust based on past experiences. Immigration is a major life event, often fraught with terror and uncertainty. Sensitivity to the multiple losses and changes newcomers must endure will enable counselors to serve clients effectively in a multidimensional transition process.

SUMMARY

Demographic projections suggest that the Latina(o) population will exceed other groups by the 21st century. The population will increase to 28.7 million by the year 2000 and to 47 million by 2020 (Sue et al., 1992). In fact, Latina(o)s are projected to become a majority-minority group in the next century. Changes introduced by NAFTA and other political forces are likely to generate a reconfiguration of the northern and southern hemispheres of this world region. Counseling practice will need to respond to these emerging markets. Already, counselors in California, the southwest states, Florida, and New York City live with clients' needs far exceeding the availability of services, particularly for immigrants. Southern Florida has experienced another influx of political refugees from Cuba. The "third wave" is creating stress on the communities of Cubans and non-Cubans alike. For as with the second wave, these refugees have limited economic resources and multiple needs.

The proposed MCT theory holds implications for research, practice, and training as these apply to working with the Latina(o) population generally and specifically. In most respects, it means having the capacity to engage from a continuum perspective—that is, operating from a flexible, Latina(o)-centered base of knowledge while being fully mindful of the fluidity of ethnic identity, levels of acculturation, socioeconomic differences, rural and urban lifestyles, and religious backgrounds. This chapter has presented the fundamental values of most Latina(o)s; however, there is still room to introduce Western counseling models. To work from a Latina(o)-centered perspective alone would be culture-bound.

Inclusion, value, self-definition, strengths (not just deficits), differences balanced with commonalities, and history to inform the present and the future are key themes that underlie the proposed MCT theory. With these premises, one has an empowerment-based model that can be a template to reengineer the fields of counseling and psychology. Investing in multicultural competency is the mandate for the counseling profession. *Más vale tarde que nunca* (Better late than never).

REFERENCES FOR CHAPTER 14

Arredondo, P. (1994). Multicultural training: A response. *The Counseling Psychologist, 22*(2), 308–314.

Arredondo, P., Orjuela, E., & Moore, L. (1989). Family therapy with Central American war refugee families. *Journal of Strategic and Systemic Therapies, 8*(2), 28–35.

Arredondo, P., Psalti, A., & Cella, K. (1993). The woman factor in multicultural counseling. *Counseling and Human Development, 25*(8), 1–8.

Arredondo-Dowd, P. M. (1981). Personal loss and grief as a result of immigration. *Personnel and Guidance Journal, 59*, 376–378.

Arredondo-Dowd, P. M., & Gonsalves, J. (1980). Preparing culturally effective counselors. *The Personnel and Guidance Journal, 58*, 657–661.

Atkinson, D., Morten, G., & Sue, D. W. (1983). *Counseling American minorities.* Dubuque, IA: Brown.

Benavides, J. (1992, October 17). Mujeres rule the roosters. *Santa Barbara News Press,* p. B1.

Bernal. M. E., Saenz, D. S., & Knight, G. P. (1991). Ethnic identity and adaptation of Mexican American youth in school settings. *Hispanic Journal of Behavioral Sciences, 13*(2), 135–154.

Bundek, W. I., Marks, G., & Richardson, J. L. (1993). Role of health locus of control beliefs in cancer screening of elderly Hispanic women. *Health Psychology, 12*(3), 193–199.

Bureau of the Census Report, U. S. Department of Commerce (1990, July). *Hispanic origin population in the United States*, p. xxii. Washington, DC: U. S. Government Printing Office.

Casas, J. M., Wagenheim, B. R., Banchero, R., & Mendoza-Romero, J. (1994). Hispanic masculinity: Myth or psychological schema meriting clinical consideration. *Hispanic Journal of Behavioral Sciences, 16*(3), 315–331.

Cromwell, R. E., & Ruiz, R. A. (1979). The myth of macho dominance in decision making within Mexican and Chicano families. *Hispanic Journal of Behavioral Sciences, 1*, 355–373.

De La Cancela, V. (1991). Progressive counseling with Latino refugees and families. *Journal of Progressive Human Services, 2*(2), 19–34.

Denton, N. A., & Massey, D. S. (1989). Racial identity among Caribbean Hispanics: The effect of double minority status on residential segregation. *American Sociological Review, 54*, 790–808.

Espin, O. (1985). Psychotherapy with Hispanic women: Some considerations. In P. Pedersen (Ed.), *Handbook of cross cultural counseling and therapy* (pp. 165–171). Westport, CT: Greenwood Press.

Felix-Ortiz, M., Newcomb, M. D., & Myers, H. (1994). A multidimensional measure of cultural identity for Latino and Latina adolescents. *Hispanic Journal of Behavioral Sciences, 16*(2), 99–115.

Giachello, A. L. (1985). Hispanics and health care. In P. San Juan Cafferty & W. C. McCready (Eds.), *Hispanics in the United States* (pp. 159–194). New Brunswick, NJ: Transaction Books.

Guarnaccia, P. J., De La Cancela, V., & Carrillo, E. (1989). The multiple meanings of ataques de nervios in the Latino community. *Medical Anthropology, 11*, 47–62.

Hall, R. (1994). The "bleaching syndrome": Implications of light skin for Hispanic American assimilation. *Hispanic Journal of Behavioral Sciences, 16*(3), 307–314

Helms, J. E. (1990). Methodological issues in racial identity. *The Counseling Psychologist, 17*(2), 227–252.

Hostede, G. (1980). *Culture's consequences.* Beverly Hills, CA: Sage.

Johnston, W. B., & Packer, A. H. (1987). *Workforce 2000: Work and workers for the 21st century.* Indianapolis, IN: Hudson Institute.

Kagan, S., Knight, G. P., & Martinez-Romero, S. (1982). Culture and the development of conflict resolution style. *Journal of Cross Cultural Psychology, 13*, 43–59.

Katz, J. (1985). The sociopolitical nature of counseling. *The Counseling Psychologist, 13*, 615–624.

Latino poverty and public policy: A guide to the literature. (1994). Boston: The Mauricio Gaston Institute for Latino Community and Public Policy, University of Massachusetts.

Levy, J. (1974). *The autobiography of Cesar Chavez.* New York: Norton.

Marin, G., & Marin, B. V. (1991). Research with Hispanic populations. In L. J. Brickman & D. J. Rog (Series Eds.), *Applied Social Research Methods Series, 23.* Newbury Park, CA: Sage.

Martinez, K. (1994). Cultural sensitivity in family therapy gone awry. *Hispanic Journal of Behavioral Sciences, 16*(1), 75–89.

Moyerman, D. R., & Forman, B. D. (1992). Acculturation and adjustment: A meta-analytic study. *Hispanic Journal of Behavioral Sciences, 14*(2), 163–200.

Padilla, A. M. (1981). Pluralistic counseling and psychotherapy for Hispanic Americans. In A. J. Marsella & P. B. Pedersen (Eds.), *Cross-cultural counseling and psychotherapy* (pp.195–227). New York: Pergamon Press.

Phinney, J. S. (1991). Ethnic identity and self-esteem: A review and integration. *Hispanic Journal of Behavioral Sciences, 13*(2), 193–208.

Ponterotto, J. G., & Casas, J. M. (1991). *Handbook of racial/ethnic minority research*. Springfield, IL: Thomas.

Stevens, E. P. (1973). The prospect for a woman's liberation movement in Latin America. *Journal of Marriage and the Family, 35*, 313–320.

Sue, D. W., Arredondo, P., & McDavis, R. (1992). Multicultural counseling competencies and standards: A call to the profession. *Journal of Counseling and Development, 70*, 477–486.

Vazquez-Nuttall, E., & Romero-Garcia, I. (1989). From home to school: Puerto Rican girls learn to be students in the United States. In C. T. Garcia-Coll & M. L. Mattei (Eds.), *The psychosocial development of Puerto Rican women* (pp. 60–83). New York: Praeger.

Zavala, I. (1981). *Mental health and the Puerto Ricans in the United States*. Unpublished manuscript.

CHAPTER 15

MCT Theory
and Women

Mary Ballou
Northeastern University

Assumption Audit

- Multicultural awareness is essential in counseling.
- MCT theory offers prescriptions for the contemporary paradigm rather than serves as a distinct theory of counseling and therapy.
- MCT theory makes culture central and demands flexibility and the liberation of consciousness.
- MCT theory demands diversity and the naming of context.
- MCT theory offers a depathologized community orientation in helping roles.
- Sometimes, MCT theory uses a shifting definition/meaning of culture, which is confusing.
- MCT theory highlights practice and training.
- MCT theory sees individuals in multiple and complex ways, although the alternatives are not well developed.
- MCT theory is in-the-making rather than already made.
- MCT theory allows for one to apply consensual principles of feminist psychology to multicultural theory.
- Like feminist theory, MCT theory recognizes an egalitarian use of power.
- MCT theory needs to expand its concern about power to training and research issues.
- MCT theory advocates a relativistic expansion of perspectives in pluralism.
- Quantitative methods have been the basis of the scientific method but also of colonial domination.
- Qualitative methods are empirical/rational and are based on phenomenology of the individual's perceptions.

- MCT theory rightly validates both qualitative and quantitative as complementary.
- Like feminist principles, MCT theory works against oppression of nondominant peoples.
- MCT theory is incomplete in its reformist or radical stance, lacking structural analysis.
- Attention to gender is not salient enough in MCT theory.
- MCT theory must give more weight to categories of difference beyond culture.
- The paradigm shift needs to explore experience as a way of knowing.
- MCT theory should use experience as a grounding for theory building and validation.

Responding to MCT theory from a women's perspective requires some clarification. I cannot speak for all women. There is, of course, much diversity among the experiences, resources/power, values, and positions of women even as sex/gender remains a powerful and fundamental characteristic. Thus, I must resist the temptation to speak for all women and instead present my own experiences and positions. I am a Yankee woman doing scholarship and practice in feminist therapy and holding a feminist analytical stance within psychology.

I shall use a feminist analysis to respond to the developing MCT theory. Feminist theory has a historical development, a fundamental analysis, and some struggles informative to the present efforts toward an MCT theory. Also, its focus on gender is similar to MCT theory's focus on culture. Indeed, one may see feminist theory as MCT theory's older sister, a bit worn by struggles but no less important than the newer member. Finally, feminist analysis insists that sex/gender as a social and biological category continues to be included in diverse human interactions in meaningful ways. Despite some cosmetic and some real gains, many women continue to be perceived and treated, and perhaps to perceive and treat others, in particular ways that most men do not. Sex/gender is one of many significant differences among people that interact in multiple and complex ways, varying with setting and time.

Given length limits, I must address the developing MCT theory selectively. That is, I get to choose what I wish to respond to and just leave the rest. In general, multicultural awareness is needed in counseling and therapy, and indeed in psychology. It is both important and laudable that Sue, Ivey, and Pedersen are committed to MCT theory development. Their current work has many strengths but some problems, too. In the end, their work may offer prescriptions for the contemporary paradigm rather than serve as a distinct theory of counseling and therapy. It is yet another voice, with its own call for substantial change in theory, practice, and research.

STRENGTHS AND WEAKNESSES
OF MCT THEORY

From a feminist point of view, the theory's strengths include the centrality of culture, the demand for flexibility, and the liberation of consciousness. These arise in the demand for diversity and the naming of context as important. They also occur in the call for acceptance of additional models of conventional practice, training content and competencies, methods of research, epistemological platforms, and the many influencing factors in personality and pathology, including sociocultural features. Self-in-relation and people-in-context are nicely, if briefly, discussed in the theory development, and their implications for research, practice, and training are drawn. Alternative helping roles and treatments, including a depathologized community orientation, are particularly noteworthy. Correspondingly, the theory presents multiple aspects of diversity, not only as varying cultures but also as characteristics of individuals, families, life events, and kinship networks. While on occasion the meaning of culture shifts confusingly, the theory does highlight the importance and complexity of diversity for theory, practice, and training. Similarly, it shows individuals in multiple and complex ways. Although some particular characteristics and phenomena (e.g., gender, spirituality, harmony with nature and ancestors) are not as well developed as they might be, ideas of context and interactive influence form part of the cogency of this work. Also, this work is distinguished by its process. Sue, Ivey, and Pedersen have combined their ideas about multicultural perspective and its impact on counseling and therapy and invited others to react to these ideas. It is an inclusive relational position that presents thinking in process.

This work is a theory-in-making rather than an already made theory. The first three chapters are more of an outline for further development and, as such, they hold promise. But they are also a tease, because just where they will go in development is not quite certain.

PERSPECTIVE OF
FEMINIST ANALYSIS

The consensual principles of feminist psychology offer a framework for viewing both the current and future directions of MCT theory. Feminist psychology has centralized gender over the past three decades just as multicultural theory centralizes culture. The history of feminist psychology holds some potential lessons for MCT theory. The consensual principles of feminist theory have by now been used in a variety of ways. For example, they have provided an analytical lens for therapy practice and theory development; for auditing and creating clinical practice, diagnosis, and assessment; for articulating research bias and paradigmatic constraints; and for addressing training and professional politics as well as guild issues. Further, the principles originally developed by the joining of feminism and therapy have proven useful in structuring feminist analysis. Such principles as developed by Carter and Rawlings (1977), Sturdivant (1980), Lerman (1976, 1986), Gilbert (1980), Greenspan (1983), Ballou and Gabalac (1985), Brown and Root (1990), and Enns (1993) may be described as including the following:

1. Egalitarian relationships, referring to a sensitivity to power and its distribution, a commitment to one's power to name, as well as to the right to bargain for nondominant persons/groups, and a belief that hierarchical forms of power distribution are inappropriate.

2. Pluralism, meaning acknowledged and equally valued differences, including complex and multiple-level diversities.

3. Working against oppression on the basis of sex, race, class, culture, religious belief, affectional/sexual orientation and life-style choice, or cosmetic or body dysfunction. Oppression profoundly influences beliefs, treatment, options/access, power structures and distribution of resources in global economies, patterns of social organization, and the professions/disciplines that serve them.

4. Emphasizing external factors, forces outside the individual, as influential in the development of the person and her or his relationships. Social/political/economic structures and cultural, institutional, and disciplinary values are critical to shaping the views of and attributions to women. Biopsycho (individual) factors are shaped by and interact with sociopolitical, environmental (external), structural, institutional, and cultural factors.

5. Valuing of women's experiences, which refers to relying on the actual experiences of women for descriptions of "reality." Because gender, class, and cultural bias contaminate both theory and research, data sources, normative standards, and images of health are not necessarily valid. Knowledge claims need to be grounded in actual women's experience, because both empirical and rational epistemologies favor Euro-American middle-class male explanatory systems. In other words, one should attribute importance to the lived experience of women rather than discounting or ignoring their experiences and assuming men's experience to be normative.

These principles offer a mode of analysis for MCT theory. One by one they will be used here to offer some thoughts about MCT theory's current status and areas in need of further development.

Egalitarian Relationships

The egalitarian relationship is a call for an equitable distribution of power with the transformation of hierarchical structures. MCT theory does attend to the power in the counselor/client relationship by essentially prescribing the power to name problems and the right to bargain in both problem definition and the direction and type of assistance rendered. This clearly is a strength of MCT. In fact, it is the first postfeminist therapy to recognize this aspect of power within the formal helping relationship. However, MCT theory has not as yet carried this power analysis into other relationships within the profession. For example, while the present MCT work addresses training, research, and practice, the attention to power is only considered in counselor-client interactions. An assessment of hierarchical power arrangements is not as yet extended to faculty/supervisor-student relationships, or to researcher-subject relationships, or to the other activities of practice (e.g., diagnosis, testing, case management.) Nor is hierarchical power analyzed at professional and disciplinary levels. Finally, hierarchy and power are not looked at within cultures themselves. For the nonhierarchical egalitarian relationship to be fully developed, the entire range of power distributions must be acknowledged. Some will require rather straightforward reforms of practice, as for example in creating and using tests that do not favor concepts of one culture, class, or gender. Others, however, will be difficult, transformative, and contradictory, such as the hierarchical power relationship inherent in some cultures' organization of kinship networks or governmental structures. Thus, the MCT theory's analysis of power structures needs extension.

Pluralism

Pluralism, or equally valid differences, provokes a complex discussion. On the surface, MCT theory takes a relativistic position. For example, the theory posits that the counselor should be aware of and accept the many forms of indigenous helping relationships and integrate them into the helping process. Another example is the acknowledgement that both qualitative and quantitative research methods have value. MCT theory certainly does acknowledge that differences exist and advocates the inclusion of diversity. It does not, however, require equal validity for all included worldviews, practices, etc. Such validity involves the power to name and the right to bargain for meaningful categories and nominative standards. Some of the views and practices (Collins, 1990) will contradict one another, requiring a deeper analysis (Ballou, 1990; Espin, 1993; Riger, 1992). For instance, to include qualitative research methods, an inclusion MCT theory calls for, is not only important but essential if the discipline is to become multicultural.

Pluralism, however, calls for equally valid differences, meaning that qualitative research methods must carry the same weight, be accorded the same power, as quantitative methods. In turn, the basic philosophical assumptions and structural requirements of the dominant forms of research design must change regarding instruction, use of research, and criteria for evaluation and selection by journals. Quantitative research rests on such notions as the following: (1) construction of reality being limited to sensory knowledge, (2) control of variables, (3) manipulation of treatment on unknowing subjects, (4) averaging group data, (5) discovering constant and unchanging universal laws, and (6) the goal of prediction and control (Harding, 1991; Merchant, 1980).

These words describe the underpinning of the scientific method, which has traditionally informed the discipline of psychology in the Western industrial world. It is, however, also the language of colonialism and domination. In contrast, qualitative methodology rests not on empiricism/ rationality but on phenomenology, which places reality squarely in individuals' perceptions. Including qualitative methods for research and making them equal requires not merely another way of gathering data but another way of thinking. It requires holding as real the perception of the people having the experience, which is essential to serving nondominant peoples. The call for qualitative as well as quantitative methods is a demand for multiple philosophical positions about what is real and what is knowledge. At the philosophic and disciplinary levels, qualitative methodology challenges the domination of the scientific method and the hegemony of rationality/empiricism. This inclusion of qualitative methods demands a basic paradigm change.

Oppression and External Structures

The two feminist principles—that one should work against the oppression of nondominant peoples and that external factors influence or cause personality—may offer future directions for MCT. These two lie at the heart of the radical critique, as opposed to the liberal revision. The case has been made (Brown & Ballou, 1992) that Western academic mental-health professions have not looked broadly enough at non-Western content, processes of interaction, and external, structural influences. Many factors besides an individual's neurotransmitters, genetics, psyche, learning patterns, and particular experiences influence human personality and psychopathology. Structures, factors, and processes external to individuals critically affect their development, functioning, and living conditions. Mainstream psychology has ignored them, however, and mostly continues to do so. When clients and counselors come from the dominant social group, they hardly notice such things as evaluative criteria, worldview, and complicity with power distribution (Ballou & Gabalac, 1985).

It is not until nondominant individuals are considered that differences in values, worldviews, and distributions of resources, with their corresponding relation to social and political structures, come into view (Espin & Gawelek, 1992; Root, 1990). In turn, if there is no awareness of external controlling structures and the particular worldviews, values, and power relations they support, then the differing individuals are denigrated. The Native-American's orientation of harmony with the natural world is discounted and named superstitious by the capitalist in search of power through control of resources.

This Eurocentric view also affects contemporary theories, such as the class and culture-biased theories of moral development by Kohlberg (1981) and Gilligan (1982). Kohlberg's theory rests on a middle-class White Western male construction of morality. Further, he places morality in a developmental hierarchy, ending in reasoning by applying universal absolutes to particular personal and interpersonal situations. Kohlberg's theory manifests inappropriate generalization of his own academic and cultural structure, class privilege, rational bias, and male experience. Gilligan's ethics of care, on the other hand, reflect her female experience of the importance of relationship and connection—an equally important addition to reasoning by universal principles and absolute rules. Gilligan's theory holds that many women and some men make moral decisions based on how they affect the people involved (ethics of care). Because she also addresses reasoning about moral principles (ethics of justice), Gilligan does not overthrow Kohlberg's work entirely. Her more recent work has also begun to question empirical/rational methods of inquiry, but she has not yet fully considered the cultural and class bias or the implications of structural contextual interactions.

Psychology has for too long held particular notions as universal, which has resulted in placing one set of arbitrary standards on all. Inevitably, some individuals are seen as better or more fitting than others. Feminist psychology has been uncovering and identifying biases concerning gender, sexual orientation, and class, and has more recently begun to examine race and culture. The content, process, structure, history, and normative criteria of Euro-American, White, male, upper-middle-class, heterosexist psychology is problematic for women and racial minorities.

Psychologies that fit and are not oppressive to nondominant people will be sometimes at odds with the particular views and values of the dominant society, as well as its supportive professions and their governing theories, methods of inquiry, and rules for practice. In this sense, a radical analysis rather than a reformist position must undergird nondominant psychology, be it feminist, antiracist, or multicultural. Radical analysis examines root structures and processes. Liberal reform addresses inclusion of and equity in content without attention to the controlling structures and power relationships expressed through hierarchical processes. MCT theory as presented at this point in its development is incomplete regarding its reformist or radical stance. The mention of gender, race, and politics in connection with culture looks promising, but the lack of structural analysis is of concern.

Two examples illustrate the needed development. Gender, race, and class govern life experiences because they determine, in part, one's placement in the hierarchy of dominance. Similarly, cognitive (rational) abilities will remain the sine qua non of school, professional, and mental-health judgments of excellence until emphasis on IQ measures, GRE scores for graduate admissions, and complicated research designs and manipulations of statistics without regard for "real life" are changed—that is, until the structures of normative criteria are changed.

Where MCT theory positions itself with regard to reformist or radical critique is enormously important. Feminist psychology has and continues to struggle with these issues. For example, the Stone Center self-in-relation model as well as the revised object-relations models, currently popular in the psychology of women, do attend to sex/gender as a category of difference. However, these reformist theories neither attend to differences of class, race, and culture nor address social, political, and economic structures and their impact on women's lives. Because class, race, and culture interact with sex/gender in the development of personality and abilities, to ignore or subsume them under sex/gender is not adequate. Ignoring the political, social, and economic context in which people live is also inadequate. At present, some feminist psychologists are grappling with how to build a theory that escapes or transcends cultural, racial, and class biases. It would seem, however, that all aspects of context and its supportive structures and processes must be seen and accorded importance for one to build theories, develop practices, and generate modes of inquiry that include the realities of lives lived through multiple and interacting categories of difference.

No one has yet developed a theory describing multiple and interacting dimensions of context and its supportive governing structures and controlling processes. Building such a theory will require several significant changes in assumptions based on Euro-American, upper-middle-class, male culture. The following list reflects just some of the points to be considered in new theory building:

- The self must not be its most important variable.
- Rational/empirical epistemologies and the resulting privilege of cognition must not be held as the pinnacle of human capacity and the best way to determine knowledge.
- Family must not be assumed to be the only form of social organization.

- One must not assume that all people or most have access to good education and adequate economic resources that enable achievement and esteem.
- The survival of children, neighbors, colleagues, partners, and kin to be in-relation with must not be assumed.
- Meritocracy and unquestioned monolithic standards must not be assumed.
- Violation and control—physical, sexual, and psychological violence—must not be assumed as unusual.
- Civil and governmental ordering of rules and services, including their continuation over time, must not be assumed.
- Developmental frameworks dependent on consistent parenting, schooling, and employment opportunities must not be assumed.

Within the radical critiques, people's lived realities are the beginning point of theory building. Reformists, on the other hand, question neither structure nor processes. They merely adapt the theory to fit one or more categories of difference and, thereby, continue to support (rather than bring to awareness and challenge) the shaping of external conditions. MCT theory must grapple with this issue.

Women's Experience

Women's experience, the final feminist principle discussed here, offers much to the psychology of the nondominant peoples, including a focus of attention and a grounding of knowledge making. In this regard, the attention to the sex/gender category is not salient enough in MCT theory. Women's experiences in cultures and kinship networks as childbearers and as objects of control and special treatment differ importantly from those of men. The cultural preparation of young men and young women for their adult roles are also meaningfully different, as well as the costs of, access to, and process of holding or losing power, status, and resources. In many cases, both obvious and subtle, one's sex and its socially ascribed gender powerfully influences what one becomes and what the culture allows and judges as normal.

Sex/gender differences are thus one of the experiences salient to understanding and describing human nature. Certainly, categories of a similar ilk (race, class, religion) are also important, and the interaction of such variables within different contexts is an axis of lived experience. In the end, any theory that does not construct itself to describe and address what is lived is off the mark, becoming someone's vision of what might be—a fiction mistaken as real. Further, it is a fiction that is diagnostic, prescriptive, and highly related to the social/economic structure within which it exists.

In addition to offering a metatheory as an organizing conceptual schema, MCT theory must also give more weight to categories of difference beyond culture. Even with its fluid and inclusive concept of culture, universals rather than multiple differences and rational processes rather than lived experiences are focal points.

This focus on experience is important also because of the cultural biases that pervade Western psychology. One system, one group's characteristics, one set of values, and one worldview become the only, the best, the right, or the healthy—that is, the reality and standard of judgment. Looking to diverse experiences is a forced corrective to this process of bias. Attention to multiple experiences in theory building leads to diverse and complex views of human nature and ways of organizing and living. Multiple normative criteria and visions of health and normal coping methods are but a few of the outcomes. Experience becomes both a grounding and a source of theory building.

Feminist theory learned this lesson with the insight that the personal was political. Personal experience reflected or was caused by the political. If a woman devalued herself, she was devalued by the larger systems governing her life. Later in feminist theory, women's experiences became the source of affirmation and value giving. The importance of caretaking and interpersonal connections became central tenets in theory building (for example, Gilligan's ethics of care, the Stone Center's self-in-relation). The grounding in experience for theory building and judging would seem an important direction for MCT theory to explore.

Experience is also being evaluated as one plank (a second is pluralism) in the contemporary epistemological platform. *How* we know is just as influenced by structure as *what* we know. The influencing structures of what we know have already been alluded to—theory and one's values, worldviews, and their interactive political/economic systems. The influencing structure of epistemology (how we know) resides in one's particular philosophic system. For instance, empiricism and rationality dominate Western intellectual traditions. Experience offers an alternative epistemology to these and other traditional influencing structures.

Finally, the paradigm change called for in MCT theory needs to explore experience as a way of knowing. Experience then becomes one of the sources of ideas for theory building, a corrective bias for evaluating existing ideas and a method of grounding knowledge claims. Currently philosophic and methodological feminist work is challenging conventional methods and control of inquiry, knowledge, and reality shaping. MCT theory would do well to focus attention on experience of cultural complexity and to use experience as a grounding for theory building and validation. Were that to happen thoroughly and consistently, MCT theory would more fully join the chorus that is creating nondominant psychology.

REFERENCES FOR CHAPTER 15

Ballou, M. (1990). Approaching a feminist-principled paradigm in the construction of personality theory. *Women and Therapy, 9,* 1–2.

Ballou, M., & Gabalac, N. (1985). *A feminist position on mental health.* Springfield, IL: Thomas.

Brown, L., & Ballou, M. (1992). *Personality and psychopathology feminist reappraisals.* New York: Guilford.

Brown, L., & Root, M. (1990). *Diversity and complexity in feminist therapy.* New York: Hayworth.

Carter, D., & Rawlings, E. (1977). *Psychotherapy for women.* Springfield, IL: Thomas.

Collins, P. (1990). *Black feminist thought.* Cambridge, MA: Unwin Hyman.

Enns, C. (1993). Twenty years of feminist counseling and therapy: From naming biases to implementing multifaceted practice. *The Counseling Psychologist, 21,* 3–87.

Espin, O. (1993). Feminist therapy not for or by White women only. *The Counseling Psychologist, 21,* 103–108.

Espin, O., & Gawelek, M. (1992). Women's diversity: Ethnicity, race, class, and gender in theories of feminist psychology. In L. Brown & M. Ballou (Eds.), *Personality and psychopathology* (pp. 88–107). New York: Guilford.

Gilbert, L. (1980). Feminist Therapy. In A. Brodsky & R. Hare-Mustin (Eds.), *Women and psychotherapy* (pp. 245–262). New York: Guilford.

Gilligan, C. (1982). *In a different voice.* Cambridge, MA: Harvard University Press.

Greenspan, M. (1993). *A new approach to women and therapy.* New York: McGraw-Hill.

Harding, S. (1991). *Whose science? Whose knowledge?* Ithaca, NY: Cornell University Press.

Jordan, J., Kaplan, A., Miller, J., Stiver, I., & Surry, J. (1991). *Women's growth in connection.* New York: Guilford.

Kohlberg, L. (1981). *The philosophy of moral development.* San Francisco: Harper & Row.

Lerman, H. (1976). What happens in feminist therapy? In S. Cox (Ed.), *The emerging self* (pp. 219–228). Chicago: Science Research.

Lerman, H. (1986). *A mote in Freud's eye: From psychoanalysis to the psychology of women.* New York: Springer.

Merchant, C. (1980). *The death of nature.* San Francisco: Harper.

Riger, S. (1992). Epistemological debates, feminist voices: Science, social values, and the study of women. *American Psychologist, 47,* 730–740.

Sturdivant, S. (1980). *Therapy with women: A feminist philosophy of treatment.* New York: Springer.

PART IV

THE FUTURE OF MCT THEORY

This last chapter will attempt to integrate key points from the contributors to this book. The main thrust will be to summarize and organize the many reactions, suggestions, and recommendations that point to the future of MCT theory and how it may change the counseling profession.

C H A P T E R   1 6

MCT THEORY DEVELOPMENT: IMPLICATIONS FOR THE FUTURE

One cannot help but be impressed by the diversity of viewpoints expressed in this book, both positive and negative. These reactions have made all the more apparent the complexity of MCT theory. It is through criticism and feedback that the theory will grow and flourish. Furthermore, it is impossible for any one person or group to capture the totality and multiplicity of helping approaches and to integrate them into a unified whole. As Parham so aptly states, "A theoretical discussion that seeks to support or correct various components of the MCT theory is an insufficient test of the theory's integrity. I, for one, have never been a fan of 'democratic sanity,' where ideas seem credible just because a group of people endorse them" (p. 189). MCT is so rich, so elaborate, and growing at such a rapid pace that it is causing major upheavals in the way many people conceptualize the helping professions.

The purpose of this chapter is to "catch the wave" of new ideas generated by the respondents and to suggest new possibilities for theory development. This final chapter has two primary purposes. First, it will attempt to identify the main assumptions of MCT theory and the reactions from contributors. Second, it will integrate the essence of these ideas toward a view of the future direction of MCT theory.

UNDERLYING ASSUMPTIONS OF MCT THEORY

All theories of counseling and psychotherapy possess multiple underlying assumptions or basic premises that guide its formulation. Theories may differ from one another in emphasizing different dimensions about people and their relationship to the world. Psychoanalysis, for example, assumes that "insight" is necessary to effect a "cure"; person-centered counseling/therapy asserts that people have an innate capacity to advance and grow on their own; rational-emotive therapy assumes that irrational thoughts lead to pathology; and family systems theory operates on the assumption that "pathology" in one member is but a reflection of dysfunction in the entire family system. The validity of these assumptions often determines the strengths and weaknesses of a given theory. For example, the early behavioral challenge to the psychoanalytic assumption that "insight leads to symptom removal" (behavior change) has forced many psychodynamically oriented practitioners to rethink their positions.

Likewise, the future impact of MCT theory resides in the validity of its underlying assumptions. Many of the MCT theory's assertions are clearly stated in the numerous propositions and corollaries of Chapter 2, but their assumptions may be less obvious. Here, 12 implicit or explicit assumptions from the first three chapters will be identified, followed by feedback from the contributors. You are encouraged to do your own "assumption audit" of MCT theory. Can you identify other assumptions being made in MCT theory? How much sense do they make? Are they valid? What evidence supports or refutes them? What theoretical, practical, research, and educational implications do they have for counseling and psychotherapy?

ASSUMPTION 1

Current theories of counseling are inadequate to describe, explain, predict, and deal with cultural elements of counseling across multiple cultures.

This assumption was generally supported by all contributors and mentioned specifically by Corey; Pope-Davis and Constantine; Nuttall, Webber, and Sanchez; Parham; Leong; and Arredondo. Because each theory is derived from its own unique cultural context, problems in generalizing theories to other contexts should not surprise one. Current theories have arisen from a predominantly Euro-American perspective and therefore tend to be limited and restrictive, particularly in their lack of attention to cultural issues. MCT theory is responding to a need among counselors working in multicultural settings for a more adequate theoretical basis.

ASSUMPTION 2

Culture is complex but not chaotic; attempts to simplify culture are likely to result in stereotyped distortions.

The assumption that culture is complex and not simple was generally supported by all and mentioned explicitly by Highlen, Leong, and Arredondo. It may be that training counselors to deal with multiculturalism results in their increased ability to manage complexity, given the inevitable complications of each cultural context. MCT theory treats complexity as a positive contribution of the multicultural perspective that links each behavior to its cultural context and combines culturally different perspectives. MCT formulations are consistent with the new science of complexity, social constructivism, and chaos theory applied to human interactions. As a result, it demonstrates how culture becomes an ideal metaphor for understanding complexity in our own lives. The encapsulated alternatives to complexity are by the same token rejected.

ASSUMPTION 3

Increased multicultural emphasis by MCT theory is a predictable consequence of increased ethnocultural diversification in society.

The recognition of ethnocultural diversification was universal, with Highlen, Corey, Daniels and D'Andrea, Arredondo, and Ballou specifically mentioning it. MCT theory addresses the complex dynamic and inclusive sociocultural aspects of the client's context. With minority groups increasing in visibility, membership problems of multiple oppressions can best be addressed through pluralistic social constructs. Social organizations are living entities where within-group as well as between-group differences and similarities require contextual interpretations that do not tolerate the ethnocentric oppression of nondominant peoples.

ASSUMPTION 4

Mental-health professionals are not well prepared in their training to deal with multicultural issues.

Most contributors acknowledged the deficiency of counselor/therapist training with regard to multiculturalism, with Lee; Pope-Davis and Constantine; Nuttall, Webber, and Sanchez; Daniels and D'Andrea; and Leong making specific mention. A psychoeducational component of MCT theory advocates changes in practice as well as in theories of counseling. The need to enlarge a counselor's skill repertoire to include indigenous helping and psychospiritual perspectives is clear. Culturally different consumers perhaps understand this need better than providers, who are likely to delay recognizing the importance of cultural factors in counseling and therapy.

ASSUMPTION 5

We are witnessing a major paradigm shift in psychology and the helping professions as multicultural and diversity concepts challenge the explanatory value of traditional social sciences.

This assumption was fairly controversial, with cautious and limited support by Lee, Corey, and Pope-Davis and Constantine, and skepticism by Casas and Mann, Parham, Leong, and Ballou. Disagreements, however, seem to arise from two lines of thinking. First, some of the contributors pointed out that theories are always changing and developing. They were not ready to accept as fact that limitations of traditional theories cannot be transcended. Second, others acknowledged the limitations of current counseling/therapy theories, but felt that the profession's ethnocentrism would prevent such a paradigm shift. Some, like Leong, showed skepticism that the field of counseling and psychotherapy are on the verge of a major paradigm shift and described that aspect of MCT theory as a "wish list" more than an established or inevitable fact.

However, MCT theory does not attempt to replace traditional/historical theories but to advocate a "culture-centered" interpretation of those theories. Taking an additive rather than subtractive view of counseling/therapy theories, MCT theory describes culture as a "fourth dimension" to helping, much as time contributes new meaning to three-dimensional space. MCT theory offers prescriptions for the contemporary paradigm rather than the overthrow of other theories.

ASSUMPTION 6

Asian, African, Hispanic, and other non-Western precursors of counseling have not been given the recognition they deserve.

There was general support for this assumption, with specific mention by Highlen, Lee, Corey, Pope-Davis and Constantine, Casas and Mann, Daniels and D'Andrea, Parham, LaFromboise and Jackson, Leong, and Arredondo. Counseling clearly needs to include non-Western theories and control the pervasiveness of Western cultural influences. This means respecting indigenous counseling/helping approaches from their historical and prehistorical perspectives, accepting the roles of traditional healers in non-Western societies, understanding the spiritual and cosmological interpretations of human existence, and expanding the epistemological foundation of counseling. LaFromboise and Jackson express reservations, however, because the adaptation of indigenous healing practices by counselors may result in misuse. Furthermore, many Native Americans perceive such an approach to indicate non-Native attempts to devalue traditional cultural traditions and ways. This is a real concern for many indigenous cultures and speaks to the need for mental-health professionals to respect the wishes of racial/ethnic communities.

ASSUMPTION 7

Individualistic assumptions have dominated the field of counseling in ways that are unacceptable to collectivistic cultures.

This assumption was generally supported and discussed in detail by Corey, Parham, LaFromboise and Jackson, Leong, and Ballou. Maintaining an individualistic perspective limits the usefulness and effectiveness of counseling in collectivist cultures. MCT theory sees individuals in multiple and complex ways within the cultural context. As such, it attempts to address the needs of both the individualist and the collectivist in a balanced and interactive perspective.

ASSUMPTION 8

All learning occurs and identities are formed within a cultural context.

The assumption seems so obvious it hardly requires proving. It is discussed by Highlen, Pope-Davis and Constantine, LaFromboise and Jackson, Leong, Arredondo, and Ballou. The cultural context gives meaning to behaviors, words, concepts, and theories. MCT theory parallels social constructivism in linking culturally learned behaviors to their cultural contexts. It takes an ecological approach to interpretation on multiple levels to demonstrate what Leong calls "incremental validity" by enriching the interpretations of reality and applications of methodologies.

ASSUMPTION 9

Unintentional racism is as serious a barrier as intentional racism.

This assumption was generally supported by all, with Casas and Mann calling for a more explicit definition and Daniels and D'Andrea outlining specific actions needed to ameliorate individual, institutional, and cultural racism. If *racism* is defined as prejudice plus the power to enforce that prejudice, then unintentional racism is perhaps more pervasive than intentional racism. MCT theory does not attribute malicious intent to counselors who disregard cultural aspects, but rather cites a lack of awareness that inhibits these counselors' effectiveness. The theory aims at helping counselors recognize bias in their assumptions and practices, so they can compensate for those biases in an appropriate interpretation or counseling intervention.

ASSUMPTION 10

Informal as well as formal counseling methods become important in different cultural contexts and with different populations.

Lee, Corey, and Parham each point out that no single helping approach or intervention strategy is equally effective for all populations or life situations. Awareness of this point has resulted in the adoption of eclectic/integrative stances or attempts to modify several theories and approaches in working with different populations. MCT theory goes beyond the eclectic adaptation of theories to a more profound culture-centered reframing or reinterpretation while seeking to avoid the problems of relativism. Counseling approaches need to adapt to the client's cultural context and respond to the salience of their cultural identities rather than force the client to adapt to the counselor's more formal and traditional perspective. Parham goes even further by stating that the models of helping must originate from the culture itself and that attempts to adapt existing models to the culture may not prove fruitful.

ASSUMPTION 11

Culture is defined inclusively and broadly rather than narrowly.

This relatively controversial assumption received cautious and limited support from most contributors. In particular, Casas and Mann; Nuttall, Webber, and Sanchez; and Parham wanted MCT theory to give a more explicit definition of culture. The MCT metatheory depends on defining culture broadly and inclusively according to the salient aspects that change from time to time and place to place. MCT theory would define culture to be relational rather than representational, subjectively dynamic as well as objectively static. Defining culture according to what is most salient is more complicated than fixed paradigms, but the inclusive definition is also more responsive to each changing and complicated cultural context.

ASSUMPTION 12

An adequate research methodology for incorporating cultural data must include not only qualitative and quantitative elements, but also the experiential aspects of existence, which might not be amenable to traditional empirical investigation.

Most contributors called for more research to test the predictive validity of MCT theory. Casas and Mann called for more empirical evidence from both qualitative and quantitative methodologies. As Lee, Parham, and Ballou each pointed out, quantitative methodology has been the basis of the scientific method but also of colonial domination. Qualitative methods are also empirical/rational but are based on the phenomenology of the individual's perceptions. Lee and Pope-Davis and Constantine demonstrated the value of case examples in testing the usefulness of MCT theory. Leong emphasized the need for clinical utility regardless of what methodology was used. Perhaps the most intriguing call, however, was made implicitly by Highlen, Lee, and to a certain extent by Ballou, who cited the need to entertain alternative ways of asking and answering questions about the human condition, ways that have been rooted in many indigenous cultures or the life experiences of specific populations. These methods are believed to operate on other levels of existence, encompassing the experiential, spiritual, and holistic dimensions.

MCT theory may be, as Ballou pointed out, a theory-in-the-making rather than an already-made theory. In any case, as she states, MCT theory needs to clarify its reformist or radical stance and develop the means for structural analysis in testing its ability to explain the past and predict the future.

A CULTURE-CENTERED PERSPECTIVE IN COUNSELING AND PSYCHOTHERAPY: THE FUTURE

Culture is one of the most important and powerful forces impacting our lives. Yet, most theories of counseling and therapy operate as if they were culture-free or, at best, culturally universal. If all learning occurs in a cultural context, then culturally learned patterns control or strongly influence nearly all facets of our thoughts, beliefs, attitudes, feelings, and behaviors. Indeed, its power may reside in the fact that it does so with or without our permission or intentional awareness. Theories of counseling and therapy that neglect this fact seriously lack explanatory power and applicability. A culture-centered approach to counseling recognizes cultural context as central and not marginal, fundamental rather than exotic. Thus, it appears that an adequate theory of MCT must contain many ingredients, as detailed in the following sections.

The Inclusive Nature of Helping

Counseling and psychotherapy must be defined in a broader and more inclusive manner than in the past. The nature of helping can take on many facets that vary across groups, societies, and cultures, including not only conventional psychological/medical treatments but also educational functions and the mobilization of culture-specific endogenous resources.

EDUCATION. A broad and inclusive definition of counseling interventions includes the use of not only psychological and medical models but also educational ones. Many cultures, for example, view helping from the perspective of education. According to the "educational model" the consumer is typically regarded as an essentially healthy, normal person with a problematic issue. The provider's task is to "teach" the client ways of dealing with the issue and the consumer's task is to "learn" new ways to deal with it constructively. Just as all counseling interventions are to some extent educative, educational change has a therapeutic dimension to it. In many non-Western cultures, the "teacher" is expected to guide a person toward appropriate personal-growth goals. Seeking help from a mental-health specialist for a "mental" problem in these cultures may reduce that person's status in the community. However, a teacher can provide almost the same functions of guidance and learning in ways that will enhance one's status.

MOBILIZING ENDOGENOUS RESOURCES. In many other situations, the client may seek help from "internal resources" using "self-righting mechanisms" such as the client's natural support system. These endogenous resources are frequently overlooked as available treatment modes. In some cultures, conditions of stress lead to a mobilization of these self-healing modes, which might result in altered states of consciousness, as in dreams, dissociated states, religious experiences, or even what appear to be psychotic reactions. Torrey (1986) cites numerous examples in which self-righting approaches have been mobilized by healers and through spirits. Prince (1976, 1980; Valla & Prince, 1989) describes the role of endorphins as a physiologically endogenous resource that one can mobilize without bringing in outside mental-health experts. Sheikh and Sheikh (1989) describe the breakdown of the Westernized "dualistic-materialistic paradigm" by a conceptual revolution in which an Easternized holistic perspective is gaining importance. "Western medicine has tended to look upon the body as a sort of machine that can be treated in total isolation from the mind, but even before the major paradigm shifts, it was becoming clear that this mechanical approach was simply not working. This was especially apparent in areas where psychosomatic linkages were showing that the mind does have a major impact upon bodily functions" (p. v).

The psychological study of altered states of consciousness has been suppressed by a behavioral bias against internal, intangible, inaccessible mental states that do not lend themselves to experimental research (Ward, 1989). In recent years, the medical model has been challenged by psychosocial approaches and the influence of sociocultural factors in the study of consciousness. Valla and Prince (1989) demonstrate, for example, how religious experiences can provide self-healing mechanisms that change the physiological as well as the psychological states. Katz (1993) describes the Fijian "straight path" as a healing tradition emphasizing the spiritual dimensions of health and their relevance to the community through healing through a way of "honorable living."

By defining therapeutic interventions broadly according to their helping functions, one develops a more inclusive framework that reflects the cultural diversity and complexity of each client's context in a global context. By enlarging one's repertoire of cultured-centered intervention resources, one becomes better able to match the right method and context.

An Inclusive and Dynamic Definition of Culture

Because all learning occurs in a cultural context, providing an inclusive definition of culture is a complicated task. It is tempting to create simple models that can be explained and understood but that don't reflect the complexity of a real-world cultural context. If one considers each learned role or meaningful relationship as a potentially salient cultural identity, then each person belongs to more than a thousand different cultures. Not all of these thousand cultures are salient at the same point in time but take turns. With these multiple cultural identities, each person can respond appropriately to different cultural contexts. The apparently overwhelming complexity of culture has, however, led many teachers, researchers, administrators, and direct-service providers to either simplify or disregard cultural similarities and differences (Atkinson & Thompson, 1992).

Lifton's (1993) "protean self," in contrast with the "fundamentalist self," demonstrates complexity with reference to the Greek god Proteus, who changed form constantly. The "postmodern person" is a shape-shifter, with multiple identities as a source of strength, making tolerance of ambiguity rather than dissonance reduction the psychological ideal. In the postmodern world, discontinuous change seems to be a permanent feature (Rosenau, 1992) but, for the "affirmative postmodernists" at least, promotes the search for meaning through complex patterns.

The inclusive definition presumes that behaviors can best be understood in the cultural context where they occurred. The culture-centered perspective therefore provides a higher degree of accuracy in judgment and assessment than alternative approaches that disregard the cultural context. The inclusive definition of culture makes it possible to identify common ground in shared salience between two persons or cultural groups who might otherwise consider their behaviors to be fundamentally different and potentially hostile. The inclusive and centralized perspective presumes that culture is not external but is within the person and is not separate from other learned competencies. Understanding culture requires a high level of self-awareness. Developing cultural awareness is a professional obligation of all practicing professionals to understand each situation from multiple cultural perspectives and prevent serious negative consequences.

The Macrorelational and Holistic Approach to Helping

A major response to the first three chapters is the call for a more ecological and systems orientation—in effect, helping systems need to take a holistic and macrorelational approach. Because most populations operate from a collectivistic worldview, they often rely more on community resources for healing and help. Euro-American individualism is clearly manifested in Western methods of scientific inquiry (analytical reductionism); concepts of normal, healthy adult development/functioning (individuation/autonomy/maturity); and therapeutic treatments (one-to-one; I-Thou relationship). Westernized notions of helping seem to have lost touch with the interconnectedness of the human condition and, as a result, underutilize the rich resources of the community. These include the extended family, neighbors, spiritual advisers, government officials, and many others. The importance and vitality of context, stressed by all authors in this book, seems to be becoming central to MCT theory. In effect, the consensus appears to be that any work with individuals or families must start with larger systems awareness and action.

Acknowledging the Sociopolitical Context of Helping

The problems of power differentials in Westernized versus non-Westernized thinking are most vivid in relationships among majority and minority cultures. As perceived by minority cultures, counseling/therapy has a history of protecting the status quo against change. These attitudes are documented in "scientific racism" and "Euro-American ethnocentrism" (Pedersen, Fukuyama, & Heath, 1989). Cultural differences were explained by a "genetic deficiency" model that promoted the superiority of dominant cultures. This was matched to a "cultural deficit" model that described minorities as deprived or disadvantaged by their culture. Minorities were underrepresented among professional counselors and therapists, the topic of culture was trivialized at professional meetings, and minority views were underrepresented in the research literature; consequently, the counseling profession was discredited among minority populations.

Walsh (1989) describes the relationship between Asian and Western psychologies as complementary. First, Asian and Western psychologies both focus on development, with the Asian systems focused on advanced stages of development in a more "transpersonal" focus and well-being and Western systems focused on psychopathology and physical/mental development.

> From a multiple-states-of-consciousness model, the traditional Western approach is recognized as a relativistically useful model provided that, because of the limitations imposed by state-specific relevancy, learning, and understanding, it is not applied inappropriately to perspectives and states of consciousness and identity outside its scope. (p. 549)

Pathologizing mystical experiences would be an example of Western models going beyond their boundaries in some cultures.

The Complexity of Culture and MCT Theory

Although culture is complex, it is not chaotic; understanding its patterns makes it possible to manage complexity. The multidimensions of culture have been addressed by a "theory of complexity." Complexity theory in the social sciences (Waldrop, 1992), which grew out of chaos theory in the physical sciences, sought to redefine conventional categories. "They believe that they are forging the first rigorous alternative to the kind of linear, reductionistic thinking that has dominated science since the time of Newton—and that has now gone about as far as it can go in addressing the problems of our modern world" (p. 13).

One promising movement in counseling is based on the concepts of chaos, nonlinear dynamics, and self-organization (Barton, 1994).

> In recent years, a new paradigm for understanding systems has been gaining the attention of psychologists from a wide variety of specialty areas. This paradigm has no single name but has been described in terms of chaos, nonlinear dynamics (sometimes called nonlinear dynamical systems theory) and self-organization. (p. 5)

These concepts are metaphorical to the qualitative functions of counseling and therapy reflecting the inherent complexity of individuals and systems outside the laboratory. When chaos theory was originally conceived to describe weather forecasting (Geleick, 1987), it described chaotic systems as unpredictable locally, although when viewed globally or over long periods of time they were essentially stable. Butz (1992, 1993) applies this metaphor to the experience of anxiety in psychotherapy and systems theories of family therapy. The convergence of hard and soft sciences toward complexity rather than simplicity, toward subjectivity rather than objectivity, constructivist rather than "discovered" reality, and a contextual rather than abstract description of human behavior promises and demands a new paradigm for counseling and therapy. It is clear from this analysis that nonlinear dynamics can be applied to MCT theory. A new paradigm is needed that can facilitate change to guide clients through the apparent chaos of their contemporary multicultural contexts.

Chaos is the starting point for most psychotherapies, in which the therapist becomes the guide and companion for encountering chaos in the client's life. Western cultures have tended to disregard or resolve chaos and thus lack conceptual tools for dealing with this level of complexity. One might well look to non-Western cultures to find conceptual tools for managing the complexity and simplicity of "organic order." The interaction of complexity and chaos suggest an emergent paradoxical and inevitably contextual explanation.

The Constructivist and Contextual View of Helping

When one makes the cultural context central to the counseling/therapy process, a new theoretical explanation of human behavior emerges. Culture-centeredness focuses on culturally learned expectations and values that define the cultural context that controls and explains behavior. The "constructivist" perspective of counseling is based on the premise that we do not have direct access to a singular, stable, and fully knowable external reality, but rather we depend on culturally embedded, interpersonally connected, and necessarily limited notions of reality. Personal reality and constructed meaning in a subjective understanding of knowledge is emphasized. For instance, McNamee and Gergen (1992) have adapted the functions of counseling and therapy to understand the client's subjective reality within its cultural context. The constructivist perspective lends itself to culture-centered approaches to counseling. Hermans, Kemper, and Van Loon (1992) promote a dialogical view of self, beyond rationalism and individualism, based on interactive stories or dialogues by which people understand themselves and construct their notion of reality. "The embodied nature of the self contrasts with conceptions of the self found in mainstream psychology, which are based on the assumption of a disembodied or rationalistic mind" (p. 23).

According to this newly emerging contextual and constructivist view, reality is based not on absolute truth but on an understanding of complex and dynamic relationships in a cultural context. Life is a narrative of stories and rules that locate the self in its cultural context. Life is not understood abstractly but through relationships in a developmental alternative to linear, stage-based convergent hierarchies (Steenbarger, 1991). As the sociocultural context changes, the self changes to accommodate and adapt as each person constructs and reconstructs meaningful reality.

Howard (1991) also documents how culture is made up of the stories we live by and have learned over our lifetime.

> A life becomes meaningful when one sees himself or herself as an actor within the context of a story—be it a cultural tale, a religious narrative, a family saga, the march of science, a political movement, and so forth. Early in life we are free to choose what life story we will inhabit—and later we find we are lived by that story. (p. 196)

Claiborn and Lichtenberg (1989) support the importance of sociocultural context for "interactional counseling," in which change is reciprocal and multidirectional, each event is both cause and effect, roles are negotiated, and the participating counselor becomes aware of and participates in constructing new environments in order to help (Pedersen, 1991).

Sampson (1993) suggests that psychology and counseling have at best accommodated add-on eclectic strategies in response to culturally different movements and special-interest groups without fundamentally transforming conventional frameworks of understanding.

> Psychology is accused of using a framework of understanding that implicitly represents a particular point of view, that of currently dominant social groups, all the while acting as though its own voice were neutral, reflecting reason, rationality, and with its ever expanding collection of empirical data, perhaps truth itself. (p. 1221)

The legitimacy of counseling psychology as a science requires more than additional data or even more inclusive samples in a defense of objective positivism; it requires the inclusion of more subjective constructivist and contextual perspectives based on the sociocultural context of culturally different people.

CONCLUSIONS

Culture-centered counseling and therapy will be guided more by adapting to culturally different clients than by following theory. Theoretical structures, however, will need to be extrapolated from examples of success with culturally different clients. It will be important to remember that the counseling/therapy clientele of the future is a globally defined population. Solutions to problems of culture-centered counseling and therapy will rely on both Western and non-Western cultures. By moving from practice to theory in the field of counseling, we can become responsive to cultural similarities and differences in each cultural context.

By making culture central to the therapeutic process, this book has attempted to demonstrate the ways that culture can facilitate the quality of helping and the effectiveness of helpers. Attempts to disregard the cultural context, on the other hand, will lead therapists toward abstract projections of their own self-referenced criteria and the fatal illusion of a monocultural future.

REFERENCES FOR CHAPTER 16

Abraham, F. D., Abraham, R. H., & Shaw, C. D. (1990). *A visual introduction to dynamical systems theory for psychology.* Santa Cruz, CA: Aerial Press.

Atkinson, D. R., & Thompson, C. E. (1992). Racial, ethnic and cultural variables in counseling. In S. D. Brown & R. W. Lent (Eds.), *Handbook of counseling psychology* (pp. 349–382). New York: Wiley.

Barton, S. (1994). Chaos, self-organization and psychology. *American Psychologist, 49*(1), 5–14.

Berry, J. W., Poortinga, Y. H., Segall, M. H., & Dasen, P. J. (1992). *Cross cultural psychology: Research and applications.* Cambridge, England: Cambridge University Press.

Butz, M. R. (1993). Systemic family therapy and symbolic chaos. *Humanity and Society, 17*(2), 200–223.

Butz, M. R. (1992). Chaos: An omen of transcendence in the psychotherapeutic process. *Psychological Reports, 71,* 827–843.

Claiborn, C. D., & Lichtenberg, J. W. (1989). Interactional counseling. *The Counseling Psychologist, 71,* 355–453.

Eenwyk, J. R. (1991). Archetypes: The strange attractors of the psyche. *Journal of Analytical Psychology, 36,* 1–25.

Favazza, A. F., & Oman, M. (1977). *Anthropological and cross-cultural themes in mental health: An annotated bibliography 1925–1974.* Columbia: University of Missouri Press.

Geleick, J. (1987). *Chaos making a new science.* New York: Viking-Penguin.

Gielen, U. P. (1994). American mainstream psychology and its relationship to international and cross-cultural psychology. In L. Comunian & U. P. Gielen (Eds.), *Advancing psychology and its applications: International perspectives* (pp. 26–40). Milan, Italy: Franco Angeli.

Glover, H. (1992). Emotional numbing: A possible endorphin-mediated phenomenon associated with post-traumatic stress disorders and other allied psychopathological states. *Journal of Traumatic Stress, 5,* 643–675.

Guidano, V. F. (1991). *The self in process.* New York: Guilford Press.

Hermans, H. J. M., Kemper, H. J. G., & Van Loon, R. J. P. (1992). The dialogical self: Beyond individualism and rationalism. *American Psychologist, 47*(1) 23–33.

Howard, G. S. (1991). Culture tales: A narrative approach to thinking, cross-cultural psychology and psychotherapy. *American Psychologist, 46,* 187–197.

Kagitcibasi, C. (1988). Diversity of socialization and social change. In P. Dasen, J. Berry, & N. Sartorius (Eds.), *Health and cross-cultural psychology: Towards applications* (pp. 25–47). Newbury Park, CA: Sage.

Katz, R. (1993). *The straight path: A story of healing and transformation in Fiji.* Reading, MA: Addison-Wesley.

Kim, U., & Berry, J. W. (1993). Introduction. In U. Kim and J. W. Berry (Eds.), *Indigenous psychologies: Research and experience in cultural context* (pp. 1–29). Newbury Park, CA: Sage.

Langs, R. (1992). Towards building psychoanalytically based mathematical models of psychotherapeutic paradigms. In R. L. Levine & H. E. Fitzgerald (Eds.), *Analysis of dynamic psychological systems: Vol. 2* (pp. 371–393). New York: Plenum.

Lefley, H., & Pedersen, P. (Eds.). (1986). *Cross-cultural training for mental health professionals.* Springfield, IL: Thomas.

Lifton, R. J. (1993). *The Protean self.* New York: Basic Books.

McNamee, S., & Gergen, K. J. (1992). *Therapy as social construction.* Newbury Park, CA: Sage.

Pedersen, P. (1991). Multiculturalism as a fourth force in counseling. *Journal of Counseling and Development, 70*(1) 5–25.

Pedersen, P., Draguns, J., Lonner, W., & Trimble J. (1989). *Counseling across cultures* (3rd ed.). Honolulu, HI: University of Hawaii Press.

Pedersen, P., Fukuyama, M. A., & Heath, A. (1989). Client, counselor and contextual variables in multicultural counseling. In P. Pedersen, J. Draguns, W. Lonner, and J. Trimble (Eds.), *Counseling across cultures* (3rd ed., pp. 23–53). Honolulu: University of Hawaii Press.

Pedersen, P., & Ivey, A. E. (1993). *Culture-centered counseling and interviewing skills.* Westport, CT: Greenwood/Praeger.

Prince, R. H. (1976). Psychotherapy as the manipulation of endogenous healing mechanism: A transcultural survey. *Transcultural Psychiatric Research Review, 13,* 155–233.

Prince, R. H. (1980). Variations in psychotherapeutic experience. In H. C. Triandis & J. G. Draguns (Eds.), *Handbook of cross-cultural psychology: Vol. 6, Psychopathology* (pp. 291–349). Boston: Allyn and Bacon.

Putnam, F. (1988). The switch process in multiple personality disorder and other state-change disorders. *Dissociation 1,* 24–32.

Putnam, F. (1989). *Diagnosis and treatment of multiple personality disorders.* New York: Guilford Press.

Rosenau, P. M. (1992). *Post-modernism and the social sciences.* Princeton, NJ: Princeton University Press.

Rosenweig, M. R. (1992). *International psychological science: Progress, problems and prospects.* Hyattsville, MD: American Psychological Association.

Sabelli, H. C., Carlson-Sabelli, L., & Javaid, J. I. (1990). The thermodynamics of bipolarity: A bifurcation model of bipolar illness and bipolar character and its psychotherapeutic publications. *Psychiatry, 53,* 346–368.

Sampson, E. E. (1993). Identity politics: Challenges to psychology's understanding. *American Psychologist, 48*(12), 1219–1230.

Schmid, G. B. (1991). Chaos theory and schizophrenia: Elementary aspects. *Psychopathology, 24,* 185–198.

Scott, N. E., & Borodovsky, L. G. (1990). Effective use of cultural role taking. *Professional Psychology: Research and Practice, 21*(3), 167–170.

Sheikh, A., & Sheikh, K. S. (1989). *Eastern and Western approaches to healing: Ancient wisdom and modern knowledge.* New York: Wiley.

Sloan, C. (1990). Psychology for the Third World. *Journal of Social Sciences, 46,* 1–20.

Steenbarger, B. N. (1991). All the world is not a stage: Emerging contextualist themes in counseling and development. *Journal of Counseling and Development, 70*(2), 288–296.

Taylor, C. (1989). *Sources of the self: The making of the modern identity.* Cambridge, MA: Harvard University Press.

Torrey, E. F. (1986). *Witchdoctors and psychiatrists: The common roots of psychotherapy and its future.* New York: Harper & Row.

Triandis, H. C. (1985). Some major dimensions of cultural variation in client populations. In P. Pedersen (Ed.), *Handbook of cross-cultural counseling and therapy* (pp. 21–28). Westport, CT: Greenwood Press.

Valla, J. P., & Prince, R. H. (1989). Religious experiences as self-healing mechanisms. In C. Ward (Ed.), *Altered states of consciousness and mental health* (pp. 149–166). Newbury Park, CA: Sage.

Waldrop, M. M. (1992). *Complexity: The emerging science at the edge of order and chaos.* New York: Touchstone.

Walsh, R. (1989). Toward a synthesis of Eastern and Western psychologies. In A. A. Sheikh & K. S. Sheikh (Eds.), *Eastern and Western approaches to healing* (pp. 542–555). New York: Wiley.

Ward, C. (1989). *Altered stages of consciousness and mental health.* Newbury Park, CA: Sage.

Wrightsman, L. S. (1992). *Assumptions about human nature: Implications for researchers and practitioners.* Newbury Park, CA: Sage.

Zohar, D., & Marshall, I. (1994). *The quantum society.* New York: Morrow.

CREDITS

This page constitutes an extension of the copyright page. We have made every effort to trace the ownership of all copyrighted material and to secure permission from copyright holders. In the event of any question arising as to the use of any material, we will be pleased to make the necessary corrections in future printings. Thanks are due to the following authors, publishers, and agents for permission to use the material indicated.

42–43: List from D. R. Atkinson, C. E. Thompson, & S. K. Grant, "A three-dimensional model for counseling racial/ethnic minorities," *The Counseling Psychologist, 21*, pp. 257–277, copyright © 1993 by Sage Publications, Inc. Reprinted by permission of Sage Publications, Inc.

46–49: Table 3.1 from "Multicultural counseling competencies and standards: A call to the profession," by Derald Wing Sue, Patricia Arredondo, & Roderick McDavis, *Journal of Counseling and Development, 20*, pp. 484–486, 1992. © ACA. Reprinted by permission. No further reproduction authorized without written permission of the American Counseling Association.

66–67: List adapted from "Elements of a Psychology of Human Diversity," by R. J. Watts, 1992, *Journal of Community Psychology, 20*, 116–151. Copyright © 1992 Clinical Psychology Publishing Company, Inc. Adapted by permission.

67: Excerpt from "Exploring the postmodern: Perils or potentials?" by K. J. Gergen, 1994, *American Psychologist, 49*, 412–416. Copyright © 1994 American Psychological Association. Reprinted by permission.

144–145: Table 9.1 from "Impacts of culture on teaching and learning," by J. Landrum-Brown, September 28, 1994. Workshop given at University of California, Santa Barbara. Adapted by permission.

195: Excerpt from "Wounding the spirit: Discrimination and traditional American Indian belief systems," by C. Locust, 1988, *Harvard Educational Review, 58*(3), 315–330. Copyright © 1988 Harvard University.

197–198: Quotation from R. Katz & E. Rolde, "Community alternatives to psychotherapy," *Psychotherapy: Theory, Research and Practice, 18*(3), 36–374. Copyright © 1981.

226: Quotation from "The prospect for a woman's liberation movement in Latin America," by E. P. Stevens, 1973, *Journal of Marriage and Family*, May, 313–320. Copyright © 1973 National Council on Family Relations. Reprinted by permission.

227: Quotation from D. R. Moyerman & B. D. Forman, "Acculturation and adjustment: A meta-analytic study," *Hispanic Journal of Behavioral Sciences, 14*(2), pp. 163–200. Copyright © 1992 by Sage Publications, Inc. Reprinted by permission of Sage Publications, Inc.

228: List from J. S. Phinney, "Ethnic identity and self-esteem: A review and integration," *Hispanic Journal of Behavioral Sciences, 13*(2), pp. 193–208, copyright © 1991 by Sage Publications, Inc. Reprinted by permission of Sage Publications, Inc.

231–233: Excerpt, copyright © 1991 by Haworth Press, Inc., Binghamton, NY, "Progressive counseling with Latino refugees and families," *Journal of Progressive Human Services, 2*(2), 19–34, by V. De La Cancela.

259: Excerpt from "Chaos, self-organization and psychology," by S. Barton, 1994, *American Psychologist, 49*(1), 5–14. Copyright © 1994 American Psychological Association.

260: Excerpt from "The diabolical self: Beyond individualism and rationalism," by H. J. M. Hermans, H. J. G. Kemper, & R. J. P. Van Loon, 1992, *American Psychologist, 47*(1), 23–33. Copyright © 1992 American Psychological Association. Reprinted by permission.

261: Excerpt from "Culture tales: A narrative approach to thinking, cross-cultural psychology and psychotherapy," by G. S. Howard, 1991, *American Psychologist, 46*, 187–197. Copyright © 1991 American Psychological Association. Reprinted by permission.

TO THE OWNER OF THIS BOOK:

We hope that you have found *A Theory of Multicultural Counseling and Therapy* useful. So that this book can be improved in a future edition, would you take the time to complete this sheet and return it? Thank you.

School and address: _____

Department: _____

Instructor's name: _____

1. What I like most about this book is: _____

_____

_____

2. What I like least about this book is: _____

_____

_____

3. My general reaction to this book is: _____

_____

_____

4. The name of the course in which I used this book is: _____

_____

_____

5. Were all of the chapters of the book assigned for you to read? _____

   If not, which ones weren't? _____

6. In the space below, or on a separate sheet of paper, please write specific suggestions for improving this book and anything else you'd care to share about your experience in using the book.

_____

_____

_____

_____

_____

Optional:

Your name: _____   Date: _____

May Brooks/Cole quote you, either in promotion for *A Theory of Multicultural Counseling and Therapy* or in future publishing ventures?

Yes _____   No _____

Sincerely,

Derald Wing Sue
Allen E. Ivey
Paul B. Pedersen

FOLD HERE

NO POSTAGE
NECESSARY
IF MAILED
IN THE
UNITED STATES

BUSINESS REPLY MAIL
FIRST CLASS   PERMIT NO. 358   PACIFIC GROVE, CA

POSTAGE WILL BE PAID BY ADDRESSEE

ATT: *Sue, Ivey, & Pedersen*

Brooks/Cole Publishing Company
511 Forest Lodge Road
Pacific Grove, California 93950-9968

FOLD HERE